CAMPAIGN MODE

Campaigning American Style

CAMPAIGNING AMERICAN STYLE

Series Editors
Daniel M. Shea, Allegheny College
F. Christopher Arterton, George Washington University

Few areas of American politics have changed as dramatically in recent times as the way in which we choose public officials. Students of politics and political communications are struggling to keep abreast of these developments—and the 2000 election only feeds the confusion and concern. *Campaigning American Style* is a new series of books devoted to both the theory and practice of American electoral politics. It offers high quality work on the conduct of new-style electioneering and how it is transforming our electoral system. Scholars, practitioners, and students of campaigns and elections need new resources to keep pace with the rapid rate of electoral change, and we are pleased to help provide them in this exciting series.

Titles in the Series

Campaign Mode: Strategic Vision in Congressional Elections
   by Michael John Burton and Daniel M. Shea

The Civic Web: Online Politics and Democratic Values,
   edited by David M. Anderson and Michael Cornfield

Forthcoming

High-Tech Grassroots: The Professionalization of Local Elections
   by J. Cherie Strachan

Campaign Polling
   by Jeffrey M. Stonecash

CAMPAIGN MODE

Strategic Vision in Congressional Elections

MICHAEL JOHN BURTON
AND
DANIEL M. SHEA

ROWMAN & LITTLEFIELD PUBLISHERS, INC.
Lanham • Boulder • New York • Oxford

ROWMAN & LITTLEFIELD PUBLISHERS, INC.

Published in the United States of America
by Rowman & Littlefield Publishers, Inc.
A Member of the Rowman & Littlefield Publishing Group
4720 Boston Way, Lanham, Maryland 20706
www.rowmanlittlefield.com

PO Box 317, Oxford, OX2 9RU, United Kingdom

British Library Cataloguing in Publication Information Available

Library of Congress Cataloging-in-Publication Data

Burton, Michael John.
    Campaign mode : strategic vision in congressional elections / Michael
John Burton and Daniel M. Shea.
        p.   cm.—(Campaigning American style)
    ISBN 0-7425-0140-X (cloth : alk. paper)—ISBN 0-7425-0141-8
(pbk. : alk. paper)
        1. Political campaigns—United States.   2. United States.
Congress—Elections.   I. Shea, Daniel M.   II. Title.   III. Series.
JK1976 .B855   2003
324.7'2'0973—dc21   2002004294

Printed in the United States of America

⊗ ™ The paper used in this publication meets the minimum requirements of
American National Standard for Information Sciences—Permanence of Paper for
Printed Library Materials, ANSI/NISO Z39.48-1992.

To our mothers

Grace M. Burton
and
Rosemary Bowers Shea

CONTENTS

PREFACE

R ON FAUCHEUX, editor of *Campaigns & Elections*—a trade magazine for the American campaign industry—has written that political campaigns "may be messy, confusing, and ephemeral, and occasionally silly, mindless, and ferocious, but they provide the pivot upon which our democracy turns."[1] Many professionals and volunteers who have worked congressional elections will agree with Faucheux's observation: "There's nothing quite like political campaigns."[2] While life offers higher callings than electoral politics, there are few vocations that can match the exhilaration of a hard-fought race for Congress.

This book represents an effort to convey the world of congressional electioneering from the professionals' point of view. The term "political professional," for the purposes of this research, encompasses all those who build their lives around the winning of American campaigns. It comprises elected officials, political staffers, congressional candidates, campaign consultants, and all the itinerant operatives who make their living off the demanding work of American electioneering. The following pages attempt to reconstruct the manner in which these professionals comprehend the political terrain around them.

In this sense, the present research is partly an exercise in self-understanding: we began our academic careers only after working as professionals in electoral politics. *Campaign Mode* started as a series of conversations about the manner in which scholarly perceptions about politics differ from professional understanding—how detached observation contrasts with strategic thinking in campaign mode. It was a dialogue that continued throughout the course of this research. Attempting to define campaign mode and investigating the manner in which the concept played out in a number of electoral contests, we found ourselves clarifying an experience of life that we had not fully appreciated at the time we were living it.

Many people have helped assemble the rendering of *Campaign Mode* that emerged from these conversations. Sharon D. Wright kindly shared her thoughts on chapter 6. Mike Radway, who supervised Michael Burton in his first paying political job, read the entire manuscript and offered a wide range of valuable comments. Chapter 3 benefited greatly from research performed jointly by Michael Burton and DeLysa Burnier as part of an electoral study undertaken by David B. Magleby and funded by the Pew Charitable Trusts.[3] The George V. Voinovich Center for Leadership and Public Affairs at Ohio University provided partial funding for the present research. Katie Nisley-Robison, Caroline Nagy, Kati Szoverfy, Danielle Sarver, Rob Soccorsi, Leigh Anne DeWine, Chris Capecci, Kevin V. Welker, Amy Tindale, and Justin McCaulley helped the authors track down factual details and clean the manuscript. Anonymous reviewers provided critical insight. Our colleagues at Ohio University and Allegheny College were extraordinarily supportive as the authors moved this project to completion. The research would not have been possible without the time and consideration granted by the candidates, elected officials, staffers, operatives, and consultants who generously shared their experiences.

We would also like to thank the folks at Rowman & Littlefield, especially the political science editor, Jennifer Knerr. Jennifer's insight and thoughtful suggestions on how to sharpen the book say a lot about her knowledge of politics and political science—and her patience in receiving the final manuscript says volumes about her good nature. Our experience with Jennifer and all the staff at Rowman & Littlefield has been splendid.

On a more personal level, we would both like to thank our families for all their support, before and during this project. In Michael's case, that means all the Drs. Burton: John, Grace, and Becky. Dan would like to send a special thanks to his wonderful family—his children Abigail, Daniel, and Brian, and his beloved wife Christine—for their unwavering support and encouragement.

Finally, we would like to thank our political mentors. Michael learned campaign mode from Thurgood Marshall Jr., Al Gore, Mike Radway, Linda Moore, David Strauss, Paul Kanjorski, and indeed, all those with whom he worked in Washington, D.C., and around the nation. Likewise, Dan extends his appreciation to those who taught him the craft on one of America's most intense political battlefields, New York State: he worked with a number of top notch professionals during his years at the Democratic Assembly Campaign Committee, including Dick Farfaglia, John Wellspeak, and John Longo. Surely the greatest strategist of the operation was Jim Murphy. Few operatives have a finer sense of nuance and timing as "Murph." We hope that this book will help scholars and students better understand the world in which these political professionals live.

Notes

1. Ron Faucheux, "Introduction," *The Road to Victory: The Complete Guide to Winning Political Campaigns—Local, State and Federal* (Dubuque, Iowa: Kendall/Hunt, 1998), ix.

2. Ibid.

3. DeLysa Burnier and Michael John Burton, "Ohio Sixth District," in *Outside Money: Soft Money & Issue Ads in Competitive 1998 Congressional Elections*, eds. David B. Magleby and Marianne Hold (Report of a Grant Funded by the Pew Charitable Trusts, 1999).

Campaign Mode and Professional Understanding   1

I N 1759, THE LEGENDARY COLONIAL OFFICER, Major Robert Rogers, set down for his expeditionary Rangers a list of tactical commands—nineteen standing orders known today as "Rogers' Rules."[1] It was the first British military doctrine written specifically for use on the North American continent. Indeed, the colonies *needed* their own set of rules. British tacticians were accustomed to open fields of battle: soldiers were trained to march forward, spot their foe, and then fire point-blank. Adversaries were separated by mere yards. But the forests around New York's Lake George were altogether different from the clearings of England and Europe. In North America, British forces campaigned against a French army that was allied with native peoples who had walked and hunted the land since childhood. Rogers needed a bold new kind of warfare. Victory, it seemed, demanded tactical creativity. Rogers took it upon himself to devise a fresh set of rules to guide his troops fighting in the New World.[2]

Rogers' Rules prescribed hit-and-run tactics. "If somebody's trailing you," Rogers said in Rule 17, "make a circle, come back onto your own tracks, and ambush the folks that aim to ambush you." Rule 3: "When you're on the march, act the way you would if you was sneaking up on a deer," by which Rogers meant, "See the enemy first." Rule 4: "Tell the truth about what you see and do," Rogers commanded; "You can lie all you please when you tell other folks about the Rangers, but don't never lie to a Ranger or officer." Rogers' Rules describe the new art of guerrilla skirmishing in the face of gentlemanly warfare—a glimpse into antiquated combat; but it is Rule 1 that good leaders struggle to keep in mind, a rule that is at once the simplest and the most complicated of them all: "Don't forget nothing."

Others have tried to locate the essence of strategy—military, political, and otherwise. Sun Tzu's *The Art of War* seems ageless ("Know the enemy and know yourself"[3]). Masters of the political art think immediately of Niccolò Machiavelli, whose classic, *The Prince*, has been studied for centuries ("[A] prudent man should always follow in the path trodden by great men and imitate those who are most excellent"[4]). Contemporary students of political science read *Plunkitt of Tammany Hall* ("[Y]ou must study human nature and act accordin' "[5]), Chris Matthews' *Hardball* ("Spin!"[6]), and David Horowitz' *The Art of Political War* ("In political warfare, the aggressor usually prevails"[7]). Former Speaker of the House Tip O'Neill named a book of political truisms after his first rule of politics, a reflection that many campaign professionals take as biblical truth: "All politics is local."[8]

Most works written by political professionals contain at least a few stern commands. *All's Fair,* a personal account of the 1992 presidential election written by feuding advisors Mary Matalin and James Carville, counsels political ruthlessness. Republican consultant Matalin summons a Vietnamese battle cry:

> Follow me if I advance
> Kill me if I retreat
> Avenge me if I die.[9]

Democratic strategist Carville adopted a rule he heard from a corporate CEO: "When your opponent is drowning, throw the son of a bitch an anvil."[10] Chilling advice, and to the political professional, inspiring—an evocation of the strategic state of mind. Politics becomes a continuation of war by other means.[11]

When one of the authors of this book (Michael John Burton) worked in the White House as assistant political director to Vice President Al Gore, he collected tactical rules under the thick glass covering his desktop. Two sets were given to him by a White House military aide: one was Rogers' Rules, and the other was "Colin Powell's Rules," taken from the general's book, *My American Journey.*[12] "Perpetual optimism is a force multiplier," Powell wrote, and "Don't take counsel of your fears or naysayers." Burton also kept under glass "Berger's Rules for White House Work," written by Bill Clinton's National Security Advisor, Sandy Berger.[13] Berger advised staffers to "Think big and write short"; also, "Never forget where you work—the White House—and for whom—the President," since, "If you lose your sense of awe about that, it's time to think about moving on." Cynics might have regarded some of Berger's directives as simplistic orders ("Wear your beeper") and hokey platitudes ("Be proud of what you are doing for your country"), but his rules, clipped from *USA Today,* were taped to the side of many staff-level computers.

Political rules are usually learned on the job. When the other author of this book (Daniel M. Shea) finished his graduate work in campaign management, he was hired as a regional coordinator for New York State's Democratic Assembly Campaign Committee (DACC). In the late 1980s, DACC was among the most sophisticated campaign organizations in the nation. Democrats controlled the assembly, so the money flowed in. DACC therefore had the best surveys, mailing lists, campaign ads, opposition researchers, and hired guns. With the onset of the campaign season, DACC operatives took leaves of absence from the state payroll to work on targeted assembly races. Much of DACC's electoral effectiveness stemmed from its willingness to go on the attack, a strategy that often defeated seemingly invincible incumbents. DACC had a tough, abrasive way of running campaigns, and many Democrats found themselves at odds with the committee's strategic and tactical decisions, but DACC's aggressive approach usually prevailed.

Smart targeting was the key. Operatives like Shea took pains to get the facts—"Know your district" was a principal rule—and DACC operatives had to know their districts inside out before they were allowed to communicate with their first voter. Data was amassed and analyzed, including electoral histories, survey results, census materials, industrial profiles, reports on local housing patterns, and more. Thorough understanding of the district was a prerequisite for the "Tony Meeting."

"Tony" was Anthony Genovesi, a veteran Brooklyn party manager, hand-picked by the speaker of the assembly to oversee DACC. Known for his domineering presence and robust use of both English and Italian, Tony's tactical wisdom was respected by Democrats and Republicans alike. In Brooklyn, Genovesi was the leader of the powerful Thomas Jefferson Club, an old-style party machine. After Genovesi's death in 1998, the *New York Times* wrote, "Gruff and beefy, Mr. Genovesi was in most ways just the opposite of a slick, focus-grouped politician."[14] According to the *Albany Times-Union*, "Genovesi succeeded in Albany by blending bare-knuckle, back-room politics with chessmaster diplomacy."[15]

Behind closed doors, in the recesses of the Capitol building, at all hours of the night, Genovesi seemed to take pleasure in berating DACC operatives who had failed to learn every tactical nuance of their assigned districts. For new staffers, the Tony Meeting was a rite of passage. Surrounded by minions and facing a table piled high with Italian foods, Genovesi would hammer out strategy for one assembly race after another. Many a graduate school hotshot left his or her first three-hour "chat" with Tony in shambles—a blank daze and a stream of stutters about the need to "get more data, get more data."

Genovesi's operatives had to "know where the angels sing and where the devils sleep." To run a cost-effective campaign, an operative needed to understand where the candidate's support was, where the opposition lay, and, most importantly, where the undecided voters could be found and what they were concerned about. Genovesi reasoned that a campaign is not won by a "silver bullet"—the greatest commercial or the latest scandal; rather, for Genovesi, the essence of campaign strategy lay in disciplined knowledge of the electorate. Genovesi took the know-your-district rule to heart, and after his first meeting with this legendary figure of New York politics, so too did Shea.

Campaign Mode

Genovesi was forcing his operatives into "campaign mode." There is no formal definition—campaign mode is a way of life more than a point of discussion—but contours can be discerned from history and experience. As electoral strategies are formulated, debated, implemented, and reformulated, an intuitive sense of political strategy takes hold on the professional mind. In Washington and on the campaign trail, one will hear political professionals say, "She understands," "He gets it," or "She knows how the game is played." A White House colleague of Burton's once described campaign mode as the ability to "think three or four moves ahead." Cold calculations must be made about the strengths and weaknesses of the candidate and the opposition, the opportunities presented and foreclosed by one's political environment, and the perils that await the candidate once the electoral season begins. Some people "get the joke," and some do not.

Campaign mode, in this sense, is a state of mind that combines a visceral drive to win elections with a deep-seated habit of strategic thinking. Ideally, strategic thinking in campaign mode is based on an understanding of political terrain that helps a professional choose the right campaign rules (see figure 1.1.) Because each element of campaign mode carries its own set of ambiguities, each deserves close attention.

Visceral Drive

Perhaps the most elusive element of campaign mode is the psychic energy that propels it. Political professionals harbor an intense commitment to electoral success. For candidates and their loyalists, campaign mode is often a singular dedication to a cause; for hired consultants, it is frequently the knowledge that success in business depends on victory in politics. Passion— even personal ego—is indispensable among candidates and operatives who run a political race day and night for little immediate gain. The election will send them hurtling through a dizzying constellation of political events, personnel conflicts, press packets, and television commercials—alternating between joy and misery—until the finish line is crossed on Election Day. In the thick of the fight, a team of political operatives might come to believe that the future of American democracy hinges on the outcome of the election, and by extension, the efforts of the campaign staff.

This is the simultaneous cost and benefit of electioneering. Dramatic films and documentaries such as *The Candidate, Power, The War Room, A Perfect*

Figure 1.1. The Elements of Campaign Mode

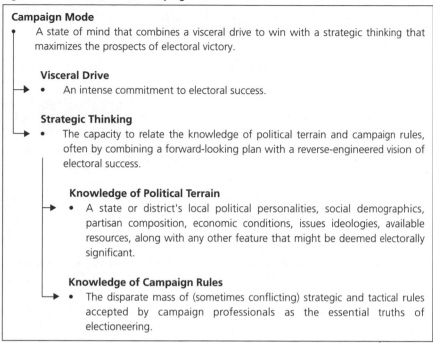

Campaign Mode
- A state of mind that combines a visceral drive to win with a strategic thinking that maximizes the prospects of electoral victory.

  Visceral Drive
  - An intense commitment to electoral success.

  Strategic Thinking
  - The capacity to relate the knowledge of political terrain and campaign rules, often by combining a forward-looking plan with a reverse-engineered vision of electoral success.

    Knowledge of Political Terrain
    - A state or district's local political personalities, social demographics, partisan composition, economic conditions, issues ideologies, available resources, along with any other feature that might be deemed electorally significant.

    Knowledge of Campaign Rules
    - The disparate mass of (sometimes conflicting) strategic and tactical rules accepted by campaign professionals as the essential truths of electioneering.

Candidate, Primary Colors, and *Bulworth* gain much of their appeal from the classic plot structure of person-against-self, as basic human needs are subordinated to the demands of electoral success. When asked what "campaign mode" means, one of the operatives interviewed for this book said it stood for "bad food and four hours of sleep"—and she did not think this condition was all bad. Operatives commonly lose themselves on the political battlefield. It is not unusual for political professionals in a tough race—candidates, consultants, and campaign staffers alike—to work sixteen hours per day during the two months preceding the election. Particularly when candidates and their staffs must traverse a wide-ranging district, they are on the job morning, noon, and night. Indeed, hard work becomes a reward in itself—and there is a perverse pride in overcoming the obstacles that would defeat mere "civilians."

The source of this powerful, visceral drive is not readily apparent—pondering its origins begs difficult questions about the human spirit—but those who have worked on hard-fought electoral contests have learned that political passion can be molded into a potent electoral weapon. Doing so requires shrewd strategic thinking.

Strategic Thinking

Strategic thinking is as much an art as it is a science. In one sense, this habit of thought is difficult to spell out in detail—it is a talent based largely on learned intuition—but some rough outlines can be discerned with the help of Richard Neustadt's distinction between "backward mapping" and "forward planning."[16]

Ideally, the two perspectives operate simultaneously. Forward planning begins with a review of current resources and future obstacles, assessing the most efficient means of advance. The value of forward planning is obvious: it promotes adaptive motion and avoids single-minded efforts to press against unmovable objects. Focus is held on that which is immediately achievable. The danger of forward planning is that the path of least resistance often leads one astray. To prevent wandering, backward mapping asks what each move contributes to the final outcome. Although sideways maneuvering and tactical retreat is sometimes necessary in the heat of battle, lateral and retrograde motions are acceptable only to the extent that a change in direction ultimately leads to success. In perfect form, strategic thinking involves looking at problems from both directions at once. It is, in other words, the merging of political means and ends into a single, orderly, unified theory of action.[17]

Neustadt was concerned with presidential power, but his interpretation of strategic thinking can be transposed onto electoral strategy. Using Election Day as an anchor point, a political operative will take account of the existing situation and then reverse-engineer a campaign victory by designating the week prior to the election for a "get-out-the-vote-drive," and the week prior to that as an opportunity to refine the campaign's voter lists, and so forth, until the plan reaches back to the present moment in time.[18] Many campaigns create wall-sized calendars that chart each significant event leading up to the day when the first ballot is cast. Everyone in the office can see what needs to be done. With Election Day looming on the horizon, there is no time to discuss anything that does not relate directly to the task at hand.

Backward mapping sets the goal; forward planning shows the way. The ideal campaign operation would begin with a strategy perfectly suited to its time and place, of course—but in the real world, the convergence of forward planning and backward mapping is usually seen in the frenzy of day-to-day progress: the campaign organization hooks its long-term vision in election-day victory, and then slowly winches forward, frequently changing its line of approach, often adjusting campaign rules to fit new developments on the political terrain.

Continuous readjustment is necessary because every political terrain presents unexpected obstacles, and because, in the world of electioneering, there is no formula for success. No mathematical algorithm can predict the winner of every election; no scientific procedure highlights all the variables on which electoral triumph might depend. Strategic thinking is a chancy proposition even for the smartest, most passionately driven political professional, and for good reason: terrain will always be open to conflicting interpretations and the rules that govern political operations will always carry a degree of uncertainty.

KNOWLEDGE OF POLITICAL TERRAIN. Strategy is governed by perception. The pressures of an electoral contest pull some features of a local political terrain to the forefront of awareness and push others toward the back. Historians of science talk about the paradigms that govern scientific communities; deconstructionists show how the evocation of one meaning displaces a variety of others; and phenomenologists talk about the manner in which fields of knowledge thematize their surroundings, carving certain features from the landscape and drawing them into view. Of the military experience, philosopher Arthur C. Danto has noted that "battle thematizes certain features of the terrain, transforming them into what soldiers call 'ground,'" bringing into view, for example, "the flanking hills of the Federal line" at Gettysburg, or "the sweep of field and meadow" that defined Pickett's Charge.[19] In this sense, ground is thematized according to its strategic or tactical value, as when Rogers reconceptualized the military situation presented by the tactical geography of the New World.

Political professionals understand a state, district, ward, or precinct in much the same way. In campaign mode, electoral victory is the axis around which the world turns. A political professional apprehends a voting district as a conglomeration of voters, demographic characteristics, media markets, neighborhoods, partisan and ideological preferences, long-standing political alliances (and disputes), and other electorally significant features. People are viewed as volunteers, staffers, base voters, swing voters, and soft partisans. Segments of the electorate that are unalterably loyal to the opposition simply recede from view. Persuadable voters, however, are said to be "on the radar screen"—they are "worth watching." Like the other electorally significant features of a district, the uncommitted voters—who, as a mass, are capable of turning the election—become the most salient characteristics of the political terrain.

The problem is that political ground tends to shift under foot. Candidates are happiest when they have reconfigured the terrain in their favor, though often the transformation is forced by the opposition—for example, by an attack ad that raises new political issues. Outside influences like national economic downturns and controversial Supreme Court decisions commonly intrude on local political arguments, and an unexpected shot from one's opponent can have much the same effect. The most dramatic instance of unexpected issue-emergence in American history came in 2001 with the terrorist assault on New York's World Trade Center, which occurred just a few hours after the voting in the city's September 11 mayoral primary had begun. The election was postponed, and several days later, the candidates resumed their work in a new world of campaign issues. Gone were ideological divides regarding social policy; in their place was a new, more pressing concern: crisis management. Lacking divine prescience, political professionals have no way to predict exactly what the terrain is going to look like on Election Day.

There is a deeper problem, however: to know a political terrain is to recognize its strategically significant features, but the prospective power of a given strategy cannot be known without knowledge of the political terrain—it's a catch-22. Of all the potentially significant features of a congressional district, which ones are most worth exploring? Variations in income? Religious values? Last year's failed highway project? Political scandal? A political operative who has recently found success by uncovering waste, fraud, and abuse in a neighboring district might look for the next incumbent's malfeasance in office, but is a scandal-based strategy really the best approach? Working with finite resources, a political professional can only investigate a limited number of options—just the ones that are most likely to affect the election's outcome—but there is no sure way for a political strategist to know which features are worth exploring until all the options have been investigated (and it is impossible to investigate them *all*).

The circle might become vicious but for the existence of presumptively critical features—a common sense that political professionals have developed through hard experience. Political operatives might read a given political situation differently, but they tend to begin their analyses with similar checklists. Professionals take account of electoral histories, ballot design, partisan leanings, social geography, national trends, candidate biographies, policy preferences, issue climates, financial resources, the distribution of media outlets, advertising costs, party organizations, bases of political support, and a host of other political features that are normally deemed relevant to understanding an electoral district.[20]

In the analysis of one political terrain, family income may be the center of attention; in another, a paucity of local television outlets may drive electoral strategy; in yet another, the changing ideological or ethnic makeup of the electorate may serve as the gravitational point that pulls together an operative's best strategic understanding. Generally speaking, political professionals find the most significant electoral features of a district to be its (1) local political personalities, (2) social demographics, (3) partisan composition, (4) economic conditions, (5) local issues and ideologies, and (6) available political resources. Whichever features might ultimately be deemed most important— and determining which ones will turn the election requires good judgment—

understanding political ground is crucial to the proper application of strategic and tactical rules.

KNOWLEDGE OF CAMPAIGN RULES. To make sense of the terrain, political professionals have to know at least a few rules of electoral strategy. Some rules are drawn as simple imperatives, like "You have to have a plan."[21] Others are statements of political fact that carry obvious strategic or tactical implications. EMILY's List, a political action committee that funds pro-choice Democratic women, named itself after the idea that "Early Money Is Like Yeast—it makes the 'dough' rise." In California, operatives commonly say "It's not real until it's on television." O'Neill's all-politics-is-local rule is among the most widely accepted principles of American politics. Thus, a California campaign organization might want to start with a plan, raise early money, get itself on the air, and address local issues whenever possible.

For political professionals, these sorts of maxims are not just hackneyed clichés; they are essential bits of knowledge. While some might debate the validity, relative priority, or general application of certain presuppositions, much of the conventional wisdom about campaigns and elections is constituted by campaign rules.

An important caveat is in order. The idea that electoral strategy is drawn from a body of rules might leave the impression that, if political operatives did everything just right—if, as Rogers advised, nothing was forgotten—then victory would be assured. But electioneering is not governed by a set of natural laws; it is merely informed by a disparate collection of ideas—lessons that are sometimes formed into the shape of universal rules even as they are nuanced by time and place. Some general truths seem clear. It is essential to "know your district" whether you work for Genovesi or not. The same goes for rules that former Republican governor and presidential candidate Lamar Alexander has offered: "Walk in parades,"[22] and "When raising money, don't forget to ask for the money."[23] Still, Democratic candidates (who wrestle with disagreements between labor Democrats and New Democrats) play the game somewhat differently than Republican candidates (who confront arguments between cultural and free-market conservatives). For that matter, many would say that the game is played differently by New Hampshirites and Iowans, Texans and New Yorkers, Northerners and Southerners, men and women, industrialists and environmentalists, Hollywood entertainers and single parents, corporate officers and Christian evangelists. There are so many subtleties that generalizations often seem impossible to make.

Those who seek a formal hierarchy of campaign rules will find disappointment. Ron Faucheux has gone so far as to say, "[Y]ou must always remember the First Rule of Political Campaigning: There are no rules."[24] It is a rhetorical overstatement meant to remind political professionals that rule-based guidance is subject to the constraints of time and place. Take, for example, the old rule of thumb holding that a challenger should not attack an incumbent until the challenger has established a firm base of support. The rule makes sense, because, according to much conventional wisdom, negative ads hurt both sides and newcomers usually have less political capital to spend. For years, the formula seemed to work. But since the mid-1980s, a number of congressional elections have taught the opposite lesson. Challengers having little name identification and even less public popularity have successfully used early negatives—though not everywhere. In some locales, the incumbents are still sufficiently respected that anti-incumbent attacks are self-defeating.

The rules of engagement are neither eternal nor universal—they change over time and must be fitted to specific theaters of operation—and there are intrinsic reasons why campaign rules resist the hierarchical model.

First, mere articulation tends to push a campaign rule toward obsolescence. A campaign organization that follows all the established rules is at risk of defeat because its movements will be predictable. A good strategist will know conventional wisdom, and then try to outsmart it. Indeed, the history of politics and warfare is an upward spiral of measure, countermeasure, and counter-countermeasure, in which new strategies give rise to new electoral environments, and vice versa—with cutting-edge rules becoming outmoded in rapid succession. Any formal hierarchy of campaign rules would be destined to change over time, with some maxims coming into conflict with others, and well-defined rules seeming to lose their strategic value as soon as they come into view.

Second, the campaign rules discussed by political professionals are generally not intended to form a well-ordered hierarchy any more than a list of tips for good writing is meant to map the structure of the English language. Unlike the rules of a formal system (arithmetic, for example), which strive for completeness and consistency, campaign rules are lessons, reminders, and nuggets of advice intended to repair an out-of-balance perspective or to reinforce a wise notion that might somehow become lost. When Genovesi stated the obvious by demanding that his staffers know their districts, he was imposing a new lesson on graduate school hotshots who had failed to dig deeply enough into the political terrain. Genovesi's novices needed a stern warning about proper research, but if they had spent too much time studying their districts and not enough time communicating with their voters, a whole different rule might have been called for: "Connect with the people!" Genovesi did not intend to diagram the width and breadth of American electioneering; rather, his know-your-district rule was meant to foster strategic equilibrium in the minds of a specific group of political operatives.

The fact that campaign rules are commonly tailored to suit a particular audience helps to explain the existence of contradictory rules. At the beginning of the twenty-first century, incumbents facing an aggressive challenger could choose either of two mutually exclusive lines of defense: (1) Never let an attack go unanswered, or (2) Do not give obscure opponents unnecessary press coverage by responding to every single charge they make. The advice that a campaign consultant might give to a client would depend largely on the predispositions of the incumbent. A skittish congressman who feels the need to reach to each negative ad might have to be restrained via the latter rule's admonition against playing up the attack, whereas a lackadaisical incumbent might need to be reminded by way of the former rule that each of the challengers' assaults brings the incumbent's reputation down another notch.

By the same token, campaign rules are intended to connect past elections with future political contests. In Virginia, Colonel Oliver North's 1994 bid for a seat in the United States Senate was notable for its profound negativity, but toward the end of the election season, the North team pulled back from its attacks in order to highlight the positive aspects of North's character. After North lost, his chief strategist believed the campaign should have "just kept pounding away." The strategist was filmed telling himself, "I'll never make that mistake again."[25] The implicit rule, which had worked well for many of North's Republican allies in 1994, and which would presumably work in future campaigns: stay on the negative.

It would seem that the value of a campaign rule is not its place in a formal hierarchy, but its use in forthcoming elections—that the rule to be learned from any given electoral contest lies at the intersection of the speaker and the listener, the case at hand and the next one to be understood. Two professionals can extract two (or more) different rules from the same case, particularly if their expectations about future elections differ in kind. Still, for professionals, the body of accepted campaign rules—incomplete, ever-changing, and internally inconsistent though it may be—offers a basket of tricks and tools that can be used to analyze each new political terrain. A broader knowledge of campaign rules means a larger number of strategic options, and tactical creativity can help a political professional find new ways to make the old rules work, or even to discard them entirely, Rogers-style, to come up with a new way of doing business.

Strategic Histories

This book illustrates campaign mode by recounting the strategic histories of five successful congressional candidates. Cases were selected according to the demands of representational balance and, to a lesser extent, research convenience. The authors sought diversity in region, gender, race, and ethnicity, as well as partisan affiliation. Two of the congressional representatives were personally known to one of the authors; operatives for another three were reached via cold calls to political consultants. The final list includes four candidates for the House of Representatives and one for the United States Senate: Representatives Ted Strickland (Democrat, Ohio's Sixth Congressional District), Bob Barr (Republican, Georgia's Seventh Congressional District), Loretta Sanchez (Democrat, California's Forty-Sixth Congressional District), Harold Ford Jr. (Democrat, Tennessee's Ninth Congressional District), and Senator Rick Santorum (Republican, Pennsylvania). By examining the manner in which each legislator found electoral success, this book hopes to illuminate the merger of campaign rules and political terrain, strategic thinking and visceral drive—the essence of campaign mode.

Each candidate's election has a unique story to tell. Some of these electoral contests were among the most-watched battles of the 1990s. Ted Strickland's efforts in rural Ohio were closely followed in the national media, as was Bob Barr's challenge to a powerful, but soft-spoken, Georgia Democrat; and Loretta Sanchez' improbable 1996 victory over a colorful GOP personality, meanwhile, took virtually every California pundit and party leader by surprise, turning Sanchez into an overnight political celebrity. Other electoral victories—those of Tennessee's Harold Ford Jr. and Pennsylvania's Rick Santorum—were never seriously in doubt. Both legislators learned how to use their position in Congress to build support back home, and by that very fact, their victories are typical of the world of congressional elections, where incumbents tend to win handily.

The matter of incumbency highlights an important aspect of campaign mode. A few of the histories recounted in this book (Strickland, Ford Jr., and Santorum) span two or more campaign cycles, encompassing the legislator's tenure between elections.[26] Political scientists have long understood the importance of the inter-election period. In the 1970s, David R. Mayhew sought to show that congressional representatives were "single-minded seekers of reelection" who organized their official activities around that all-important goal.[27] Morris P. Fiorina soon argued that the bureaucratic structure of Capitol Hill—indeed, much of the federal bureaucracy—had been bent to the re-election needs of congressional incumbents.[28] While some scholars, Richard F. Fenno among them, have persuasively argued that legislators are less single-minded than purist versions of the re-election thesis implied,[29] legislators have an undeniable political interest in cultivating voter support even when elections are not imminent.

The point is well stated by Anthony King, whose book, *Running Scared*, is critical of a political system that fosters "an acute awareness among members of Congress of the fact that they endlessly face the possibility of electoral defeat."[30] Writes King:

> Politics and government in the United States are marked by the fact that American elected officials have, in many cases, very short terms of office *and* face the prospect of being defeated in primary elections *and* have to run for office primarily as individuals rather than as standard-bearers of the party *and* have continually to raise large sums of money in order to finance their own election campaigns.[31]

The result, according to King, is a "Darwinian" adaptation of congressional behavior that involves "their roll-call votes, their introduction of bills, their committee assignments, their phone calls, their direct-mail shots, their speeches, their press releases, their sound bites, who they see, how they spend their time, their trips abroad, their trips back home and frequently their private and family lives—to their environment."[32] For the congressional representative who wants to survive, campaign mode has value, not just on the campaign trail, but in congressional office as well.[33]

The pages that follow illustrate campaign mode by way of semi-structured case studies. With respect to political terrain, the presumptively significant features discussed above are analyzed: local political personalities, social demographics, partisan composition, economic conditions, issues and ideologies, the political resources available to candidates, along with other factors that seemed electorally significant in a given race. With respect to campaign rules, the authors drew out (what they believed to be) the most important lesson taught by the election (or series of elections) under examination, and then organized the electoral narrative accordingly. Each chapter carries that rule as its title, and as a group, the stories offer a small sample of the electoral rules that inform political professionals:

- Build Strong Connections with the Electorate (Strickland)
- Hammer at the Opponent's Weak Point (Barr)
- Defy Conventional Wisdom (Sanchez)
- Gain the Center without Losing the Base (Ford Jr.)
- Preempt the Challenge (Santorum)

The argument for case study research of this sort will be elaborated in chapter 2, but the approach can be demonstrated by a brief strategic history that shows the importance of local politics—one that reiterates a campaign rule that most congressional representatives already know: "Pay attention to your district."

A Strategic History

In 1984, the year of Ronald Reagan's presidential landslide, only a handful of Democrats won first-term election to the House of Representatives. Among them was Paul E. Kanjorski from the Eleventh Congressional District of Pennsylvania, elected to represent Wilkes-Barre and the Wyoming Valley region, which lies in the northeastern part of the state.

The seat had long been held by Daniel J. Flood, the inimitable Democratic chairman of the House Appropriations subcommittee on Health, Education, and Welfare. Flood, a dramatic artist by training (he once opened a hearing by calling out, "The curtain is rising; the actors are in their places"[34]) was known for his cape, cane, top hat, sharply-waxed mustache, and his astounding ability to secure federal aid for his constituency. Flood was a true character, but he was also an *effective* character. When tropical storm Agnes swept over northeastern Pennsylvania in 1972, sending the Susquehanna River over its banks and submerging downtown Wilkes-Barre, Flood aggressively used his legislative powers to bring federal relief. "Stand by! This is going to be one Flood against another,"[35] he said. Locals recall that Flood mandated federal procurement of the region's anthracite coal long after the government needed it. Some of Flood's achievements still affect travelers who drive through the region: as the federal government was laying out the thousand-mile route for Interstate-81, the Congressman made sure the highway would run along the outskirts of Wilkes-Barre.

Flood was a textbook example of the pork-barrel congressman. Elected in 1944, he represented the Eleventh for thirty-two years, sitting out for a term after defeats in 1946 and 1952. He left in early 1980 after a federal grand jury indicted him on corruption charges. Without Flood, nothing about the Eleventh Congressional District was certain.

Kanjorski learned of Flood's indictment when a local television reporter called him for comment. Kanjorski had been raised in a Republican home, and he had, in fact, been a congressional page selected by a GOP member of Congress in the 1950s. A few years after Army duty, Kanjorski began legal practice with his father. Richard Nixon's so-called "Southern Strategy"—the president's use of social conservatism to bring the white South firmly into the GOP camp—led Kanjorski to the Democratic side of politics. As an attorney practicing trial and corporate law, he took on a number of pro bono cases, representing military veterans and flood victims trying to get their full benefits. As a worker's compensation referee, he dealt with countless injured employees. As solicitor for the city of Nanticoke, his hometown, Kanjorski counseled public officials on the law and became familiar to the local political community. And as a member of the Board of Directors for the Wyoming Sanitary Authority, Kanjorski pursued allegations of corrupt practices in a nearby municipality, further raising his public profile. A political base was taking shape.

Kanjorski ran in the April 1980 special election, but he did not fare well, coming in fourth. The first post–Flood congressman would be Raphael Musto, a Democrat whose congressional career was cut short when he lost the November general election. Republican newcomer James Nelligan beat Musto, with Kanjorski rising to third place. In 1982, Kanjorski declined to enter the field of candidates (his father was ill) and another Democrat, attorney Frank Harrison, took office. Harrison had linked Nelligan to the economic policies of Reagan, which were judged harshly in that election year, and so Harrison returned the Eleventh to Democratic hands. However, Harrison's tenure in Congress was ill-fated. The district was accustomed to Flood's legislative muscle, but Harrison was surrounded by stories that his office could not even handle constituent mail. Harrison just did not seem to be there for his people. The revolving door was set to spin once more.

With less than two months to go before the primary, Kanjorski filed his candidacy and made a substantial personal loan to his campaign organization. He would use the money to focus on Harrison's seeming lack of attention to the district. The grassroots campaign, with posters, flyers, and all the rest, would be organized by Kanjorski's wife, Nancy, with the help of people Kanjorski had assisted over the years. Political consultant Ed Mitchell would execute the media campaign, including radio and television. Kanjorski and Mitchell determined that they would advance the perception that Harrison had forgotten his constituents.

Kanjorski's "boiling water" commercial crystallized the message that Harrison was out of touch. In January of 1984, Harrison was part of a congressional delegation that left for South America and the Caribbean Basin with the stated purpose of reviewing foreign assistance. It proved to be a fateful trip. While Harrison was gone, giardia contamination placed water supplies around the district under a boil order. Few other problems could have affected modern life more directly, and the water issue was constantly in the news. Mitchell produced a now-legendary television spot that hit Harrison hard. Scenes of a luxurious beach opened the ad, with a voice-over that asked where Harrison had been during the crisis. The next visual showed constituents from a nearby congressional district receiving good clean water, trucked in by the U.S. military—a tribute to the effectiveness of congressmen who had not been in the Caribbean. Then came Mitchell's devastating close: a shot of a teakettle sitting atop a stove, steaming on the burner, with the voice-over intoning, "It's enough to make you boil." It was a dead-bang case for change.

Kanjorski beat Harrison in the primary, 47 to 43 percent. The day after the election, the Associated Press offered a blunt analysis: "Freshman Democratic Rep. Frank Harrison, accused by an opponent of neglecting his constituents, was defeated in his bid for renomination."[36] In the general election, Kanjorski defeated a Republican attorney, 59 to 41 percent, exceeding Democratic presidential candidate Walter Mondale's total by a full 16 percent. When Congressional Quarterly's political reference book, *Politics in America*, was published the next year, it said, "Kanjorski owes his presence in the House largely to an intestinal parasite and a sunny beach."[37]

Professional Understanding

To understand campaign mode, scholars must think like professionals. The authors learned through experience that decision-making responsibility burns away insignificant information. A professional version of political realism sets in. It is not the realism described by political theorist Hans Morganthau, who believed that "politics . . . is governed by objective laws that have their roots in human nature."[38] Rather, it is the more practical realism taught by Genovesi, Shea's one-time mentor, and Paul Kanjorski, for whom Burton once worked, in which the search for strategic plausibility is of the utmost concern. Indeed, the manner in which Kanjorski's story is told shows how a strategic history is recounted from a political professional's point of view.

The fact that Kanjorski's 1984 victory was a product of local concerns is highlighted by reference to the important features of the political terrain—its political personalities, its economic conditions, and a key issue in the life of that part of northeastern Pennsylvania, namely, federal aid. As the story is told here, Flood had eased the region's economic woes by funding infrastructure projects and requiring federal acquisition of local coal. The electorate insisted on federal money; Nelligan and Harrison could not match Flood's record. Although the passage of time lowered the district's unrealistically high demand for federal assistance, the constituency was used to serious attention. Kanjorski, whose past work had demonstrated that he would defend the interests of working families, stood a decent chance against an incumbent who seemed to ignore the district. Hence the strategic lesson: pay attention to your district.

Note that some presumptively significant features simply fell from view. There were no major ideological differences between Kanjorski and Harrison, and while some analysts might find Kanjorski's Polish heritage was meaningful in this largely ethnic district, race was simply not a factor (the district was 99 percent white). In the parsimony of professional understanding, the political terrain was characterized by only those factors that related directly to the pay-attention-to-your-district rule.

This manner of analyzing campaigns and elections differs from aggregate-level research techniques, by which scholars look for empirical regularities in masses of political data. Quantitative methods have shown that Americans tend to vote less than citizens of other Western democracies, but when they *do* vote, they tend (like others) to cast their ballots along party lines, though less and less so at the beginning of the new millennium than a few decades earlier. Empirical research has demonstrated beyond question that elections are highly predictable—so predictable, in fact, that many political scientists tend to discount the statistical significance of political campaigns on electoral outcomes.[39]

Political professionals also appreciate the tight mathematics of electoral success. Statistical work done on behalf of those running for office can be exhaustive. Campaign consultant Dick Morris has written about the "mother of all polls"—a 259-question survey meant to advise President Clinton just before the 1996 State of the Union Address—a survey so detailed that it "had to be divided into five parts, since no one would willingly stay on the phone for the hours it would have taken to answer every question."[40] Unlike "horse race" surveys that show who is ahead and who is behind, campaign polls examine myriad patterns of gender, race, ethnicity, income, geography, ideology, social status, and a variety of other features. Voter groups are ranked by degrees of persuadability, and more finely still, according to the media expense of reaching out to them. The key question: What is the most cost-efficient cluster of people that can be persuaded to vote for the candidate? For political professionals no less than political scientists, electioneering is a numbers game.

But there is an important difference. Where scholars look for tectonic movement in the electorate, candidates work along the fault lines—sometimes operating on little more than an untested confidence that the trends of history can be changed through sheer force of will, and sometimes appearing to succeed against all odds. Political professionals tread on unsettled ground, where leadership can make or break the odds of victory; operatives look for opportunity within—and sometimes despite—the larger trends. Elections seem far less determined on the ground than they do from on high. Too many races have been decided by a mere handful of votes and too many upset victories have drifted into campaign lore. George W. Bush's razor-thin (and in some quarters, still contested) victory over Al Gore will hold this notion in memory for decades to come.

When a congressional candidate has mapped out her strategy over a period of two or three years, spending the last year working full-time on the campaign, devoting double-time in the final three months approaching Election Day, it becomes very difficult to tell her that the numbers just do not add up. For professionals, politics comes to appear as an outgrowth of personality, skill, imagination, artistry, and the sheer ability to work harder and longer than the opponent, doing so with less and less sleep every night.

The pressures of electoral contests affect the way operatives look at political data. A careful social scientist would develop a hypothesis grounded in the literature of his or her field; data will be collected and some reasoned conjecture would be tested accordingly. For the most part, it is not considered scientifically appropriate to pick through the data for interesting facts, the legitimate fear being that data-mining generates post hoc contrivances. A political professional, however, will think nothing of digging through a mountain of data points to find curious patterns, pulling disparate facts into a workable theory of the district. Candidates are not trying to confirm or disconfirm hypotheses; they are gambling on strategies and tactics. As such, a candidate might stare at a map for long periods of time waiting for an answer to present itself. She will meet with the people that the numbers represent, bouncing around ideas, hoping that someone knows what her opponent did to become so strong in the outskirts of some rural county.

Virtually every decision a political professional makes is imbued with notions of terrain and the rules that may or may not operate on it. Electoral strategy as practiced in American politics is virtually incomprehensible without some notion of campaign mode. Even if electoral strategy does not truly decide the outcome of elections, or if political operatives are mistaken about the electoral significance of the particular factors they plug into their analyses, the study of strategic thinking still has much to offer because it drives political decision making. Those who seek to understand the relationship between electioneering and electoral outcomes can benefit from knowing the specifics of strategic thinking.

The specifics can only be found by studying congressional elections in depth. Short case studies—like the Kanjorski story related earlier—tend to highlight a small number of electoral factors. A chief premise of the present research is that electoral strategizing is a thorny task, owing to the variety of campaign rules from which political professionals can choose and the complexity of political terrain on which they operate. Brief accounts risk oversimplification. If only two or three electorally significant features can be discussed in any detail, readers might be left with the impression that the "right" strategy was obvious all along. By examining five congressional elections in depth—the authors have analyzed the documentary record; interviewed candidates, consultants, and key staffers; and related their findings to the broader academic literature—this book hopes to show that the task of finding the right strategy is a difficult project, requiring a comprehensive understanding of the opportunities and constraints specific to each election.

Plan of the Book

The introduction to this book has endeavored to sketch the broad outlines of campaign mode. Political professionals commonly look at states and congressional districts in terms of political personalities, social demographics, partisan composition, economic conditions, issues and ideologies, available political resources, and other electorally relevant features. Knowing the political terrain, and being familiar with some of the basic rules of electoral strategy, candidates and political operatives attempt to figure out which strategies will work and which will not. They look at the immediate situation in terms of the desired result, and "act accordin'." The quality of electoral strategizing is largely demonstrated by the outcome reported on Election Night.

The notion that political strategy can make or break a candidate is a matter of some controversy. Chapter 2 reviews the literature on "campaign effects," much of which holds that campaigns have only a marginal impact on electoral outcomes. It will be argued that this literature tends to understate the power of electoral strategy, partly because the quantitative methods commonly used to study American elections tend to overlook its value. The chapter will conclude by explaining the necessity of case study research in the study of strategy.

The next five chapters examine individual candidates and their electoral contests. Chapter 3 follows Ted Strickland through four electoral cycles, as he built strong connections with his southern Ohio constituency. Chapter 4 examines the 1994 campaign of Georgia's Bob Barr; it shows how Barr successfully deployed an issue-based strategy against a well-liked incumbent. Chapter 5 traces Loretta Sanchez' 1996 ambush of a long-serving incumbent in southern California. Chapter 6 demonstrates the expansion of Harold Ford Jr.'s political support in racially divided Memphis, Tennessee. Chapter 7 shows how Rick Santorum used his position in the Senate to preempt any serious challenge to his incumbency. The book will conclude with chapter 8, which revisits the notion of campaign mode and clarifies some of the conceptual issues raised by the preceding case studies.

While this book deals with campaign rules, it does not comprise a set of timeless precepts; rather, it is a collection of strategic histories—each of them teaching a lesson in the tradition of Robert Rogers. Readers should be aware that this sort of analysis carries with it all the difficulties that confront the task of political strategizing. Judgments must be made about the electorally significant features of each political terrain and the effectiveness of each political strategy; this in an environment where information is limited, often hidden from view, and where the interpretation of past events is its own competitive sport.

Each story bears a variety of morals. In fact, the authors have chosen to draw the lessons of each narrative in two directions. First, there is the strategic rule that professionals might apply to similarly situated candidates—the rule by which each chapter is named. Second, in the conclusion to each chapter, the authors will relate the individual narrative to a broader context—principally, the academic literature on campaigns and elections—showing the extent to which each case study speaks to a segment of current scholarship. The telling of Barr's success in Georgia, for example, seems to deepen the scholarly understanding of southern politics in the 1994 congressional elections, and the story of Sanchez' unexpected victory two years later points up a new dimension of candidate quality. Indeed, because the book is premised on the notion that political terrain is subject to competing interpretations, the reader is invited to ask whether the lessons gleaned by the authors are the only ones that could be learned from a given story.

Individually, each case illustrates a campaign rule as applied to a given electoral contest; as a group, these strategic histories demonstrate the complexity of electoral strategy. Even if the lessons offered here are neither as grand nor as simple as Rogers' overarching principle—"Don't forget nothing"—perhaps they will help sustain a serious discussion about the nature of electoral strategy in congressional contests.

Notes

Source Materials: Unless otherwise noted, newspapers, magazines, and wire services are cited to the *LEXIS-NEXIS* database. Print editions are indicated by the inclusion of page numbers in the text of the citation. Electoral data are drawn from *Politics in America* (CQ Press) and *The Almanac of American Politics* (National Journal Group), along with reports from the Federal Election Commission, the Bureau of the Census, local boards of elections, and secretaries of state. Additional data was retrieved from the Center for Responsive Politics at www .opensecrets.com. Personal and telephone interviews cited herein were conducted by the authors.

1. See U.S. Army, United States Army Infantry School, *Ranger Handbook,* April 2000, Part II. Military historians will note that Rogers' Rules come in two forms: the "Standing Orders" noted here and the twenty-eight maxims listed in Rogers' "Plan of Discipline." (For the latter, see Robert Rogers, *Journals* (New York: Corinth Books, 1961.) For the purposes of this book, "Rogers' Rules" will denote the "Standing Orders."

2. See John R. Cuneo, *Robert Rogers of the Rangers* (New York: Oxford University Press, 1959).

3. Sun Tzu, *The Art of War*, Samuel B. Griffith trans. (London: Oxford University Press, 1963), 84.

4. Niccolò Machiavelli, *The Prince*, Luigi Ricci trans. (Oxford: Oxford University Press, 1935), 48.

5. William L. Riordan, *Plunkitt of Tammany Hall: A Series of Very Plain Talks on Very Practical Politics* (New York: Signet Classics, 1995), 25.

6. Christopher Matthews, *Hardball: How Politics Is Played Told by One Who Knows the Game* (New York: Harper & Row, 1988), 168.

7. David Horowitz, *The Art of Political War and Other Radical Pursuits* (Dallas, Tex.: Spence Publishing, 2000), 11.

8. Tip O'Neill (with Gary Hymel), *All Politics Is Local and Other Rules of the Game* (Holbrook, Mass.: Bob Adams, 1994).

9. Mary Matalin and James Carville (with Peter Knobler), *All's Fair: Love, War, and Running for President* (New York: Random House, 1994), *front matter*.

10. Ibid.

11. See John J. Pitney, Jr., *The Art of Political Warfare* (Norman: University of Oklahoma Press, 2000).

12. Colin L. Powell (with Joseph E. Persico), *My American Journey* (New York: Random House, 1995), 613.

13. Barbara Slavin, "World Will Be Samuel Berger's Stage," *USA Today*, 27 March 1997.

14. Elizabeth Kolbert, "For Albany, Losing a Piece of Its Past," *New York Times*, 13 August 1998.

15. John Caher, "Fellow Lawmakers Recall Genovesi as a True Marauder," *Albany Times Union*, 12 August 1998.

16. Richard E. Neustadt, *Presidential Power and the Modern Presidents: The Politics of Leadership from Roosevelt to Reagan* (New York: Free Press, 1990), 215.

17. Ibid.

18. See Catherine Shaw, *The Campaign Manager*, 2d ed. (Boulder, Colo.: Westview, 2000), 250.

19. Arthur C. Danto, "Gettysburg," *Grand Street* 6 (spring 1987): 98, 109; see also the discussion of conceptual "lenses" in Graham Allison and Philip Zelikow, *Essence of Decision: Explaining the Cuban Missile Crisis*, 2d ed. (New York: Longman, 1999).

20. See Daniel M. Shea and Michael John Burton, *Campaign Craft: The Strategies, Tactics, and Art of Political Campaign Management, Revised and Expanded Edition* (Westport, Conn.: Praeger, 2001).

21. Lawrence Grey, *How to Win a Local Election*, rev. ed. (New York: M. Evans and Co., 1999), 89.

22. Lamar Alexander, *Little Plaid Book* (Nashville, Tenn.: Rutledge Hill Press, 1998), 44.

23. Ibid., 42.

24. Ron Faucheux, "Introduction," *The Road to Victory: The Complete Guide to Winning Political Campaigns—Local, State and Federal* (Dubuque, Iowa: Kendall/Hunt, 1998), ix.

25. Mark Goodin in *A Perfect Candidate*, Icarus Films (1996).

26. See David Brady and Morris Fiorina, "Congress in the Era of the Permanent Campaign," in *The Permanent Campaign and its Future*, eds. Norman J. Ornstein and Thomas E. Mann (Washington, D.C.: AEI Press, 2000).

27. David R. Mayhew, *Congress: The Electoral Connection* (New Haven, Conn.: Yale University Press, 1974), 5.

28. Morris P. Fiorina, *Congress: Keystone of the Washington Establishment* (New Haven, Conn.: Yale University Press, 1977).

29. Richard F. Fenno, Jr., *Senators on the Campaign Trail: The Politics of Representation* (Norman: University of Oklahoma Press, 1996), 12–14.

30. Anthony King, *Running Scared: Why America's Politicians Campaign Too Much and Govern Too Little* (New York: Martin Kessler, 1997) (italics in original).

31. Ibid., 29–30.

32. Ibid., 73–74.

33. The authors thank an anonymous reviewer for noting that the original manuscript left the place of inter-election campaign mode ambiguous.

34. Robert Williams, "PostScript," *Washington Post*, 25 July 1977.

35. William C. Kashatus III, " 'Dapper Dan' Flood: Pennsylvania's Legendary Congressman," *Pennsylvania Heritage* 21 (summer 1995): 4–11.

36. Associated Press, 11 April 1984.

37. Alan Ehrenhalt, ed., *Politics in America: Members of Congress in Washington and at Home, 1986*, (Washington, D.C.: Congressional Quarterly, 1985), 1339.

38. Hans J. Morgenthau and Kenneth W. Thompson, *Politics among Nations: The Struggle for Power and Peace*, 6th ed. (New York: Alfred A. Knopf, 1985), 4.

39. See chapter 2.

40. Dick Morris, *Behind the Oval Office* (New York: Random House, 1999), 93.

Strategic Effects 2

THE VIRTUAL TIE between George W. Bush and Al Gore in the 2000 presidential election has prompted a great deal of speculation about the American electorate. The candidates were separated by only a half million votes nationwide (with Gore voters in the popular majority) and by just one state in the electoral college (where Bush won the only majority that counted). How could the electorate have been so evenly divided? Perhaps the left wing of the Democratic Party and the right wing of the Republican Party had moved an equal number of voters to the political extremes. Perhaps voters had converged at the center of the ideological spectrum, placing roughly the same numbers on both sides of the middle line. Or perhaps the outcome was nothing more than a statistical fluke.

There is another way to understand the outcome. From the political professional's point of view, the sum of electoral conditions, resources, and strategies turned out to be roughly even on both sides. If, as seems to be the case, Bush and Gore were aided by some of the best operatives in the business, then a close race might have been expected. Throughout the 2000 electoral cycle, each side constantly shifted plans and resources to confront changing political conditions. Strategic motion by one campaign organization led the other to change its angle of attack. Like the stalemated trenchlines of World War I, advantages were gained only temporarily, as leads shifted back and forth. Bush was up going into the summer, Gore was ahead after the party conventions, Bush reemerged after the debates, and Gore pulled even in the final week. It was hand-to-hand combat until Election Day, and then it continued after that. Because neither campaign's strategy overwhelmed the other, professional hindsight makes the near tie on Election Day seem almost inevitable.

In September of 2000, however, many political scientists had not expected a draw. Statistical models presented at the annual conference of the American Political Science Association predicted that Gore would easily defeat Bush. Looking at economic conditions and public opinion surveys, political scientists showed a Gore advantage of up to twenty points. A journalist wrote that "the formulas reflect the continuing tendency of political science to seek numerical precision by relating disparate facts."[1] Electoral strategy was not seriously considered.

In fact, during the second half of the twentieth century, political scientists generally disregarded the effects of strategy because "campaign effects"—the net impact of campaign activities on the outcome of an election—were deemed subservient to larger structural factors. That is to say, campaigns did not seem to matter much. Political partisanship and the state of the economy towered over the short-term, small-scale handiwork of candidates and their operatives. There seemed to be little point in exploring electoral strategy because it was assumed that campaign operations had only minimal effects on the final outcome.

The Minimal Effects Argument

The scholarship on American elections has shown beyond a reasonable doubt that political campaigns have only a marginal impact on electoral outcomes. Forces like partisanship, incumbency, and economic conditions commonly explain much of the vote. The effects of a candidate's campaign efforts are comparatively small, as documented by scholarly research that began to emerge in the middle of the twentieth century.

The notion that campaigns are of little consequence is largely rooted in the work of Paul F. Lazarsfeld, Bernard R. Berelson, and Hazel Gaudet, whose 1944 book, *The People's Choice*, found that the vast majority of Erie County, Ohio, voters had chosen their presidential candidate in the 1940 presidential election well before earnest campaigning began.[2] The authors showed how a voter's religion, socioeconomic status, and place of residence consign the voter to a specific station on an "index of political predisposition."[3] For example, "Of all rich Protestant farmers almost 75 [percent] voted Republican, whereas 90 [percent] of the Catholic laborers living in [the city] voted Democratic."[4] The connection between political partisanship and voting behavior allowed scholars to predict how any given social group would vote on Election Day. Campaign flyers, political events, and news stories had scant impact on the final outcome. To the extent that voters converted from one party to another, they were shown to have switched *between* the 1936 and 1940 elections, not *during* the 1940 election season. The campaign season merely accelerated preexisting conversion trends.[5]

The People's Choice encouraged a cynical view toward the electorate, and it did so explicitly:

> There is a familiar adage in American folklore to the effect that a person is only what he thinks he is, an adage which reflects the typi-

cally American notion of unlimited opportunity, the tendency toward self-betterment, etc. Now we find that the reverse of the adage is true: a person thinks, politically, as he is, socially. Social characteristics determine political preference.[6]

Political science thus suggested that voters were not issue-driven. The electorate appeared to be doing little more than ratifying predetermined social forces.

In 1960, *The American Voter*, written by Angus Campbell, Philip E. Converse, Warren E. Miller, and Donald E. Stokes, confirmed the minimal effects argument with a more sophisticated model.[7] *The American Voter* reasoned that people use party cues to interpret campaign messages. The political parties give voters a framework for understanding the issues and arguments presented in campaign appeals and news accounts. While short-term forces sometimes overtake partisanship—Dwight D. Eisenhower was elected president despite the fact that there were more Democrats than Republicans at the time—*The American Voter* concluded that such "deviations" were usually predictable, insofar as most people had made up their minds before the party conventions were gaveled to a close.[8]

The American Voter reinforced the notion that partisan predisposition was the dominant factor in U.S. elections. Partisanship framed the issues and images that would aid the voters' candidate selection. The new model was more flexible than the strict, socially driven voting patterns demonstrated in *The People's Choice*, but partisanship remained the key to electoral prediction.

A decade and a half later, Norman H. Nie, Sidney Verba, and John Petrocik found that the electorate was still guided by partisan attachments.[9] Researching the nature of partisanship and its impact on the electoral process during the 1960s, *The Changing American Voter* suggested the following:

> Party affiliation is transmitted from generation to generation not because parties adjust to suit the issue preferences of social groups but because the attachment to parties is a habitual, somewhat sentimental attachment, not unlike the religious preference that most citizens inherit from their parents. . . . One might defect [from one's party] by voting for a candidate of the other party (as many Democrats switched to vote for Eisenhower), but the voter remained Democrat or Republican and party affiliation remained the key to the voting decision.[10]

In the 1956 Eisenhower re-election, roughly 80 percent of those who identified with one of the two major parties voted for its presidential candidate, and the number of loyalists was even greater in congressional elections.[11]

The Changing American Voter was published at a time when political scientists were reexamining voter motivations. In 1966, V. O. Key's book, *The Responsible Electorate*, suggested that past events operate as a voter guide.[12] If the party in power is doing a good job, then it is rewarded; if it is failing, then it is punished. People are willing to vote against their own party, according to Key's analysis, if the party has not performed well. As such, "The impact of events from the inauguration of an Administration to the onset of the next presidential campaign may affect far more voters than the fireworks of the campaign itself."[13] Voters respond to what they know, assessing their interests and casting their ballots accordingly. Wrote Key, "Voters are not fools."[14] Key believed that voters made real choices, but their choices were not based on political promotion: "As voters mark their ballots they may have in their minds impressions of the last TV political spectacular of the campaign, but, more important, they have in their minds recollections of their experiences of the past four years."[15]

Morris Fiorina built on Key's argument in his 1981 book, *Retrospective Voting in American National Elections*.[16] Fiorina argued that a voter compiles a "running tally of retrospective evaluations," and that this calculation directly shaped a voter's choice on Election Day just as it helped shape a voter's party identification, which then played a powerful role in future voting decisions.[17] Voters have choices in Fiorina's model—partisanship is not purely habitual—but not much room was left for campaign effects.

Fiorina's work drew from David Mayhew's examination of congressional incumbency. In the mid-1970s, Mayhew argued that congressional representatives want to be reelected, so they spend a good deal of time working toward that end—and, as public officials, they have a disproportionate ability to make their views heard and to claim credit for the good things that government does. The "electoral connection" reduces campaign effects relative to the power of incumbency.[18] Likewise, Edward R. Tufte modeled 98 percent of the variance in congressional elections by combining two factors that are largely outside the control of congressional candidates—the state of the economy and presidential popularity.[19] According to Fiorina, the increasing safety of congressional incumbents stemmed largely from the bureaucratic trappings of Congress: the ability to endear one's self to the voting public by way of constituent casework, free mailings, and locally focused grantsmanship, all of which is maintained by a growing establishment of congressional support services, and all of which helps incumbents win re-election.[20]

After Tufte and Mayhew, and into the 1990s, the literature on elections came to include a growing body of predictive models. Michael Lewis-Beck and Tom Rice showed that a handful of variables can be combined to predict the number of seats each party will hold after the election: growth (or decline) in disposable income, presidential popularity, the number of seats exposed, and the length of time the president has been in the White House.[21] Beyond political science, historian Allan Lichtman and journalist Ken DeCell developed a set of questions the two authors call the "Thirteen Keys to the Presidency."[22] According to Lichtman and DeCell, the fate of the incumbent-party presidential candidate can be determined by asking a series of true/false questions (e.g., "The economy is not in recession during the election campaign" and "The incumbent-party candidate is charismatic or a national hero") then checking to see which way the "keys" lean.[23] The forces of political destiny seemed all-powerful.

Campaign lore is rich with victories snatched from the jaws of defeat, but even dramatic swings can be explained by the scholarly literature. It has been suggested that changing "patterns of public support for [Ronald Reagan] can be largely accounted for by short-run fluctuations in prices, income, and unemployment" as opposed to "something special" about Reagan's personal appeal.[24] Others have argued that the ebbs and flows of the political polls are almost meaningless. As noted by James E. Campbell in *The American Campaign*, "[A] significant portion of [polling volatility] reflects merely fleeting changes in national preferences and differences caused by various measurement and sampling errors in the surveys. To no small degree, poll volatility, especially several months before the election, is noise."[25]

Residual Impact

Statistical research demonstrates that elections are highly predictable. At most times and in most races, campaigns do not matter. Still, some elections are too close to call, and a number of outlier cases—candidates who beat the odds—imply that campaigns might sometimes have a powerful effect. As evidence, one can point to a Pennsylvania story that follows Paul Kanjorski's victory by seven years: the events ensuing the April 1991 death of Republican Senator John Heinz. After Heinz died in a plane crash, the Democratic governor appointed a little-known former college administrator, Harris Wofford, to fill Heinz' seat pending a special election in November, setting the stage for one of the most surprising electoral victories of the decade.

Wofford had not been Governor Robert Casey's first choice. In fact, Wofford was well down the list. President of Bryn Mawr College before taking a job in the Governor's cabinet, Wofford had been present at the creation of the Peace Corps and had built a distinguished record of public service, but he had never run for elective office. The Republican candidate was expected to be former Pennsylvania Governor and sitting U.S. attorney general Richard L. Thornburgh. Thornburgh seemed a perfect candidate: experienced, tough, well-spoken, and widely known—everything pundits thought Wofford was *not*. Some observers expected that Thornburgh would enjoy an easy coronation. But Wofford did a few things right. He hired James Carville and Paul Begala to run his campaign, and the pair helped Wofford figure out how to tap into deep-seated fears that Pennsylvania's ailing economy was eroding middle-class security.[26] Message seemed to be everything.

The most celebrated line of the Wofford campaign comes from a television spot. "If criminals have a right to a lawyer," Wofford proclaimed, "I think working Americans should have the right to a doctor."[27] Linking Thornburgh to the economic policies of George H. W. Bush, while painting Thornburgh as an aloof Washington insider, the Wofford campaign sawed away at the attorney general's lead. Candidates once separated by nearly fifty points were getting close. Mary Matalin later wrote of Thornburgh's decline, "Cardinal rule 101 of politics is: *Never let the other side define you.*"[28]

The morning after Election Day: political upset. Wofford had beaten Thornburgh by ten points. President Bush's attorney general had been trounced by an obscure academic—a political amateur who smothered the former Pennsylvania governor under the perceived economic failings of an otherwise popular president. Shockwaves bolted across political Washington. Republicans were reeling in disbelief and Democrats were giving each other high-fives. In the *Washington Post*, columnist David Broder wrote that Wofford's victory contained "important cautionary messages to President Bush."[29] Columnists Jack Germond and Jules Whitcover wrote that "Wofford's success in painting his opponent as [a Washington] insider on the basis of his three years as attorney general, and [Wofford's] advocacy of national health insurance for all Americans, gave the Senate race a national character that can be a blueprint for the Democrats' challenge to Bush next year."[30] Health care reform was boosted high up the Democratic campaign agenda, and Bush, constantly on the defensive, never shook the notion that he failed to understand the insecurities of the American middle-class.

Wofford's triumph was exceptional. The Senator would lose his seat to Congressman Rick Santorum three years later, but Wofford's 1991 victory tends to suggest that political campaigns can influence electoral outcomes.

It is difficult to explain Wofford's victory without reference to campaign strategy. The partisan split in Pennsylvania was roughly even, and as far as the powers of incumbency were concerned, Thornburgh, as a former governor and then a high-profile Bush appointee, had built stronger connections with his Pennsylvania constituency. With respect to Pennsylvania's declining economy, liability might have cut either way. The downturn could have been blamed either on Wofford, an incumbent senator, or on Thornburgh, a cabinet secretary in the incumbent administration. Here one finds the essence of political strategy: recessionary economic conditions came to favor Wofford because the Democratic team found a way to direct public ire at Thornburgh.

A political professional would say Wofford beat Thornburgh by making a fixed social condition work to his advantage.

Campaign Effects and the Research Agenda

Wofford's come-from-behind win turned on the power of his campaign. While the scholarly literature on U.S. elections shows that campaign effects are marginal, there is reason to believe that the dynamics of political campaigns are still important. First, campaign effects seem to have been underappreciated. A close look at long-term, broad-scale electoral factors shows the importance of electoral strategy. Second, significant changes in the electoral environment have intensified the role of strategy in American elections. The new electoral environment tends to reward smart strategic maneuvering.

Without quantitative methods, scholars might not know the degree to which campaign effects are shunted aside by larger forces. "The problem," as Thomas M. Holbrook writes, "is that campaign effects are unlikely to be found by analyzing only ultimate vote decisions or election outcomes."[31] Says Holbrook, "A political campaign must be understood to be a process that generates a product, the election outcome, and . . . one cannot expect to understand the process by analyzing only the product."[32] The use of quantitative research methods has led many political scientists to neglect intervening electoral strategies—leaving researchers subject to Murray Edelman's caution that using the wrong investigative tool "is rather like looking under the lamppost, where the light is good, for the quarter one dropped in a dark section of the street."[33]

Overreliance on readily available numerical data can produce an incomplete picture of the political world. At the practical level, political scientists who wish to study campaign effects by way of quantitative methods face a variety of technical obstacles. Most prominently, the National Election Study (NES)—the cornerstone of election-centered behavioral research—asks very few questions dealing with potential campaign effects. Respondents are asked about the timing of their voting decision; the number of articles or stories they read, saw, or heard about the campaign; and whether or not they were visited by a party/campaign worker during the race, but not much more. The NES does not ask respondents which campaign events they recall or find meaningful; respondents are not asked if there was anything they particularly liked (or disliked) about any of the candidates; and with a survey as broadly based as the NES, it is virtually impossible to relate the messages that candidates were trying to convey with the messages that voters actually received. In other words, many elements of electoral strategy are simply missing from the NES.[34]

New Scholarly Insight

A growing number of scholars have begun to look at campaign effects, and political scientists have been developing a deeper appreciation for the value of electioneering. John W. Kingdon and Marjorie Randon Hershey wrote about campaign strategy in the 1970s, and scholars would later begin to take campaign effects even more seriously.[35] Kingdon and Hershey understood that campaigns are subject to powerful outside forces, but they found some free play in the system.

In his aptly titled 1986 book *Do Campaigns Matter?* Holbrook found that "[e]lection outcomes and voting behavior are easily explained with just a few variables, none of which are related to the campaign," and yet, according to Holbrook, "Campaigns *do* matter."[36] "[P]revailing attitudes toward the economy and the incumbent administration" merely create a predicted "equilibrium"—the outcome that would be expected without campaign effects.[37] Candidate support at the beginning of a race is often *out* of equilibrium, failing to match predictions. A predicted frontrunner who has somehow fallen behind expectations has to "move public opinion toward the expected outcome."[38] Campaign effects are minimal, but they do exist.

Through a comprehensive exploration of vote totals, trial-heat polls, and individual-level survey data, Campbell has shown that the "fundamentals" in presidential elections—such as incumbency and the election-year economy—explain much of presidential vote, but that they do not always determine all of it. Every election sees idiosyncratic campaign effects such as candidate gaffes, strategic blunders, and campaign events gone awry. In postwar presidential elections, Campbell found that the net impact of idiosyncratic campaign effects is roughly 1.5 percent of the popular vote. The finding has profound significance: with seven "near dead heats" within the 1.5 percent margin since 1876 (not including the 2000 Gore-Bush race),[39] Campbell believed that "a significant number of presidential elections have been . . . close enough that some unsystematic factors of particular campaigns may have made the difference to the election's outcome."[40]

Other scholars have found limited campaign effects, as well. Paul R. Abramson, John H. Aldrich, and David W. Rohde note that a great deal of the party defection that occurred in 1996 happened just prior to Election Day—evidence, the authors suspected, that "the choices of some voters were affected by the campaign."[41] According to Stephen Medvic, campaigns that hire a wide range of consultants tend to do better than campaigns that do not—a conclusion that holds particularly true for challengers.[42] Although disentangling campaign effects and contextual forces is a difficult process—the ability to pay for expensive consultant fees, for example, might represent not a cause of victory, but the effect of donor optimism—the power of campaigns has received increasing scholarly attention.

In fact, evidence of campaign effects had been there all along. The presidential contest between Republican Wendell Willkie and Democrat Franklin Delano Roosevelt was never in doubt, of course, but a close reading of *The People's Choice* seems to suggest that campaigns can be powerful. "The whole business of the campaign," it was argued, "accelerated trends that hurt the Democrats.[43] Campaigns, the researchers found, played a critical role in activating partisans, and indeed, a full 8 percent of the voters who had backed the Democratic candidate in 1936 withdrew their support in the midst of the 1940 campaign season.[44]

A Changing Electoral Context

One of the greatest challenges to the party-centered interpretation of voting behavior is the declining partisan affiliation among American voters. Throughout the 1960s, political parties lost ground as the era of patronage politics came to a close and as caucuses and primaries began to deny political parties the power to choose their own candidates. Far fewer voters identified with the two major parties at the end of the twentieth century than at its beginning. In 1972, Broder was moved to declare, "The Party's Over."[45]

The diminished importance of party identification is an important change. The number of Americans who identify with a political party declined from the mid-1950s through the early 1980s. Although the popular impression of the parties improved somewhat over the next two decades, party identification has never returned to the levels that existed when the minimal effects literature first emerged.[46] Martin P. Wattenberg has noted that, in 1992, the pool of nonpartisans had grown larger than the pool of Democrats: "38 percent Independent, 36 percent Democrat, 25 percent Republican, and 1 percent apolitical."[47]

The devaluation of party labels can be seen across the board. The number of voters willing to split their vote between the parties nearly doubled in the last half of the twentieth century. Between 1952 and 1964, about 10 to 15 percent of the electorate cast split-ticket ballots; this number shot up to between 20 and 30 percent in the 1970s and 1980s. By the late 1990s, split-ticket voting seemed to have become a permanent feature of the American landscape.[48] This tendency is especially pronounced among younger voters, suggesting increased volatility in the years ahead.[49] In 1944, the Roper Center asked voters if they were satisfied with the two existing parties, and 78 percent said that they were; by 1994, however, this number had dropped to 40 percent. Over the same half-century, the number of people who said that they would like to see a "strong new party" join the fray jumped from 14 percent to 53 percent.[50] Ross Perot's 19 percent showing in the 1992 presidential race speaks to this change, as does Jesse Ventura's successful 1998 independent gubernatorial bid in Minnesota.

Not only is the American electorate feeling less loyal to the major political parties, it is increasingly apathetic toward electoral politics in general.[51] Some contend that voter indifference provides fertile ground for manipulative political imagery. Dan D. Nimmo's 1970 book, *The Political Persuaders*, argued that candidate image making targets the apathetic voter because "[h]is relatively low involvement makes him the primary target of professional campaigners. They bombard his weak perceptual defenses, attempting to effect modest shifts in perception. . . . [The candidate's] image remains sufficiently ambiguous to permit the gradually politicized voter to 'fill in the gaps' by projecting his own private needs."[52] A competing argument holds that low-interest voters will not pay attention to campaign messages,[53] but Nimmo's argument seems at least plausible.

Changes in the electoral environment highlight the potential importance of campaign strategy. Political campaigns are evolving in ways that make strategy more important at the beginning of the new millennium than they were fifty, or even just twenty years previous. With partisanship declining, media consultants on the rise, and campaign operations seeming to pay more and more attention to the demands of the voting public, strategy may well play a heightened role in deciding electoral outcomes.

In the first part of the twentieth century, party leaders communicated political orders to the masses below through a rigid organizational hierarchy. The only strategy that mattered was the prospective candidate's battle to gain the party's imprimatur. In the new millennium, party power is diminished as campaigns connect with voters more directly. Candidates and their supporters must figure out how best to use television, radio, direct mail, and the Internet. In the early days, the partisan press would offer favorable reports on its party's candidates; in the new millennium, mainstream newspapers pride themselves on their nonpartisanship. A smart congressional campaign now implements a well-planned media strategy with relatively little help from the party apparatus. The heavy lifting of contemporary electioneering has been entrusted to individual candidates, their consultants, and their staffs.

In the middle of the twentieth century, party leaders screened candidates, built coalitions, and ran campaigns. Now, candidates select themselves. Anyone who can raise money, build a strong organization, and generate a plurality of votes on Election Day has a shot at winning the nomination, whether or not the party leadership approves. In fact, state and local party organizations, which once chose nominees at their own discretion, now regularly state their neutrality in primary contests. The parties let the best candidate win and then back the victor in the general election. It is a new theory of party operations: where political parties once mobilized the electorate, the job has been left to a cadre of independent professionals who now strategize the vast majority of high-level political campaigns, and even some races in sparsely populated rural counties.

Given that voter partisanship has long been the principle factor in deciding American elections, any decline in party identification suggests the possibility of an increase in electoral volatility, and, by extension, the persuadability of individual voters. Indeed, some research that appears to back the minimal effects argument can be reinterpreted to support the opposing point of view. Among political partisans, scholars have found *declining* defection rates, even among voters who disagree with their party and their party's candidate.[54] On one hand, this finding demonstrates the continuing power of partisanship to decide American elections, but there is an alternative explanation. The real test of political prowess might be the capacity to keep partisans in line when other forces are pulling them away. At a time when most voters deny that they cast their ballots "straight-ticket," when few Americans view party politics kindly, and when the news media castigate any claim that sounds vaguely partisan, the continuing maintenance of party loyalty might be the ultimate demonstration of campaign effects.

The focus on strategy and tactics has sharpened. Graduate schools of campaign management have appeared, and a professional organization, the American Association of Political Consultants—complete with its own ethical code—binds campaign professionals on both sides of the aisle. And, with ever-increasing specialization, a candidate might hire different firms for general strategy, polling, direct mail, radio and television production, media buying, opposition research, web design, telephone solicitation, database management, accounting, and fundraising. Electioneering has become a sophisticated enterprise. In an electoral environment where millions of dollars are at stake and political professionals are working for the opposition candidate, a campaign that relies on "seat-of-the-pants" strategizing seems doomed to failure.

The main objective of electoral strategy is to reinforce a candidate's base, persuade voters who are not committed either way, and perhaps even win a few converts. All this seems possible because elections have become more volatile than they once were. In the early twentieth century, candidates and voters were almost exclusively white and male. In the new millennium, candidates are still largely white and male, and a disproportionate number of lawyers and business professionals hold office, but the political arena includes candidates of increasing diversity. The same is true of the electorate. Women were granted universal suffrage in 1920. The 1965 Civil Rights Act massively increased the number of African Americans on the voting rolls. In 1971, eighteen-year-olds were granted the right to vote. In the 1990s, both major parties actively courted Spanish-speaking voters. Throughout all this time, migration and immigration, ideological change, shifting wealth, changing issues, and other electorally significant factors have altered the American political landscape, demanding ever-evolving strategies and tactics.

Implications for Research

The emerging picture is well represented in Paul S. Herrnson's book, *Congressional Elections*.[55] People enter the voting booth in possession of only a negligible amount of information about the candidates. Though many recognize the candidates' names—incumbents more than challengers—most voters cast their ballots for incumbents, and most use party cues to guide their decision. When the nation is doing well, the president's party is rewarded; when the nation seems to be on the wrong track, the president's party is punished. In addition, people generally vote just as they did in the previous election, confirming the advantages of incumbency and partisanship. Short of crisis or scandal, elections are fairly predictable: "Situations in which voters have little information . . . usually work to the advantage of incumbents and of candidates who belong to the district's or state's dominant party."[56]

And yet, strategy appears to matter. Political professionals "try to set the campaign agenda so that the issues that politically informed voters use as a basis for casting their ballots are the most attractive issues for their candidate."[57] Incumbents try to render challengers invisible; challengers, who are usually underfunded, work hard to gain media attention; open-seat contests, which remove the incumbency advantage, offer the best chance of an even playing field. Political professionals build coalitions that begin with a corps of loyalists and reach out to uncommitted "swing" voters, and sometimes even members of the other party. Herrnson has found that "[s]ixty-two percent of all House campaigns target demographic, geographic, or occupational groups," and targeting one's own base along with persuadable voters greatly enhances a challenger's odds.[58] By using polls, electoral history, and political judgment, campaign professionals merge candidate imagery and issues to build a general strategy for electoral victory.[59]

If strategy matters, then political scientists must pay attention to it. Herrnjyson has written that "[t]he best way to examine congressional election campaigns is from the inside out, first by examining the motives and goals of those who participate in campaigns, next by analyzing how they mount their campaign efforts, and only after that assessing the campaigns' impact on contributors and voters."[60] A general understanding of contemporary electioneering can be gathered from books like *Campaign Craft*,[61] or Dennis W. Johnson's *No Place for Amateurs*.[62] David Menefee-Libey's *The Triumph of Campaign-Centered Politics* looks inside the machinery of Democratic campaign organizations on Capitol Hill.[63] James A. Thurber and Candice J. Nelson's edited work, *Campaign Warriors*, concentrates on the business of campaign consulting.[64] Robert V. Friedenberg's *Communication Consultants in Political Campaigns* examines media consulting, an important segment of the campaign industry.[65] Finally, Herrnson has published an edited volume, *Playing Hardball*, in which leading scholars discuss strategic issues in congressional campaigns.[66]

Campaign Mode studies the strategic motion of congressional contests. The word "strategy" is derived from military affairs. Political scientist John J. Pitney, in *The Art of Political Warfare*, notes that one military manual has called strategy "the process of interrelating ends and means."[67] This definition, Pitney says, raises three questions: "What goals do we want to achieve? What resources can we use? In light of goals and resources, what is our best course of action?"[68] For political professionals, the end is clear: their candidates must win! Successful strategy requires serious consideration of a "[l]eader's qualities," the "[c]oordination of forces," "[p]erceptions and intentions," "[m]oral resources," and the "lay of the land."[69] Operatives must think about the manner in which each of these factors will play out during the campaign cycle, and they must prioritize electoral targets in order to maximize the tactical impact of campaign expenditures. Electoral strategy typically refers to the art and science of building coalitions—efficiently mobilizing resources in the service of electoral victory.[70]

Research into political strategy necessarily bears a resemblance to that which is based on game theory and rational choice theory, both of which assume that individuals and institutions seek to achieve predetermined goals by efficiently organizing the resources persuadable to them. For example, the two major political parties both play to centrist voters when, as is often true in American politics, the middle ground holds the bulk of available voters.[71] Some political scientists have developed sophisticated mathematical models to explore this political axiom.[72] While game theory and rational choice modeling have been criticized for producing simplistic depictions of political phenomena, there remains an intuitive appeal to the notion that political actors are engaged in a careful effort to maximize the odds of electoral victory.[73]

The difference between formal theorizing and strategic historiography lies in the choice of evidence and approach. Most works of game theory and rational choice theory rely, at bottom, on mathematical models; the methods used for this book, however, are inspired by political memoranda we drafted as political professionals, as well as Richard F. Fenno's firsthand studies of congressional representation.

Fenno's 1978 classic, *Home Style*, introduced "soak and poke" research techniques to political science.[74] In Fenno's highly personalized investigative mode, a researcher "watches, listens to, and talks to one congressman morning, noon, and night for several days" in pursuit of "open-minded exposure to events in the milieu and to the perspectives of those with whom they interact."[75] Fenno has acknowledged that this sort of research is subject to criticism—"too subjective, too episodic, not enough cases, too few angles of vision, unsystematic collection of evidence, insufficiently susceptible to testing."[76] Still, Fenno notes that "there is something to be gained by occasionally unpacking our analytical categories and our measures to take a firsthand look at the real live human beings" who run for Congress.[77]

Campaign Mode attends to congressional candidates, but its sights are trained less on candidate style and more on election strategy; it is a search for strategy in the wild. Electoral events are examined in light of their seeming strategic value; conventional rules of electioneering are explored in order to find the strategic thinking held in the details of political events. Like Fenno's work, the findings of this research were derived partly from conversations with political professionals, but a larger organism is under examination here: the candidate's electoral strategy—how it came to life, what motivated key decisions, and how various tactics played out over the course of one or more electoral cycles. *Campaign Mode* tracks five members of the United States Congress—four who ran for the House of Representatives and one who ran for the Senate—documenting the electoral strategies deployed by each candidate's team in the search for electoral victory. (A challenger who lost a bid for the House is briefly discussed in the concluding chapter.)

Participant interviews are important to this sort of research, but not sufficient. Tactical information is generally held close to the vest and is rarely made available to academic researchers. Although many professionals are surprisingly open about their tactical blunders, and although seasoned investigators can develop what Fenno calls a "low gullibility quotient,"[78] scholars who rely too heavily on nonpublic data effectively insulate their work from peer critique.

Campaign Mode looks at documentary evidence, including demographic, economic, governmental, electoral, and media-generated information, and in one case, original survey data. All of the districts have been visited by at least one of the two authors and at least one major strategist was interviewed for each race. Some candidates were accompanied in their travels, while some campaign consultants were interviewed at length. Election returns were examined, district maps were scrutinized, and thousands of newspaper articles were studied—everything from announcements of upcoming town meetings to analyses of electoral strategy. One congressional representative was interviewed over a few games of pool. In each case, we, as authors, sought to become leading experts on the congressional district (or state), the major political actors in the election (or elections), and the means by which each team sought to gain electoral success (or to preempt a serious electoral challenge altogether).

While this research had a preplanned foundation—for instance, case selection demanded an emphasis on geographic, ideological, and partisan diversity—the methods used to study each electoral contest evolved through the course of the investigation. A variety of research techniques was necessary principally because (1) some early assumptions turned out to be wrong, but more importantly, (2) the elections often demanded the use of specialized research tools.

With respect to the first reason, an example is in order. Research on Harold Ford Jr. of Memphis, Tennessee, was originally designed to show the power of the congressman's personal style. The popular media had suggested that the source of Ford's electoral power was to be found in his charisma—and without doubt, much of Ford's success is due to his intense personal character—but close scrutiny of Memphis and its political history showed that there were far more interesting forces at work. Ford is an African American in a southern city that remains deeply polarized by race. As chapter 6 explains, the most significant strategic factors in Ford's rise to overwhelming popularity lie in his deeply held policy convictions and his adroit manner of communicating a middle-of-the-road political philosophy across racial lines. Sticking to the original research plan would have produced a lopsided account of Ford's political accomplishments. New findings demanded new sources of information.

With respect to the second point, research on each candidate was tailored to its political context. There is little point in focusing on media strategy when the real story is grassroots organizing, as was the case in Loretta Sanchez' victory in Orange County, California. If issues are critical, as they were in Bob Barr's Georgia campaign, survey research offers a powerful way to understand what made the district tick. In Ohio, Ted Strickland's success was a product of his personal connection to the district, so this aspect of his political life was studied in depth. In the case of Rick Santorum, Harris Wofford's successor in Pennsylvania, the story is less the 2000 campaign than the years leading up to it, during which the Senator built a reputation for political prowess that prevented his opponent from gaining a foothold in the electorate; much of the focus is therefore directed at the months and years preceding the election season.

We hope that our research flexibility has increased the value of these case studies. On one hand, the investigations lack the benefit of uniform structure; on the other hand, the researchers gained new insights along the way. Navigational corrections are common in exploratory research. Fenno has written, "The idea of home style had never occurred to me until I had taken quite a few trips around the country."[79] In much the same way, the present research originated with the notion that campaign mode was an elusive concept that would not be readily susceptible to clear-cut definition. During the investigation, however, it became apparent that many aspects of strategic thinking *can* be defined. The realization is remarkable, given that we had more than a dozen years of political experience between us. Only after several contests were examined did a well-defined understanding of campaign mode reveal itself. (Some backtracking on prior research was required.) Thus, we found midway through our analysis that campaign mode has a number of distinct, describable features.

We hope that further research into campaign mode will document the concept by way of formal and quantitative methods. Qualitative research often generates hypotheses for quantitative analysis and it can discern some of the goals and resources central to candidates' rational choices. At the same time, a more structured assay of the subject at this early stage might not have been profitable—the trees are not yet known well enough to start appraising the whole forest—and there are features of electoral strategy that make aggregate-level analysis less attractive than a set of individual-level case studies.

First, sequence is an important part of electoral strategy, and case studies are highly sensitive to the time factor in electoral strategy.[80] Campaign spending shows the importance of timing. A basic rule of thumb holds that candidates must buy radio and television ad slots for the last days of the election before they buy time early in the cycle, lest the opposition drive everyone else off the air in the final hours of the election. For Strickland's 1998 re-election, media expenditures were followed week-by-week. It was found that the opponent's campaign organization failed to purchase its late-cycle ads in a timely manner, leading to a disorderly flurry in the two months preceding the election. The challenger's ads were placed, pulled, and repositioned across the district. The incumbent, meanwhile, was able to hone his message, narrowly tailoring radio ads for maximum effect. Although both sides spent a lot of money on media advertising, it was found that the incumbent received a better return on his investment because his campaign paid better attention to political timing.

Second, case analyses comprehend idiosyncratic strategies and tactics. Any search for "the norm" will be frustrated by the wide variety of strategic options that political operatives have at their disposal. Indeed, strategy thrives on ingenuity. Barr was able to defeat an incumbent by playing to the incumbent's strengths, using a jujitsu maneuver that left his opponent defenseless. Sanchez' entire campaign was based on clever violations of accepted rules. Textbooks can be written about strategy and tactics, but the dynamism of political elections calls for an understanding of the process through which electoral strategy unfolds.

Third, strategic historiography can find tactical nuances that are deliberately hidden from view. The Sanchez campaign employed a strategy based on stealth. Partly out of poverty and partly out of strategy, the campaign maintained a low profile. Doing so lulled the incumbent into complacency. When Sanchez emerged from the shadows with a powerful, well-funded campaign, it was too late for the incumbent congressman to respond. Political campaigns are proprietary operations by necessity, in part because strategic operation demands that secrets be kept from the opposition. If researchers draw the range of acceptable data too narrowly, the secrets will be kept from political scientists as well. *Campaign Mode* aims to complement aggregate-level analysis by looking in-depth at the manner in which electoral strategies unfold.

Strategic Effects

Electioneering is difficult work. Building an alliance with one group of supporters often requires alienating another; rich lodes of swing voters sometimes go unmined because the neighborhoods in which they reside lie beyond the reach of local media; sticking to an effective message often means downplaying equally important policy issues; and holding all the organizational, political, financial, and human resources together over the course of an electoral contest—making sure that political messages are consistent and campaign operations are within budget—is a daunting task at which more fail than succeed.

Campaign Mode attends to the electoral effects of strategic motion. It tries to assess the manner in which political professionals maximize their impact on a given electoral district, designing strategies and tactics to make the most of their own opportunities while minimizing the options available to the opposition. In Wofford's 1991 election, for example, strategy was decisive. Pennsylvania's economy was in trouble and Wofford crystallized middle-class discontent by directing voter fury at Thornburgh. Strategic failure by Wofford's team would have spelled defeat. *Campaign Mode* assumes the professional point of view: strategy can make a difference in American elections.

Strategic decisions are not confined to the campaign season proper. As Mayhew and Fiorina understood, congressional representatives do not draw a clean line between time in office and time on the campaign trail. The whole idea of retrospective voting is premised on the notion that elections depend on pre-campaign events. In this sense, "campaign effects" might be a misnomer, insofar as electoral contests are rarely hemmed in by the campaign season. Incumbents and challengers do not confine their strategic activities to the campaign period (though the pressures may be somewhat less intense in the off-season). Fenno's *Home Style*, for example, follows congressional representatives around their districts as they do their best to mobilize and maintain their electoral constituencies during their term of office. Challengers begin organizing their efforts well before the campaign season begins. Strategic effects should therefore be viewed as a long-term continuum rather than a short-term phenomenon—and more importantly, putatively structural factors like national economic conditions are, in a sense, the result of innumerable strategic decisions.

To speak of strategic choice is not to say that decision making always proceeds from a conscious evaluation of feasible options; sometimes it just follows from the logic of the political world. The "fundamental political perception" that Fenno discovered among congressional representatives had a profoundly strategic quality: "As they move about 'the district,' House members continually distinguish between those people who vote for them and those who do not: 'I do well here'; 'I run poorly here'; 'This group supports me'; 'This group does not.' "[81] If voters are not fools, then politicians must think strategically. Staffers, consultants, and campaign operatives—whose ideals and livelihoods rest partly on the success of the congressional representative—must also view the world from a strategic point of view. In campaign mode, political professionals base their decisions on an understanding of political terrain that is focused on electorally significant factors, so it is reasonable to assume that day-to-day decisions would take on a strategic cast—everything from an incumbent's approach to the national economy to the manner in which a campaign consultant describes an incumbent's legislative vote.

As such, strategic effects are the net impact of decisions made by political professionals on the outcome of an election. It matters little whether any given strategic choice was raised to a conscious decision point or was simply the product of a strategic perception of the electoral environment. Indeed, in campaign mode, strategic decisions are made almost without thinking: the "right thing to do" seems obvious. Moreover, a good deal of strategic maneuvering occurs before any attention is paid to the campaign, as candidates seek to position themselves for a congressional bid. They build a solid list of contacts, appraise their fundraising abilities, nuance their language on controversial subjects, and turn down speaking engagements that would not be helpful in the long run.

Strategic effects are best sought at the individual rather than the aggregate level of analysis, looking at the options that were presented to any given campaign organization, its strategic actions, and, of course, the result—taking into account expectations offered by aggregate-level calculations. In aggregate-level research, the behavior of any individual electoral effort tends to become lost in the sheer number of cases examined, and the specific identity of winners and losers has little or no bearing on research findings. As a result, the effects of any single strategic maneuver disappear from view, leaving only the clean outlines of a seemingly predetermined electoral cycle. Strategic investigation, however, leads to an altogether different perspective, one that highlights the contingent nature of American politics. Particularly when the focus is held on marginal races, electoral outcomes seem far from determined by structural factors.

Strategic analysis does not always render easy answers, but strategy remains important. The Bush-Gore contest led to electoral postmortems that tried to pinpoint Gore's strategic failure. Was the problem Gore's decision not to use President Clinton in his campaign, or the inherent inability of a vice president to distance himself from his president? Did a centrist administration fail to rally the base, or did a populist approach lose the center? In Florida, where ballot recounts became dramatic ordeals, controversy over the outcome will likely continue for generations. Second-guessing arises after any defeat, particularly close calls. Indeed, the elections of 2000 split the Senate in half. So close was the election in Washington State that the results were not known until weeks after the polls closed; Democrat Maria Cantwell was declared the winner over Republican Slade Gorton by just over two thousand votes. The even split later gave Senator Jim Jeffords of Vermont the power to hand control of the Senate over to the Democratic Party by declaring himself an Independent. Minor tactical shifts in Washington or Florida might have changed the course of history.

An old rhyme holds that, for want of a nail, a shoe was lost, and so the horse, the rider, the message, the battle, and finally the war were lost as well, "all for the want of a nail." The 2000 election surely left operatives in the Gore and Gorton campaigns with an unshakable certainty that tactical and strategic decisions can make all the difference in the world. It is a notion that grips political operatives in the heat of battle, one that is brought into view when researchers study electoral politics from a strategic perspective.

The following chapters of this book relate five strategic histories. Its point is not to prove conclusively that strategy has an effect on congressional elections—though we will try to show supporting evidence—but rather to illustrate the manner in which electoral contests are seen from the professional's point of view. It is a perspective that highlights the contingent, ever-evolving, frequently surprising character of American elections, viewed from the ground level. In the professional mind, structural factors frame the race, but they do not decide it. In campaign mode, a candidate's electoral fortunes are largely influenced by the rules of engagement that strategists bring to bear on the political terrain.

Notes

1. Adam Clymer, "And the Winner Is Gore, If They Got the Math Right," *New York Times*, 4 September 2000.
2. Paul F. Lazarsfeld, Bernard Berelson, and Hazel Gaudet, *The People's*

Choice: How the Voter Makes up His Mind in a Presidential Campaign (New York: Columbia University Press, 1944).

3. Ibid., 16–27.

4. Ibid., 26.

5. Ibid., 102.

6. Ibid., 27.

7. Angus Campbell, Philip E. Converse, Warren E. Miller, and Donald E. Stokes, *The American Voter* (New York: John Wiley & Sons, 1960).

8. Ibid., 78–80.

9. Norman H. Nie, Sidney Verba, and John R. Petrocik, *The Changing American Voter*, (Cambridge, Mass.: Harvard University Press, 1976).

10. Ibid., 29.

11. Ibid., 30.

12. V.O. Key, Jr., *The Responsible Electorate: Rationality in Presidential Voting*, 1936–1960 (Cambridge, Mass.: Belknap, 1966).

13. Ibid., 9–10.

14. Ibid., 7.

15. Ibid., 9.

16. Morris P. Fiorina, *Retrospective Voting in American National Elections* (New Haven, Conn.: Yale University Press, 1981).

17. Ibid., 106–29.

18. David R. Mayhew, *Congress: The Electoral Connection* (New Haven, Conn.: Yale University Press, 1974); David R. Mayhew, "Congressional Elections: The Case of the Vanishing Marginals," *Polity* 6 (1974): 295–317.

19. Edward R. Tufte, "Determinants of Outcomes of Midterm Congressional Elections," *American Political Science Review* 69 (1975): 812–26.

20. Morris P. Fiorina, *Congress: Keystone of the Washington Establishment* (New Haven, Conn.: Yale University Press, 1977).

21. Michael S. Lewis-Beck and Tom W. Rice, *Forecasting Elections* (Washington, D.C.: Congressional Quarterly, 1992), 57–75.

22. Allan J. Lichtman and Ken DeCell, *The Thirteen Keys to the Presidency* (New York: Madison Books, 1990).

23. Ibid., 7.

24. D. Roderick Kiewiet and Douglas Rivers, "The Economic Basis of Reagan's Appeal," in *The New Directions in American Politics*, eds. John E. Chubb and Paul E. Peterson (Washington, D.C.: Brookings Institution, 1985), 87–88.

25. James E. Campbell, *The American Campaign: U.S. Presidential Campaigns and the National Vote* (College Station: Texas A&M, 2000), 56.

26. Dale Russakoff, "The Bulldozer behind Wofford's Landslide; Consultant Carville Showed Candidate How to Marshal Middle-Class Discontent," *Washington Post*, 7 November 1991.

27. Dale Russakoff, " 'The Right to See a Doctor When You're Sick'; Wof-

ford's Appeal for Access to Medical Care Creates 'Wildfire' in Senate Race in Pennsylvania," *Washington Post*, 19 November 1991.

28. Mary Matalin and James Carville, with Peter Knobler, *All's Fair: Love, War, and Running for President* (New York: Random House, 1994), 72 (emphasis in original).

29. David S. Broder, "Cautionary Messages," *Washington Post*, 7 November 1991.

30. Jack Germond and Jules Witcover, "Wofford's Victory Boosts Democratic Hopes," *Atlanta Constitution*, 8 November 1991.

31. Thomas M. Holbrook, *Do Campaigns Matter?* (Thousand Oaks, Calif.: Sage, 1996), 153.

32. Ibid.

33. Murray Edelman, *Constructing the Political Spectacle* (Chicago: University of Chicago, 1988), 5.

34. A more technical problem with the NES data is respondent turnover. The principle means for assessing campaign effects has been a comparison of time-series data, called "trial-heat data." Survey results from one stage of the campaign are compared with results at different points in the campaign. Shifts in support might suggest campaign effects. But because a new group of voters is interviewed for each survey, precise measures of these changes are difficult—leading scholars rely upon aggregate-level explanations. Panel studies, which interview the same voters at different points in the campaign, allow for greater precision with respect to strategic effects, but they are difficult and expensive to conduct, so they are also rare.

35. John W. Kingdon, *Candidates for Office: Beliefs and Strategies* (New York: Random House, 1968); Marjorie Randon Hershey, *The Making of Campaign Strategy* (Lexington, Mass.: D.C. Heath, 1974).

36. Holbrook, *Do Campaigns Matter?* 43, 158, emphasis added.

37. Ibid., 156–57.

38. Ibid., 157.

39. Campbell, *The American Campaign*, 76, 165.

40. Ibid., 182.

41. Paul R. Abramson, John H. Aldrich, and David W. Rohde, *Change and Continuity in the 1996 and 1998 Elections* (Washington, D.C.: Congressional Quarterly, 1999), 39. See accompanying table on page 40.

42. Stephen K. Medvic, "Professionalization in Congressional Campaigns," in *Campaign Warriors: The Role of Political Consultants in Elections*, eds. James A. Thurber and Candice J. Nelson (Washington, D.C.: Brookings Institution, 2000), 104.

43. Ibid.

44. Lazarsfeld, Berelson, Gaudet, *The People's Choice*, 102.

45. David S. Broder, *The Party's Over: The Failure of Politics in America* (New York: Harper & Row, 1972).

46. See Martin P. Wattenberg, *The Decline of American Political Parties, 1952–1996* (Cambridge, Mass.: Harvard University, 1998), 174. But see also Larry M. Bartels, "Partisanship and Voting Behavior, 1952–1996," *American Journal of Political Science*, 44 (2000): 35–50.

47. Wattenberg, *The Decline of American Political Parties*, 173.

48. John Kenneth White and Daniel M. Shea, *New Party Politics: From Jefferson and Hamilton to the Information Age* (Boston: Bedford/St. Martin's, 2000), 157–60.

49. Ibid., 159.

50. Christian Collet, "Third Parties and the Two-Party System," Public Opinion Quarterly 60 (1996): 431–49.

51. Since 1952, the NES has asked respondents about their interest in the "current campaign." That year, some 37 percent noted that they were "very interested," a level that was maintained, more or less, until the early 1970s. It then dropped to about 30 percent for the rest of the 1970s and 1980s, and by the 1990s it had shrunk to about 25 percent.

52. Dan Nimmo, *The Political Persuaders* (Englewood Cliffs, N.J.: Prentice Hall, 1970), 193.

53. See Campbell's discussion of the "minimal effects conundrum," in *The American Campaign*, 10–12.

54. David G. Lawrence, "On the Resurgence of Party Identification in the 1990s," in *American Political Parties: Decline or Resurgence?* eds. Jeffrey E. Cohen, Richard Fleisher, and Paul Kantor (Washington, D.C.: Congressional Quarterly, 2001).

55. Paul S. Herrnson, *Congressional Elections: Campaigning at Home and in Washington*, 3rd ed. (Washington, D.C.: Congressional Quarterly, 2000).

56. Ibid., 184.

57. Ibid., 185.

58. Ibid., 190, 232, 234.

59. Ibid., 225–48.

60. Paul S. Herrnson, *Playing Handball: Campaigning for the U.S. Congress* (Upper Saddle River, N.J.: Prentice Hall, 2001), vii.

61. Daniel M. Shea and Michael John Burton, *Campaign Craft: The Strategies, Tactics, and Art of Political Campaign Management*, rev. and exp. ed. (Westport, Conn.: Praeger, 2001).

62. Dennis W. Johnson, *No Place for Amateurs: How Political Consultants are Reshaping American Democracy* (New York: Routledge, 2001).

63. David Menefee-Libey, *The Triumph of Campaign-Centered Politics* (New York: Chatham House, 2000).

64. James A. Thurber and Candice J. Nelson, eds., *Campaign Warriors: The Role of Political Consultants in Elections* (Washington, D.C.: Brookings Institution, 2000).

65. Robert V. Friedenberg, Communication Consultants in Political Campaigns: Ballot Box Warriors (Westport, Conn.: Praeger, 1997).

66. Paul S. Herrnson.

67. John J. Pitney, Jr., *The Art of Political Warfare* (Norman: University of Oklahoma Press, 2000), 21, citing U.S. Marine Corps, "Strategy," Marine Corps Doctrine Publication 1–1, 1997.

68. Ibid, 22.

69. Ibid., 26–27.

70. In contrast to strategy, "tactics" are the maneuvers employed to implement strategy. Thus, a general strategic plan will have numerous tactical elements, each one aimed at turning strategic vision into hard reality. Although strategy and tactics are conceptually distinct, the line is easily blurred. At the highest levels of the Wofford organization, for example, the strategic plan called for the use of economic issues against Thornburgh; one implementing tactic was the production of television advertisements like the health care commercial. Among those who dealt with campaign communications, however, the ad campaign was a strategy to connect the candidate with middle-class Pennsylvanians, whereas the implementing tactics included an effort to buy ad time on television programs that would reach these voters. Strategy and tactics are thus distinguished by the level of one's perspective: strategy is developed from above and tactics are applied down below.

71. Anthony Downs, *An Economic Theory of Democracy* (New York: Harper & Row, 1957).

72. See Ken Kollman, John H. Miller, and Scott E. Page, "Political Parties and Electoral Landscapes," *British Journal of Political Science*, 28 (1998): 139–58.

73. See Donald P. Green and Ian Shapiro, *Pathologies of Rational Choice Theory: A Critique of Applications in Political Science* (New Haven, Conn.: Yale University Press, 1994); see also Jeffrey Friedman, ed., *The Rational Choice Controversy: Economic Models of Politics Reconsidered* (New Haven, Conn.: Yale University Press, 1996).

74. Richard F. Fenno, Jr., *Home Style: House Members in Their Districts* (Glenview, Ill.: Scott Foresman, 1978).

75. Ibid., 249–50.

76. Richard F. Fenno, Jr., *Senators on the Campaign Trail: The Politics of Representation* (Norman: University of Oklahoma Press, 1996), 8.

77. Ibid., 8–9.

78. Ibid., 13.

79. Fenno, *Home Style*, 250.

80. See Richard F. Fenno, Jr., "Observation, Context, and Sequence in the Study of Politics," *American Political Science Review* 80 (March 1986): 3–15.

81. Fenno, *Home Style*, 8.

Build Strong Connections with the Electorate   3

TED STRICKLAND
D-OHIO
SIXTH CONGRESSIONAL DISTRICT

O N THE NIGHT OF August 5, 1993, Congressman Ted Strickland returned to his Capitol Hill office, having just cast a historic vote. At issue was President Clinton's comprehensive economic package. The Omnibus Budget Reconciliation Act was a Democratic effort to shift government spending away from the priorities of Republican presidents Ronald Reagan and George H. W. Bush, and toward a budgetary agenda more suited to the new Clinton administration. Spending was cut and taxes were increased in an effort to reduce the federal deficit. Grave uncertainties surrounded the bill's prospects, however. Republicans were unified in opposition and Democratic support was wavering. Strickland's vote was not in doubt—he was already committed to passage—but the question for Strickland was whether support for the president's bill would unravel the congressman's ties with his southern Ohio constituency.

The legislative debate was portrayed as a political death struggle. For more than a decade, Washington had been embroiled in the politics of deficit spending. Ever since Reagan's first budget was enacted, the federal deficit had been running in the hundreds of billions of dollars. In 1990, Bush broke his famous presidential campaign pledge—"Read my lips: no new taxes"—to staunch the ever-increasing debt load. In 1992, Ross Perot called the federal deficit "a crazy aunt you try to hide in the basement." Clinton, for his part, issued a campaign promise to cut the deficit in half over a period of four years. Clinton's pledge would come to the House of Representatives in the form of a five-year economic plan—a complicated mix of spending cuts, loophole closures, user fees, and tax increases. Just seven months into Strickland's first term and Clinton's new presidency, Congress was voting on a bill that would reverse a Bush-era tax-cut for upper-income families and add about four cents to a gallon of gas.

With many old-bull Democrats voting against their president, the evening's drama focused on a handful of freshman legislators. When the legislation passed 218 to 216, with every Republican voting against it, the evening's political significance was unmistakable: every Democrat who voted for the bill could be said to have cast the deciding vote for "the largest tax increase in history." Strickland spent hours that night discussing the vote with constituents who phoned his Washington office. One woman was desperately concerned that her income taxes would go up. Strickland patiently explained that, although everyone would see an increase in the price of gasoline, only those who earned more than $100,000 a year would see their income taxes go up. It was the first test of Strickland's post-vote connections with the Sixth Congressional District of Ohio.

The Candidate

Ted Strickland's staff was not surprised to see their boss spending so much time with a single caller. In the 1970s, with a Master of Divinity in hand, Strickland went on to earn a doctorate in counseling psychology from the University of Kentucky. His official biography shows service "as a minister, a psychologist, and a college professor," noting that the congressman was "a director of a Methodist children's home, an assistant professor of psychology at Shawnee State University, and a consulting psychologist at the Southern Ohio Correctional Facility."

Strickland sometimes says he aspires to be a "Roosevelt Democrat." Born in Lucasville, Ohio, Strickland's political base is in the nearby city of Portsmouth, a small industrial town along the Ohio River. With an easygoing, friendly style, he greets constituents by calling out "Hey, brother," or simply, "Friend!" It is an air of thoughtful self-possession, utterly unpretentious. Asked a policy question, he will pause before answering, refraining from glib, canned answers. At the podium, Strickland exudes confidence in his commitments. From his personal manner as much as anything else, Strickland has gained a following of dedicated foot soldiers who would, as a political operative might put it, "lie on the tracks" for him. It is a personality that fits his constituency. Not flashy, not highbrow—Strickland conveys a sense of warmth and sincerity, and a sense of mission.

The District

Strickland's southern Ohio congressional district—drastically reshaped in 2002—was, in the 1990s, largely defined by Appalachian foothills. It held less in common with Cleveland and Toledo than it did with Huntington, West Virginia, on the other side of the Ohio River. The district ran along the banks of the Ohio, absorbing some of the state's southern interior, and then lifted awkwardly toward the suburbs northeast of Cincinnati. The region's largest city is Portsmouth, with a population of 24,000. Rolling wooded hills surround aging towns and villages. A skein of two-lane highways links diners, gun shops, strip mines, cornfields, and mobile homes. This is old Appalachia, with a Scots-Irish "country accent." The district was 97 percent white and generally conservative on social issues. Tourists from the northern part of the state might be surprised to see an occasional rebel flag tattoo. There is irony here: southern Ohio was well-traveled by the Underground Railroad, and it was the scene of a decisive Union victory against a Confederate raid in 1863. Still, southern Ohio is a slice of Dixie in this Great Lakes.

The Sixth Congressional District encompassed a troubled region. The economic staples of the area are energy, building materials and petrochemicals, some manufacturing, institutions of higher education such as Ohio University and Shawnee State, and a uranium enrichment plant in the middle of the district (a major regional employer for the duration of the Cold War)— but there is little economic growth. Sparsely populated Vinton County has unemployment in the 10 percent range—twice the state average—with almost 20 percent of families living below the poverty level. The county's secondary school dropout rates, like many other counties in the district, are painfully high. Few graduates attend college. Although two of the district's counties draw relative wealth from Cincinnati and Dayton, southern Ohio is the poorest region in the state, and as such, it had long relied upon the economic assistance provided by GOP congressmen.

Strickland's 1992 victory had been launched by a battle between the two Republicans who represented southern Ohio. After the 1990 Census, the state legislature merged the districts of Bob McEwen, who represented south*western* Ohio, and Clarence Miller, who represented south*eastern* Ohio. The brutal primary race between the two long-time incumbents pitted Miller's supporters from the eastern side of the district against McEwen's supporters from the western side. Lacking substantive disagreement, the political battle focused on the "House Bank" scandal.

In one of the many convoluted embarrassments to hit Congress in the 1990s, hundreds of congressional representatives were found to have "bounced" checks at the House Bank. The "bank" was not really a bank (since it operated more like a shared checking account) and some members had no idea that their accounts were being mismanaged (since many so-called "overdrafts" arose from shoddy internal bookkeeping); nevertheless, the idea that congressional representatives were allowed to cut rubber checks at a financial institution contrived for their own personal benefit was anathema to many voters. Miller, who had no bounced checks to his name, started ruminating about the seriousness of McEwen's overdrafts: "If it's big numbers," Miller said, "it could be a very big issue."[1] When McEwen admitted to 166 bad checks, Republicans in southern Ohio had to choose sides in a primary battle that pitted one GOP congressman against another.

McEwen survived Miller's personal attacks, but the congressman's narrow, 286 vote win—the product of recounts and legal challenges—left McEwen with just four months to unify the new district's Republican base against their Democratic opposition. Strickland, who had breezed through the Democratic primary, simply adopted Miller's campaign message: he slammed McEwen for his overdrafts even after the congressman was exonerated by the Justice Department. ("There ought to be a higher standard than illegality for a congressman," Strickland claimed.[2]) McEwen, burdened by his 166 overdrafts, unable to garner a strong endorsement from Miller, and having difficulty converting Miller's supporters to his own cause, was pushed on the defensive. Strickland won by only a few thousand votes—122,720 to 119,252—but the slim 51 to 49 percent margin was enough to make Strickland one of the 110 new Members of Congress elected that November.

Strickland's 1992 victory was more a referendum on the incumbent than a vote of confidence in the challenger. Strickland's campaign exploited key weaknesses in McEwen, concentrating the public's anti-incumbent mood on the incumbent's overdrafts and congressional privileges. The unfortunate result of negative campaigning, however, was that Strickland had little opportunity to introduce himself to the electorate. He had talked about his vision for the future, of course, but those who followed the race mostly saw a confrontation between an insider (McEwen) and an outsider (Strickland). The new congressman's beliefs were deeply held, but the Sixth Congressional District, which had been represented by Republican congressmen for decades, would soon find itself uncomfortable with Democratic talk of increased taxes and abortion rights, not to mention the new Clinton administration's "don't-ask-don't-tell" policy toward gays and lesbians in the military.

Defeat

Weaving a host of political connections—relationships that will last from one election to the next—demands time and attention. In Strickland's case, the mission would focus on southern Ohio employment. For Jackson County, Strickland's first bill was an effort to ease restrictions on growing businesses, like a sizable local employer that used Industrial Development Bonds. Strickland fought repeated threats to the uranium enrichment facility in Piketon— locally called the "A-plant." He secured a temporary exemption from environmental law that averted massive coal mine layoffs in Meigs County, and he enlisted the federal government to clean up an environmental hazard in Lawrence County. For Washington County, he protected a defense contractor from government competition. In Strickland's hometown of Lucasville, where a deadly prison riot made national news, Strickland offered legislation to extend federal death benefits to penitentiary workers. For the district as a whole, Strickland pressed for new roads and increased tourism, rural health care, economic development, and the protection of U.S. markets from unrestrained imports. And, for constituents all over the district who were frustrated with their dealings with the federal government—everything from lost Social Security checks to slow passports—Strickland and his staff worked hard to keep up with their obligations to constituent service.

Having ousted his predecessor for enjoying the perks of office, Strickland linked up with the congressional reform movement. He introduced a bill to end tax-paid mass mailings from congressional offices. He declined a cost-of-living increase and said that he would not accept the generous congressional health insurance plan until Congress had guaranteed equivalent coverage for all Americans. He kept his office expenses down by paying some bills out of his own pocket. Strickland even caused a stir among congressional colleagues with a bid to prevent the funding of new elevators for a congressional office building as well as an effort to bar members of Congress and their staffs from putting government frequent-flyer mileage to personal use.

The Republican attack on Strickland, however, would not revolve around the congressman's work for the district, or even his modest efforts to reform Congress. The GOP would spin its campaign around a larger issue: Bill Clinton. Strickland's vote for Clinton's economic package would, for many southern Ohioans, define the congressman's term of office. Shortly after the 1993 vote, the National Republican Congressional Committee, the Christian Coalition, and a conservative antitax group, Citizens for a Sound Economy, each bought ads targeting Strickland. The congressman denounced the effort, and the chairman of the Democratic National Committee, David Wilhelm, a southern Ohio native, told a Christian Coalition audience, "There is nobody in the U.S. House of Representatives who casts his ballot more . . . closely informed by his faith than Ted Strickland."[3] But the conservative threat remained. In September 1994, National Public Radio reported, "The Strickland worry [is] that in September and October [groups like the Christian Coalition and Citizens for a Sound Economy] will resume their targeting, then there could be an avalanche and in this basically conservative district even some of the Strickland volunteers could bow to peer pressure."[4]

The president was an issue in the Strickland campaign because larger forces were at work. The Democrats, who had controlled the House of Representatives for all but four years since 1931, and who had controlled much of the national political agenda since Franklin D. Roosevelt's 1932 election,

had, through the long-grinding friction of governance, worn itself into disparate factions. Differences cut along sectional, demographic, and ideological
lines. Rural Democrats were pitted against urban Democrats. Democrats of
the North found themselves at odds with Democrats of the South and West.
Roosevelt-style Democrats were running up against upwardly mobile New
Democrats.

Instability within the Democratic Party spelled Republican opportunity.
Newt Gingrich understood the strategic situation: "the 'next great offensive
of the Left,' as he put it, would be 'socializing health care,' because the Left,
as he put it, was 'gradually losing power on all other fronts, and they had to
have an increase in the resources they controlled. We had to position ourselves in the fight before they got there or they might win.'"[5] The 1994
Republican strategy, coordinated by national GOP leaders, was played out
with Napoleonic precision across the country.

Strickland was targeted for defeat, but a stroke of luck came in May, when
he drew a weak Republican opponent. State Senator H. Cooper Snyder had
been the Republican Party favorite, but in a surprising victory, businessman
Frank Cremeans edged Snyder out. Cremeans would prove to be an excep-
tionally poor candidate. His message went to the concerns of small business—taxes are too high and the government is bent on regulation—but
Cremeans was given to off-hand comments that suggested a social conservatism that drifted to the rightmost segments of the movement. At one point,
Cremeans wondered out loud whether the fall of Greece and Rome may have
been caused by AIDS. Toward the end of the campaign, the GOP was
unhappy with the way things were going and even one of Cremeans' own
advisers confided to a newspaper reporter that his candidate's "political skills
don't quite match up to his business skills."[6] The *Dayton Daily News* called
Cremeans a "bad joke," adding that a Cremeans victory "would constitute a
mockery of democracy itself."[7]

An early spring campaign poll showed Strickland up by eighteen points.
People seemed to like Strickland's personable, earnest, straightforward style,
but there were ominous signs. First, Cremeans had personal wealth, and he
was ready to spend a large portion of it to get elected. Second, at the top of
the state's Democratic ticket were strong GOP candidates for governor and
senator, as well as a southeastern Ohioan, Nancy Hollister, whose bid for
lieutenant governor would likely energize the Republican base in the eastern
part of the congressional district. Third, for all the reformist hopes that
accompanied the 1992 congressional freshman class, no great transformation
had been achieved. Although there was progress on Democratic issues—the
passage of the Family and Medical Leave Act and expansion of the Earned
Income Tax Credit, for example—the institution remained pretty much as
the freshmen had found it.

When, late in the summer, Democrats could not even pass anticrime legislation, it seemed proof that the party could not govern. As Marine One carried the president out of town on the afternoon of the failed crime bill vote, some White House staffers wondered if Clinton's presidency could ever recover.

Democratic members of Congress seemed doomed. They were hopelessly divided while their Republican opponents were coalescing around a unified message. The GOP issued a ten-point legislative statement they called the "Contract with America." The Contract promised that a Republican-controlled House of Representatives would bring to a vote a variety of measures aimed at fiscal restraint, crime reduction, welfare reform, family values, national security, tort reform, and term limits.

Cremeans was on board. He criticized Strickland for being out of step with the people—for sticking with Clinton when he should have been listening to his district. Television ads linked the congressman and the president: "Are they too liberal for Southern Ohio?" Although Strickland had opposed his president on the North American Free Trade Agreement, on gun control, and on the crime bill, Cremeans wanted to make sure that voters knew about Strickland's support for the president's 1993 economic package and against a constitutional amendment to balance the federal budget. If there was any doubt as to Cremeans' electoral strategy, it was erased when Cremeans declared, "This is a referendum on Clinton."[8]

Strickland hoped that, "When it gets down to it, people aren't voting on a presidency. They are choosing between two people."[9] Frances Strickland, who was running her husband's campaign, said that Clinton would not be invited to stump in the Sixth Congressional District. It was not that Ted was ashamed of the president, she was just listening to common sense: "We don't think that he is being . . . well received here."[10] Indeed, just being a Democrat was a problem.

Surveys had the congressman running double-digit leads, but a generic poll—one that matches Democrats against Republicans without naming specific candidates—was showing a 12 percent preference for Republicans.[11]

Then came the quote that would crystallize Cremeans' message. It came, not from Cremeans, nor from a Cremeans supporter, nor even from a Cremeans media firm: it came from Strickland himself. Strickland had wanted to debate Cremeans, perhaps hoping that voters would conclude, as did the *Dayton Daily News*, that Cremeans "doesn't have a clue."[12] But the debate would be remembered for a Strickland line:

> *Debate Moderator:* Mr. Strickland, as you mentioned earlier, you have been a strong supporter of health care reform. How would you fund reform without raising taxes?

> *Rep. Strickland:* Well, we may need to raise some taxes. We may
> need to raise some taxes.[13]

Frances Strickland sensed the problem immediately,[14] and the congressman later thought "[i]t may not have been a politically wise thing to do."[15] Even if the remark was, as Strickland called it, "an honest feeling," the damage was done. Cremeans immediately aired campaign ads that used Strickland's own words against him.

Strickland was to suffer one last blow. On the Sunday before the election, the Christian Coalition distributed voter guides saying that the congressman was for abortion, against the death penalty, for gays in the military, against the Balanced Budget Amendment, and for "taxpayer funding of obscene art." From Strickland's point of view, the death penalty claim was just plain wrong and the mention of "obscene art" was an absurd reference to his support for the National Endowment for the Arts. The Christian Coalition flyers, the tax remark, the perceived connection with Clinton, the 1993 vote for the economic package—all these factors combined to defeat Strickland in November. It was another 51 to 49 percent election. With the candidates separated by a mere 3,402 votes, any one of these factors might have accounted for the margin of defeat.

Redemption

Strickland seemed to face an inauspicious political future. He had succumbed to a gaffe-prone challenger who was now in a position to build his own connections with the district by doing constituent casework and racking up legislative accomplishments. Further, Strickland's 1992 victory had come after a hard-fought primary between two Republicans, whereas, looking forward to 1996, Cremeans would likely go unchallenged in his party. Finally, after the 1994 election, there was every indication that Clinton would continue to be a drag on the Democratic ticket.

But there was also reason for hope. Nationwide, the 1992 campaign had been a referendum on Democratic incumbency—thirty-four incumbent Democrats lost their seats—but in 1996, Strickland could make himself the "outsider" once again. And just as Strickland had little chance to establish a separate identity for himself during the 1992 campaign, Cremeans had yet to connect with the voters. Examined closely, Cremeans' victory was anything but solid. If, in the year of the "Republican Revolution" (when the GOP captured the House and Senate, along with a mass of governorships and state legislatures), spending large sums of money in a historically Republican district—if, in this situation, Cremeans could pull only a 2 percent margin of victory, he might well lose the next time around.

But in the first half of 1995, this was mere speculation. The new Republican Congress was ascendant, and Cremeans set about earning his stripes as a Gingrich Republican. He voted for every point of the Contract with America, working tirelessly in aid of the GOP leadership during the first hundred days of the Revolution. At home, he made serious efforts to protect the A-plant and he fought to ensure that the Sixth Congressional District was given necessary transportation funding. For those of a more socially conservative bent, he wrote legislation intended to allow the Vinton County courthouse to display a cross during the Christmas season, even though many argued that the courts would strike down any such law. Most prominently, Cremeans battled a federal effort to expand the region's Wayne National Forest, because local school districts might lose a considerable portion of their tax base if the land moved out of private ownership. At year's end Gingrich attended a fundraising breakfast for Cremeans and one of his colleagues.

Still, Cremeans seemed hapless. A left-liberal magazine ranked Cremeans fourth on its list of "The Ten Dimmest Bulbs in Congress," noting that the congressman's chief of staff was "viewed in Washington as Cremeans' baby sitter."[16] Even Cremeans' investment in the new Republican majority was going bad. As the House of Representatives spearheaded a thorough reprogramming of federal priorities, the president was prepared to use his veto authority in a new budgetary battle royale. Gingrich assumed that Clinton would give in to the Republican agenda rather than shut down the government for lack of funds. Events worked out differently, however. The Republicans passed their budget; Clinton vetoed it; and the public blamed the GOP for the ensuing government shutdown. By the time the issue was resolved (on Clinton's terms), Gingrich and the House Republicans had ceded much of their strategic advantage to Democrats and the Democratic president. With confidence in the economy increasing along with the president's popularity, Cremeans' status as a Gingrich Republican was no longer a campaign asset.

For a time, Cremeans was the only sitting Member of Congress who supported wealthy publisher Malcolm S. "Steve" Forbes in his bid for the presidency. This move not only put the congressman out of step with establishment Republicans, who were standing behind Senate Majority Leader Bob Dole, but stumping for one of the richest men in America seemed to pit Cremeans' political ambition against his populist rhetoric. Bob Kelley, a teacher who ran against Cremeans in the 1994 primary, went after him again in 1996, based almost solely on the Forbes issue: "Cremeans is playing up to corporate America instead of the people who elected him."[17] Forbes eventually pulled out of the presidential race, and Cremeans fell in line behind Dole, but Kelley kept after Cremeans. Following a resounding defeat in the GOP primary, Kelley seemed to endorse Strickland, saying,

"I'm conservative and [Strickland's] liberal, but he's a good man and has a feeling for the people of this district. I really respect him."[18]

The political climate had changed so much in the two years since the Republicans unveiled their Contract with America, that Strickland could say publicly, "I believe in government."[19] Perhaps the most remarkable moment in the campaign occurred when President Clinton, on a train headed to the Democratic Convention in Chicago, stopped in Chillicothe, in the north-central part of the district, to address a gathering of 10,000 people (a crowd about half the size of the city's population). The 1993 budget vote was now a badge of honor. The president opened his stump speech with an aside to Strickland:

> I want to thank you for having the courage—and I think it proba-bly cost you your seat in '94—to vote for that economic plan when our friends in the opposition said it was tax-and-spend. . . . Four years later, we have 10 million more jobs, the deficit has gone down four years in a row under the same administration for the first time since before the Civil War. Ted Strickland was right, and his oppo-nent was wrong.[20]

As the election drew to a close, the *Cincinnati Enquirer* reversed its 1994 endorsement of Cremeans, deciding that, in 1996, Strickland was the lesser of two evils.[21] The *Dayton Daily News* continued its assault on Cremeans: "He is an embarrassment to Ohio, to Congress and to democracy."[22] But not for long: The official tally had Strickland winning the election with yet another 51 to 49 percent victory—the third two-point margin in a row for Ohio's Sixth Congressional District.

Consolidation

Strickland's 1996 victory was big-league politics. Cremeans had raised almost $1.8 million against Strickland's $680,000. Some of Cremeans' new money went to pay back old debts, but even so, great sums were being spent on Cremeans' behalf. Counting the outside interests that invested in television advertising, phone calls, and voter guides, among other things, the total cost of the election may have run up to the $4 million mark.[23] Political Washing-ton had come to know the Sixth as one of the most volatile congressional districts in the nation. It was no longer assumed to be Republican; it was now considered "swing." The 1998 election would bring even greater attention.

Strickland would have to move aggressively to win again. In 1992, he won in large part due to the bloody Republican primary. In 1994, he had lost in a mid-term election, a dangerous time for incumbents of the sitting president's party, especially freshmen like Strickland, because the electorate has a chance to punish the president by voting against congressional representatives of the president's party. In 1996, Strickland had run alongside a president who had regained fallen popularity, and although presidential coattails are usually short,[24] the massive, enthusiastic rally for President Clinton in Chillicothe likely helped get Strickland supporters out to vote. But the next election, 1998, would be six years into the president's term, traditionally the *most* dangerous year for congressional representatives of the president's party.

In the middle of a president's second midterm, voters cannot cast judgment on the president, but they *can* vent their frustrations (some of which have been pent up for more than half a decade) on the next best thing: the president's congressional allies. Reagan's party lost the Senate in 1986. In 1974, just after Nixon had resigned from office, much the same thing happened, as Democrats greatly widened their majority in the House of Representatives. Sixth-year punishment was a time-honored tradition. Strickland, once again a new member of Congress, could expect to face a tough re-election fight. He would need to take full advantage of the relationships he had been cultivating over the years.

Early on, it became clear that Lieutenant Governor Nancy Hollister was seriously thinking about a run for Congress, and Republican leaders were pushing her in that direction. Hollister seemed perfect for the Sixth Congressional District. In statewide office, she had earned name recognition; as a woman, she had the opportunity to minimize any gender gap that might crop up; as a hesitant supporter of abortion rights, she might be able to remove that divisive issue from play; and as a political moderate, she would not offer the right-wing rhetoric of the Cremeans campaign.

More important than all of this, however, was the district's political geography. Much of Strickland's strength came from the more moderate eastern part of the district—Miller's old constituency—where Hollister had served as mayor of Marietta. With such ties to the region, she could neutralize Strickland's support in the eastern half of the district, and then pummel him in the more conservative western half. Further, Hollister had previously directed the state's Office of Appalachia, which was helpful to this part of the state, and later, as lieutenant governor, when Spring floods hit the area in 1997 it was Hollister who was dispatched by the governor to handle the problem. In fact, Hollister's boss, Republican governor George V. Voinovich, was running for the U.S. Senate, allowing Hollister to follow on his coattails.

But the Republican primary turned a dream candidacy into a nightmare. Hollister, the party-backed candidate, would find herself opposed by four other GOP contenders. Two of the four, an English professor and an accountant, never stood a chance, but the other two candidates tested Hollister's mettle. Cremeans got into the race a few days after the lieutenant governor's announcement, calling himself the "conservative alternative" to Hollister, and he later hired former Christian Coalition director Ralph Reed as his top consultant. In August, insurance agent Michael T. Azinger, a conservative son of a West Virginia state legislator, positioned himself to the right of Cremeans. Both would hammer away at Hollister's position on abortion. The three serious contenders were splitting southern Ohio Republicans in as many directions, while Strickland enjoyed a clear Democratic field, continuing to get good press for his work on behalf of the district.

Although Strickland's voting record in Congress had moderated somewhat—he broke ranks with his Democratic colleagues on issues like partial-birth abortion—the congressman's second term of office would have the same focus as the first: jobs for southern Ohio. Strickland said he would protect Social Security and Medicare, of course, and he stressed the importance of education and rural health care, especially for children. He even became involved in an effort to impose sanctions on foreign countries that persecuted religious minorities. But most of Strickland's initiatives were intended to strengthen employment in his distressed part of Ohio. Increased funds for road construction meant jobs. Opposition to proposed air pollution standards meant jobs. Constant attention to the A-plant meant jobs. Almost everything Strickland did in Congress revolved around the notion that southeastern Ohio should be handled with special care because its good people were hard-pressed to make a living.

Support *for* the district was earning Strickland support *from* the district. The unions liked him for his pro-labor voting record. Political action committees associated with labor groups provided considerable backing for Strickland, and union members made up a critical segment of Strickland's base. Scattered throughout the district were party loyalists in each county who worked along side a cadre of supporters who had met and liked Strickland. Most just called him "Ted." In addition to union members and Democratic activists were student volunteers in Athens County who symbolized the intense loyalty Strickland had inspired. Although the congressman was pro-gun, had protected a uranium enrichment plant, had worked hard to allow a coalmine to empty drainage water into nearby streams, and had opposed antipollution guidelines, Strickland's support among liberal Democrats was enthusiastic. Part of the reason, surely, was that liberals had nowhere to turn, but another reason, in the words of one volunteer, was that Strickland is "a good person—a member of Congress who carries his own lunch," adding, "He's someone you can believe in."[25]

With the Democratic base holding firm, Strickland had no primary opposition. The Republicans, on the other hand, were in the middle of internecine warfare that was reminiscent of the 1992 Miller-McEwen battle. At first, it looked like Cremeans was getting little traction and Azinger was getting even less. Azinger was young, politically inexperienced, and new to the state. Without enough money to pay Reed, Cremeans was left to run the campaign for himself—yet as time passed, Cremeans and fellow conservative Azinger seemed to pick up steam. Each was trying to outflank the other's right. Republicans in the state's congressional delegation quickly moved into Hollister's corner, and Governor Voinovich sent a letter expressing his support. As if to underscore the cold depths to which the primary election had sunk, Cremeans re-aired sound bites from a 1996 radio spot in which Hollister and Voinovich endorsed Cremeans' candidacy, without ever mentioning that it was an old endorsement—that neither official was backing Cremeans' 1998 bid.

The May primary gave Hollister an ambivalent win. She received only 39 percent of the vote to Cremeans' 35 percent and Azinger's 21 percent, with the remainder going to lesser candidates. Azinger "wonder[ed] whether the voters will get out of bed and go vote for somebody who's just like the incumbent."[26] Noting that the majority of the vote went to Cremeans and Azinger, David Azinger (Mike's brother) said, "The conservatives won the election, but lost the nomination."[27] Mike Azinger would not endorse Hollister until late October. Some antiabortion activists never fell in line.

As Hollister moved to connect with a weakened base, Strickland concentrated his efforts on district jobs. The A-plant needed constant attention, and Strickland was credited with one more save in late summer, when he and a Kentucky Republican sponsored legislation to build new uranium recycling facilities in Piketon and in Peducah, Kentucky. For the Rocky Shoes & Boots manufacturing facility in Athens County, Strickland persuaded the U.S. Postal Service to open up its procurement procedures. Strickland was later able to use both accomplishments in campaign ads. With Clinton embroiled in the Monica Lewinsky controversy and Hollister calling for the president's resignation, Strickland maintained his focus on jobs for the Sixth Congressional District.

As the closing days drew near, Hollister played to her own strengths—a southern Ohio daughter made good, and, in her words, "a lady who gets results, who gets things done"[28]—but the lieutenant governor never seemed to connect with the voters. A television spot highlighted her achievements for southern Ohio, but for the most part, Hollister focused on moderate fiscal conservatism: lower taxes and less government regulation. Strickland, meanwhile, criticized the lieutenant governor for failing to look after problems closer to home. He ran a television ad that said, "While southern Ohio schools have been crumbling, Nancy Hollister recommended using our tax dollars to build [urban] sports stadiums." Over the course of a dozen debates, Hollister pressed a generalized Republican message, backed up by one-size-fits-all ads purchased by the Republican National Committee. The message did not seem to have much local bite, however—at least, it did not seem to have the same power as Strickland's ads, which featured strong endorsements from southern Ohio workers who testified that the congressman had saved their jobs.

The Hollister campaign finally put a scare into Strickland supporters when Hollister focused on a local issue: transportation funding. In a daring political maneuver, Hollister persuaded two congressional Republicans to insert language in a $500 billion appropriations bill that would reprogram federal highway money away from a plan developed by an independent commission and toward a plan favored by Hollister. Hollister claimed that the realignment would leverage existing funds. Strickland saw the change as a political gimmick that had no real money behind it; it was just a shift in funding from one part of the district to another. Strickland persuaded President Clinton to threaten a veto of the entire spending package if the provision was not removed. Speaker Gingrich let the matter drop. Hollister, although she lost her road plan, gained a campaign issue. A television ad proclaimed, "Strickland kills a plan to help southern Ohio." Strickland, who said he had already procured the money Hollister was now trying to reprogram, made the issue a matter of credibility—"She's not a trustworthy person"[29]—but Hollister's message, combined with heavy pro-Hollister spending by the Republican National Committee seemed to pose a serious threat.

The *Cincinnati Enquirer* endorsed Strickland once again, but campaign polls, which had been showing double-digit strength for Strickland, were slipping. A small-sample survey by respected Zogby International showed a statistical dead heat, with Strickland at 42.0 percent and Hollister at 40.5 percent. Strickland supporters had reason to be afraid: a full 17.5 percent of the electorate was undecided. The poll's generic ballot looked even worse for Strickland. An unnamed Republican was getting 38.7 percent to the unnamed Democrat's 32.2 percent. National and state pundits became wary of making predictions in such a close race. At a rally with First Lady Hillary Rodham Clinton a few days before the election—part of Strickland's fourteen-county bus tour—Strickland sermonized about the importance of the ballot, beseeching one thousand Ohio University students to get out and vote. *The (Cleveland) Plain Dealer* predicted yet "another photo finish."[30]

Strickland was counting on Election Day turnout, but the weather was cold—and it rained. The night before, the congressman was heard giving thanks to his supporters, no matter what might happen. As the polls came in, however, Strickland took the lead. Shortly after ten o'clock, the race was called in his favor. Hollister, it turned out, could not hold her own people, losing twelve of the fourteen counties, even her home base of Washington County. In contrast, GOP Governor Voinovich, running for U.S. Senate, beat his Democratic opposition in all but two counties in the Sixth Congressional District, outrunning Hollister's vote totals by an average of about 40 percent in each. The final tally was 57 to 43 percent for Strickland.

Hollister had run a good campaign, but she never really seemed to find Strickland's weak point. After-election analyses focused on the relationships the candidates had built with the Sixth. *The (Cleveland) Plain Dealer* reported on one GOP activist who said, "[Strickland] really worked the district. You've got to take your hat off to him."[31] A Republican elected official attending one of the debates said, "We're interested in local issues and who can represent this district best," adding, "That will decide this race."[32] Strickland himself was quoted as saying, "I have felt for a long time that I do have a connection with the people who live here that transcends partisan politics."[33] While the conventional wisdom held that 1998 would be a close election, there were cracks in the GOP coalition. One pro-life activist told a reporter, "Secretly, a lot of pro-lifers are hoping Strickland will win to send a message."[34] Another said, "We're going to leave that [race] blank on the ballot," because, "We see little difference between her and Ted Strickland other than their gender and their party."[35] Indeed, there remains a nagging question among supporters of both candidates as to whether Republicans in this rural, conservative district were ready to accept a woman as their representative in the United States Congress.

Strickland had consolidated his support in the Sixth Congressional District. Campaign 2000 was a nonevent that saw only sporadic campaigning by Strickland and Azinger, who unleashed a barrage of attack ads at the end of the campaign and garnered 40 percent of the vote against Strickland's 58 percent. Soundly beating a conservative Republican two years after doing the same against a moderate Republican showed that the bond between Strickland and his district had strengthened. In no small way, Strickland's deepening relationship with the Sixth Congressional District of Ohio illustrates the importance of constituent connections.

Electoral Constituencies

Strickland won over the Sixth Congressional District by building strong connections within it. Possessing unbridled passion for the job, the congressman allied himself with his constituency by protecting its chief interest—jobs. Using an unassuming, highly personal style, Strickland instilled among his supporters a firm confidence that he would do his best for the people. He accomplished this mission partly by reaching out to his constituents one-on-one. Just before the 1994 election, it was reported that Strickland had been personally seen by 28 percent of the district's voters.[36] But the secret to Strickland's success went beyond sheer numbers: Strickland was able to secure the Sixth because, over time, he had developed a well-formed hierarchy of support.

Richard Fenno has argued that congressional representatives see concentric circles within their constituencies: "geographical" ("the district"), "re-election" ("the supporters"), "primary" ("the strongest supporters"), and "personal" ("the intimates").[37] "Representation," Fenno has said, "is a process of continuous negotiation between politicians and citizens."[38] Candidates must negotiate connections between themselves and their supporters—personal, primary, and re-election—in order to build an Election Day majority. The story of Strickland's electoral resilience is readily understood in terms of Fenno's concentric circles.

Strickland's personal circle of supporters is made up, principally, of family. His wife Frances, in addition to being a key campaign advisor, served during Strickland's first term as an unpaid chief of staff in the congressman's congressional office. Constituent service was one of her chief concerns. Strickland's brother Roger, a bona fide southern Ohio "good ol' boy," often travels around the district with the congressman, chatting with volunteers and supporters. In addition, a small number of senior staffers make it into the inner circle, including Frances Strickland's successor as chief of staff, John Haseley, a native of the district who keeps close tabs on its interests. The importance of this sort of inner circle cannot be overstated. As Fenno understood, candidates need a devoted personal constituency that will allow the candidate to speak his or her mind without fear of press leaks.

In addition to those who have a personal connection to Strickland, there is a wider group of die-hard loyalists who form the core of the primary vote. They support Strickland because they believe in him. Whether union members or student liberals—Strickland has shown an uncanny ability to connect with both groups at the same time—activists are solidly committed to their candidate, chiefly because Strickland seemed to be working hard for his constituency. After the 1994 defeat, Strickland supporters immediately started to build a county-by-county organization that effectively prevented a primary challenge in 1996. In contrast, Republican candidates after 1994 could not bridge the gap between conservative and moderate supporters, so they lacked a unified team of Republican activists and split their core vote.

Once divided, the GOP vote was conquered by Strickland's deeply committed campaign organization. Strickland's broader re-election constituency was built over time. Strickland had run for Congress in 1976 and 1978, when he earned 39 and 35 percent of the vote, respectively, and again in 1980, when he moved his numbers up to 45 percent. In 1992, Strickland drove his share of the vote up to 51 percent. When support stalled in 1994 at 49 percent—a slim losing margin—Strickland simply continued his campaign efforts: "For two years, he'd turn up at parades and festivals, just like he was a congressman."[39] And while support among the union rank and file seemed to falter in 1994,[40] it moved back into Strickland's camp in successive years, helping Strickland regain his 51 percent margin in 1996 and then pull well ahead with 57 and 58 percent in 1998 and 2000, respectively. The clear trend was upward, as Strickland traveled his district and received credit for protecting southern Ohio jobs. While Strickland's first victory relied heavily on the eastern part of the district, on Democratic partisans and Democratic-leaning swing voters, Strickland's later victories show support among voters and counties that otherwise vote Republican. The record suggests a continual strengthening of connections with a stable re-election constituency.

In 1993, after the budget vote, the level of attention Strickland gave to a single tax-weary constituent phoning into his office exemplified Strickland's representational style. Broadening and deepening connections to the district allowed Strickland, over time, to recover from electoral defeat and to move the Sixth back into the Democratic column. Even after his resounding victory in 1998, the congressman remained accessible to his constituents. He continued to meet with union officials and to promote the cause of southern Ohio jobs in any forum he could find. Virtually anyone who wished to speak to the congressman, elected officials and concerned citizens alike, were given the opportunity to do so. Pockets of conservative discontent notwithstanding, Strickland successfully built a "durable connection," as Fenno might say,[41] with his southern Ohio district.

Notes

1. Roger K. Lowe, "Miller-McEwen Contest Is Likely," *Columbus Dispatch*, 1 April 1992.

2. "Farlow Declares Plan in Bid for Prosecutor," *Columbus Dispatch*, 23 September 1992.

3. George Embey, "Democrats, Too, Welcome Religious, Says Party Leader," *Columbus Dispatch*, 19 June 1994.

4. Edward Lifson, "Report on Re-election Campaign in Ohio's Sixth District," National Public Radio, *All Things Considered*, 6 September 1994.

5. Haynes Johnson and David S. Broder, *The System: The American Way of Politics at the Breaking Point* (Boston: Little, Brown, 1997), 39–41.

6. Kevin Merida "Many Freshmen Are Looking Less Vulnerable," *Washington Post*, 4 November 1994.

7. Editorial, *Dayton Daily News*, 16 October 1994. See also Cremeans' reply, 27 October 1994.

8. Howard Wilkinson, "Taking U.S. Temperature; Sixth District Election Watched as an Indicator, *Cincinnati Enquirer*, 19 October 1994.

9. Ibid.

10. Lifson, "Report on Re-election Campaign."

11. Cited in Kevin Merida, "Challenger Burned Learning the Ropes; Sound Bites Can Bite Back," *Washington Post*, 5 October 1994.

12. Editorial, *Dayton Daily News*, 16 October 1994.

13. Edward Lifson, "Ohio Congressman Loses Race to Political Novice," National Public Radio, *All Things Considered*, 10 November 1994.

14. Ibid.

15. Merida, "Many Freshman are Looking Less Vulnerable."

16. Ken Silverstein, "The Ten Dimmest Bulbs in Congress," *The Progressive*, September 1995, 29, 31.

17. Pamela Brogan, "Kelley Challenging Cremeans Because of Tie to Forbes," *Gannett News Service*, 29 February 1996.

18. Pamela Brogan, "Cremeans Wins GOP Primary, Now Faces Strickland," *Gannett News Service*, 19 March 1996.

19. Robert Shogan, "Ohio Race Offers Window onto National Election," *Los Angeles Times*, 3 June 1996.

20. U.S. President, *Public Papers of the Presidents of the United States: William J. Clinton*, 1996, vol. 2 (Washington, D.C.: Government Printing Office), 1352.

21. Editorial, "Nose-Holder: In Strickland vs. Cremeans Race Give Strickland One More Chance," *Cincinnati Enquirer*, 24 October 1996.

22. Editorial, "Strickland Can End Ohio Embarrassment," *Dayton Daily News*, October 13, 1996.

23. Jonathan Riskind, "Big Money Fueled Campaign," *Columbus Dispatch*, 9 March 1997; Jonathan Riskind, "High Dollar Campaigning," *Columbus Dispatch*, 9 March 1997.

24. See Gary C. Jacobson, *The Politics of Congressional Elections*, 5th ed. (New York: Longman, 2001), 146–53.

25. Faith Dickerhoof, personal interview, 20 September 2000.

26. Pamela Brogan, "Hollister's Win Leaves Questions of GOP Support," *Gannett News Service*, 6 May 1998.

27. Ibid.

28. Jonathan Riskind, "Hollister to Battle Strickland," *Columbus Dispatch*, 6 May 1998.

29. Robert Schlesinger, "Roads Are Hot Issue in Ohio's 6th District Race," *The Hill*, 28 October 1998.

30. Joe Frolik, "Foes Battle for Even a Thin Edge in 6th District," *The (Cleveland) Plain Dealer*, 1 November 1998.

31. Joe Frolik, "Jackson County GOP Boss Will Be Glad When It's All Over," *The (Cleveland) Plain Dealer*, 3 May 1998.

32. Jonathan Riskind, "Voters: Local Issues, Not Scandals, Will Decide Race," *Columbus Dispatch*, 29 August 1998.

33. Jonathan Riskind, "Strickland Has Easy Win in 6th," *Columbus Dispatch*, 4 November 1998.

34. Jonathan Riskind, "Voters: Local Issues, Not Scandals, Will Decide Race."

35. Joe Frolik, "Foes Battle for Even a Thin Edge in 6th District."

36. Lifson, "Report on Re-election Campaign."

37. Richard F. Fenno, Jr., *Home Style: House Members in Their Districts* (Glenview, Ill.: Scott Foresman, 1978), 1–29.

38. Richard F. Fenno, Jr., *Senators on the Campaign Trail: The Politics of Representation* (Norman: University of Oklahoma Press, 1996), 238.

39. Joe Frolik, "Candidates in Race for Ohio's 6th District Speed Up," *The* (Cleveland) *Plain Dealer*, 22 October 1998.

40. See Thomas B. Edsall, "Grass-Roots Organizing Tops TV Ads in AFL-CIO Political Agenda," *The Washington Post*, 20 May 1998.

41. Fenno, *Senators on the Campaign Trail*, 238.

Hammer at the Opponent's Weak Point

4

BOB BARR
R-GEORGIA
SEVENTH CONGRESSIONAL DISTRICT

TED STRICKLAND is a quiet politician; Bob Barr is a congressional firebrand. On the floor of the House of Representatives, Barr's hands wave and his fingers jab as if he were delivering a fiery sermon. His language is strong, precise, and deeply conservative. A former attorney, the congressman is best known for his blistering attacks on President Clinton during the Senate's 1999 removal trial, the culmination of an impeachment effort Barr had helped initiate almost a year before the public had ever heard Monica Lewinsky's name. An advocate of traditional matrimony, Barr sought a prohibition on same-sex unions with the "Defense of Marriage Act." Congressional Quarterly's political reference guide, *Politics in America*, has quoted one of the congressman's most extreme statements: "The very foundations of our society are in danger of being burned. The flames of hedonism, the flames of narcissism, the flames of self-centered morality are licking at the very foundations of our society: the family unit."[1]

Barr's ideological passion tolerates few entangling alliances or creature comforts. According to *The Almanac of American Politics*, Barr "says he has no close friends on Capitol Hill and usually sleeps in his office."[2] First elected to represent his northwestern Georgia district in 1994, Barr ranks among the nation's most uncompromising conservatives. As a freshman legislator, Barr shepherded a bill favoring assault weapons to the House floor without benefit of a committee hearing. He argued, "[T]his is an issue the American people know. . . . It is high time [the House] stood up, unafraid, undefensive."[3] In 1997, when Barr called for hearings aimed at the impeachment of Bill Clinton and Al Gore for alleged campaign finance violations, he did so without the consent of House Speaker Newt Gingrich or Judiciary Committee Chairman Henry Hyde, both of whom distanced themselves from Barr's effort. In late 1998, the House impeached Clinton over the Lewinsky matter, and Barr became one of the "House managers" who prosecuted the case before the Senate. In January of 1999, just before the Senate's vote, with the case against Clinton faltering, Barr took a swipe at Republican senators: "Every time you turn around, they're placing restrictions on us."[4] Whether protecting the interests of Georgia veterans or seeking authorization for a Washington, D.C. monument to honor Ronald Reagan, Barr is a congressman on a mission.

Barr's tenacity serves to rally the nation's conservatives. A *New York Times* reporter has observed:

> On Capitol Hill, Mr. Barr's more unsettling shows of temper are well known among colleagues on both sides of the aisle, who whisper about the committee meetings where he had to be talked down and about aides who seemed to fear his tongue-lashings. But if he is not Mr. Congeniality in the Class of '94, he is an important figure for members of his party's conservative base.[5]

While some analysts have maintained that southern conservatism has diminished the Republican Party's appeal to moderate voters,[6] there is little doubt that crusaders like Barr have nurtured the conservative grassroots.

Barr's electoral base lies in northwest Georgia, a part of the state which had been Democratic as far back as the 1830s.[7] Over time, new issues, changing priorities, and shifting alliances undermined Democratic power in Georgia politics while transforming American political geography. The nation's electoral map was undergoing a rapid transformation. Northern states like Maine, the home of "Rock-Ribbed" Republicanism, and southern states like Georgia, a mainstay of the Democratic Party's "Solid South," were abandoning their traditional partisan loyalties. In 1996, Clinton, an Arkansas Democrat, won the state of Maine by more than twenty points while narrowly losing Georgia. In 2000, Gore lost the entire South, including his home state of Tennessee and the usually reliable Democratic border state of West Virginia. In Barr's home, the Seventh Congressional District of Georgia, Clinton and Gore were easily defeated by Republicans Bob Dole and George W. Bush in 1996 and 2000, respectively.

Still, old voting habits die hard. In the early 1990s, even as the Seventh Congressional District was moving into the GOP column, it was represented by a moderate Democrat, George "Buddy" Darden, who had served the district since 1983. Darden enjoyed public visibility, fundraising prowess, and a high-placed legislative position that brought a great deal of federal money into the district. Barr, however, overcame the powers of incumbency in 1994 with a hard-hitting congressional campaign that demonstrates some of the electoral advantages of an ideologically based, anti-incumbent strategy.

The District

Georgia's Seventh Congressional District stretches from the distant suburbs of Atlanta to the Alabama border. In 1994, the district was made up of eleven counties in the state's Upper Piedmont: ten of them mostly rural counties, and part of another, Cobb County, which the Seventh shares with the Sixth (Gingrich's former district). Although Georgia pride is rooted in its pastoral heritage, the vast majority of Seventh district residents live in the cities of Marietta (in Cobb County, on the distant outskirts of Atlanta) and Rome (near the Alabama state line).

During the nineteenth century, the region was a microcosm of the Old South. Cotton plantations used slave labor to extract wealth from the soil; yeoman farmers tried to scratch out a self-sufficient living. General William Tecumseh Sherman drove his Union troops through this part of Georgia, burning cotton and foodstuffs that once formed the heart of its agricultural economy. (The Confederacy is still honored in Cobb County by the Kennesaw Mountain National Battlefield Park.) During Reconstruction, farming declined as Northern textile mills relocated to the South. In the twentieth century, the area grew into a manufacturing powerhouse. Textile mills, once the leading employers but now becoming unprofitable, were replaced by more technologically advanced industries, particularly defense manufacturing. By the early 1990s, Atlanta's suburban sprawl had engulfed Cobb County, helping to make the district largely white, upscale, and conservative.

The area's partisan predisposition changed dramatically in the last four decades of the twentieth century. Until the 1980s, the western Upper Piedmont of Georgia was reliably Democratic, but it was not liberal.[8] The 1960s saw conservatives like presidential candidate George Wallace and segregationist governor Lester Maddox do well in this part of the state.[9] Buddy Darden's Democratic predecessor, Congressman Larry McDonald, was an outspoken member of the ultra-conservative John Birch Society. As the Democratic Party became more identified with political liberalism and as the Republican Party followed Nixon's anti-integrationist "southern strategy," GOP values became more appealing to white, middle-class southerners. The Republican Party was gaining a foothold in Georgia. Reagan's 1980 campaign for president accelerated the GOP march through the South.[10] Still, Democrats have maintained some strength among the surviving textile communities such as Rome, in Floyd County, where former governor Jimmy Carter won in 1980 even as the surrounding region voted for Reagan.

By 1983, when Congressman McDonald was killed on the Korean Air

Lines jet shot down by the Soviets over the Sea of Japan, several Republicans had gained elective office in Georgia, and ten years later, Georgia Republicans held seats at every level of government. By 1994, most Seventh District voters—rural farmers and white-collar suburbanites—were solidly GOP in both statewide and national elections. The trend would upset the long-standing reign of the Democratic Party in Georgia politics.

Darden had entered politics as a young district attorney. A brief stint in private practice was followed by election to the state legislature. After McDonald's death, Darden ran against the congressman's widow in the nonpartisan special runoff that had been called to fill the empty seat. Darden billed himself as a "responsible conservative."[11] He was a model incumbent. After his election, Darden kept his distance from the liberalism expressed by some of his Democratic colleagues, building a centrist voting record that frequently backed Reagan's legislative agenda. In 1984, one analysis showed Darden's legislative votes siding with Reagan 48 percent of the time while giving his own party just 58 percent support.[12] One Washington observer noted, "Darden has one of those middle-of-the-road to conservative records, which are common in southern delegations. You wouldn't mistake him for a northern big-city Democrat, but you wouldn't mistake him for a Republican either."[13] Ideology aside, Darden helped sell the material interests of his district. On the Armed Services Committee, he helped the Lockheed Corporation gain defense contracts for military aircraft built at its Marietta plant, where the company was consolidating its far-flung manufacturing operations. Elevated to the Appropriations Committee in the 1990s, Darden enhanced his power to bring home federal money. Aside from the district's increasingly Republican tilt, there was little reason for Darden to believe that a political newcomer like Barr could pose a serious challenge.

The Candidate

Barr is an Iowa-born graduate of the University of Southern California and George Washington University, earning a law degree from Georgetown. After working as a legislative analyst for the Central Intelligence Agency and later as a trial lawyer in Atlanta, Barr was appointed U.S. attorney for the Northern District of Georgia. He was a tough prosecutor, racking up a string of high-profile victories, including the successful prosecution of a GOP congressman. In 1990, Barr was named president of the Southeastern Legal Foundation, a conservative watchdog group that would later play a central role in several of the investigations that dogged Bill Clinton. One wall of the Foundation's headquarters would later bear photographs of Barr, Gingrich, and Maddox.[14]

Barr's first attempt at elective office came in 1992, when he joined four other Republicans vying for a seat in the U.S. Senate. Paul Coverdell won the nomination, but Barr's strong showing—he lost a runoff by just over 1,500 votes—boded well for the future. Barr's support for Coverdell's victorious general election campaign earned Barr respect from the new senator. In the meantime, Barr maintained his own political apparatus, which included passionate supporters of his conservative cause, and he began using local op-ed pages to attack Darden and Clinton. In May of 1993, when Darden voted for the president's budget plan, Barr told an audience of small business owners what he thought of the "Clinton-Darden tax-and-spend program": "Apparently, [Darden's] strings are being pulled by the president and not the people of the 7th District."[15] In August, immediately after Darden voted for the final version of the president's budget bill, Barr announced his candidacy. "The people are angry at Buddy because he has lost the grass-roots touch with his district," Barr's campaign manager proclaimed. Darden had "voted with the largest tax increase not only in American history, but the history of the world."[16]

To meet Darden head-on, Barr had to win the Republican nomination—not a sure thing. His opponent was gynecologist Brenda Fitzgerald, a fellow conservative whose only notable policy disagreement with Barr involved U.S./China trade.[17] The contest devolved into a series of personal attacks as each side jostled for the right-most position. Fitzgerald charged that Barr had defended a "cop-killer" in court and she insinuated that Barr had protested the United States' involvement in Vietnam. Barr returned fire. As a defense attorney, he said, it was his responsibility under the Constitution to provide counsel for the accused. Against the charge of anti-draft activism, a college roommate affirmed that Barr had never protested the Vietnam War.[18] Indeed, Barr noted, "I won't even go to a Jane Fonda movie today. The peace symbol is very offensive to me."[19] (In the middle of the controversy, Barr "admit[ed] having attended a couple of Young Democrats meetings at the University of Southern California but says his parents found out and threatened to pull him out of school."[20])

On Election Day, Barr won the primary with 57 percent of the vote to Fitzgerald's 43 percent. Barr then laid out his strategy for winning the general election: "We're going to hammer [Darden] for supporting the Clinton administration. . . . We're not going to pull any punches with him."[21]

Southern Strategies

Once an unswerving bastion of Democratic politics, the American South was slowly transforming into Republican stronghold. Franklin Delano Roosevelt had long-ago forged a coalition of farmers, organized labor, liberal intellectuals, racial and ethnic minorities, and the urban political machines of the

North, along with the apparatus of racial oppression that maintained segregation in the South. The "New Deal Coalition" could hold itself together so long as the Depression and World War II dominated the national agenda. When civil rights became a powerful political force in the 1950s and 1960s, the Democratic Party was compelled, in effect, to choose between two of its core constituencies: white voters in the South and black voters across the country.

The party's judgment was rendered slowly—and not without political cost. In 1948, states' rights Dixiecrats, objecting to the Democratic Party's burgeoning advocacy of civil rights, nominated South Carolina Governor Strom Thurmond for president. When Lyndon Baines Johnson signed the Civil Rights Act of 1964, the partisan restructuring was accelerated. The decision to move with the tide of the civil rights movement left the Democratic Party vulnerable to white southern disaffection. It was an electoral weakness that manifested itself in Wallace's 1968 campaign for president, Nixon's "Southern Strategy," an increasingly Republican southern vote for presidential candidates, and a string of losses by Democratic gubernatorial and Senate candidates in the South.

Still, the Republican takeover was far from complete. Even as Reagan swept the South in the 1984 presidential elections, the Republican Party occupied only a third of the seats in the southern congressional delegation.[22] George H. W. Bush carried the South in 1988, but moderate House Democrats were holding their own.[23] Reagan-era momentum had stalled: while national and statewide contests favored the Republican Party, most congressional elections returned southern Democrats to Washington.[24] The momentum of congressional incumbency held sitting members in place, and the lack of a well-organized Republican Party structure rendered grassroots organizing difficult. To continue its southern expansion, the Republican Party needed ground-level support—some of which eventually came from the Christian Coalition[25]—and it had to make sure that the party's message would resonate with white voters in the American South.

The change would come in 1994. Joseph A. Aistrup, in *The Southern Strategy Revisited*, notes two key features of the southern political terrain that favored Republican gains: (1) the Clinton administration's seeming tolerance of gays in the military, eventually formalized as the "don't-ask, don't tell" policy on homosexuality in the ranks, and (2) passage of the "Brady Bill," a waiting period imposed on the purchase of handguns.[26] Conservative Christian radio stations and right-wing commentators like Rush Limbaugh used these issues, along with allegations of financial wrongdoing and rumors of marital infidelity, to show that "Clinton was too immoral, too liberal, or both."[27] Southern voters were poised to attack Clinton and the Democratic Congress.

Lacking a presidential contest to unify the party's message, the GOP cobbled together an assortment of long-stalled Republican policies into its "Contract with America." The Contract, which would help candidates across the country (including Cremeans in Ohio), was developed under the direction of southern House leaders, including Georgian Newt Gingrich and Texan Dick Armey. Some moderate Republicans in the Northeast felt that they had been excluded from the Contract's writing,[28] but on September 27, 1994, the party unveiled the Contract on the steps of the Capitol Building. The signing ceremony, which involved hundreds of GOP candidates, had been scripted and staged to spread the Republican message nationwide. Live video and audio feeds made the signing available to news producers across the country.[29] (GOP organizers later ran "highlights" for the benefit of radio stations that had somehow missed the live event.[30]) The visuals were strong, the message was clear, and the footage was widely distributed.[31] Few staged events in contemporary political history have had a greater impact on congressional elections than the signing of the Contract with America.[32] Even without a presidential candidate, the Republicans would be running a national campaign.

The General Election

While southern electoral terrain shifted in favor of the Republican Party, Barr's run for the Seventh Congressional District of Georgia would be fought uphill. Barr had moved to the state just over a decade earlier, while Darden was a likeable Georgia native who had used his congressional office to protect the interests of the district since 1983. As a result, voters saw Darden as a competent, intelligent, hardworking congressman who brought the Seventh its fair share of federal spending. Barr's resume was impressive—his service as a U.S. attorney earned him a measure of prominence in northwestern Georgia; he had gained conservative allies through his presidency of the Southeastern Legal Foundation; his 49.5 percent showing in the 1992 Senate runoff against Coverdell gave Barr electoral respectability—but compared to Darden, Barr was a political novice.

Darden had been accumulating the powers of incumbency for more than a decade. As a member of the Appropriations Committee, Darden could expect that his war chest would be filled by well-heeled political action committees, ensuring that he would have lots of money to advertise his accomplishments on radio and television. Like most congressional representatives, Darden had paid close attention to his district. He had spent most of his congressional life in Georgia (instead of Washington), and he had always attended to constituency casework (building a base of satisfied voters). If Tip O'Neill was right that all politics is local, Darden was strategically positioned for re-election in 1994.

Darden's odds were improved by some of Barr's unique shortcomings. A twice-divorced father of four who had reportedly testified on behalf of gun control and who had not always been firmly opposed to abortion, Barr was running on a pro-life, pro-gun, pro-family agenda that left him in an awkward position to begin charging Darden with ideological inconsistency. With a famously severe personality, Barr could not even hint that he would be a more likeable congressman than Darden. Darden had successfully weathered the House Bank scandal that defeated Ohio's Bob McEwen in 1992, and there were no hints of pending troubles, so Darden could not reasonably be accused of corruption. Furthermore, Darden's on-the-job competency had been clearly demonstrated in the careful attention he paid to the district, so there was little chance that Darden could be accused of forgetting the district's material needs.

Perhaps the only realistic strategy that remained at Barr's disposal was an issue-based attack that would offer conservative policies as an ideological alternative to legislative liberalism. But even here, there were potential problems. At least one analyst questioned the political wisdom of conservative groups that backed Barr in the GOP primary. Fitzgerald, it was reasoned, was slightly less strident, and she might therefore have been less offensive to middle-of-the-road voters than Barr.[33]

Despite Barr's disadvantages, the Republican undercurrent was strong. Darden had been fighting for his political life ever since he assumed the seat of his ultra-conservative Democratic predecessor. Numbers tell the story. The old (pre-1992) Seventh Congressional District gave Reagan 73 percent of its vote in 1984, and it gave Bush 70 percent in 1988; when Bush lost to Clinton in 1992, the new Seventh gave the Republican 47 percent of the vote to the Democrat's 38 percent (15 percent went to Perot). Darden had won handily in 1988, with 65 percent, but he slipped to 60 percent in 1990 and 57 percent in 1992 when he outspent his Republican opponent more than twelve times over. It was a gloomy trend for the Democrat.

Although Darden was a well-liked person, he was allied with Clinton much of the time—and Clinton was growing unpopular in Georgia. The slack in Darden's electoral support could be seen in an early poll: roughly two-thirds of the electorate said it would consider voting for someone else.[34] Significantly, the two GOP candidates in the 1994 congressional primary had used staunchly conservative themes, seemingly without fear that moderate voters would punish them in the upcoming general election.

Barr's strategy for the general election would replicate the approach he used in the GOP primary. Barr would show that he was more conservative than his opponent. It was an issue-based strategy that would require the Barr campaign to overcome two formidable obstacles.

First, issue-based strategies ask voters to abandon a representative they once supported in favor of a largely unknown quantity on the basis of a few "bad votes." Some lines of anti-incumbent attack—those that go to ideological inconsistency, corruption, and ineptitude—are potent because they imply a violation of fundamental expectations: members of Congress should be dependable, ethical, and competent. Failing to meet these standards is sufficient reason to throw a bum out. But with policy, the issues are usually more complicated. Every story has at least two sides and journalists are disinclined to run with only one perspective. In fact, the news media tend to cover personalities more than policies. When issue statements are actually reported, lengthy explanations are clipped into brief sound bites. To make matters worse, illuminating the details of a complicated program is rarely a good use of expensive radio and television advertising. And even if an issue is presented in depth—by the news media and paid ads—few voters take the time to make a thoroughgoing policy comparison. The trick to policy-based campaign strategy lies in the ability to crystallize voter discontent into a single, sharply pointed theme of the sort that Paul Kanjorski had used in his "boiling water" commercial.

Second, drawing attention to policy often means sensationalizing divisive issues for tactical effect, a technique that risks political blowback. An ideologically extreme attention-grabber frequently alienates middle-of-the-road voters. In Barr's case, the district's conservatives were already in the fold; the moderates held the balance of power. An extremist policy agenda might drive swing voters toward Darden. Barr needed a theme that could show, in the simplest possible terms, that Darden was out-of-step with the district's values. The case would have to be made in a way that tapped preexisting political beliefs.

The solution for Barr and many other GOP candidates in 1994, including Cremeans in southern Ohio, was to turn the midterm election into a "referendum on President Clinton."[35] In 1992, the Seventh Congressional District had given Darden 57 percent of the vote while offering Clinton only 38 percent. At least a third of Darden's supporters had voted against Clinton. By mid-1994, taxes, gun control, gays in the military, and allegations of financial and personal wrongdoing weighed heavily on Clinton's image. By the 1994 general election, many southern voters saw Clinton as the embodiment of Democratic excess. The president had become a divisive political symbol. With southern ground already sloping toward the GOP, opposition to Clinton seemed to have become a sensibly moderate position. Hence, the Republican Party's nationwide, anti-Clinton strategy was tailor-made for Georgia's Seventh Congressional District, where the Democratic incumbent had paid meticulous attention to local concerns.

The battle for the Seventh would call the all-politics-is-local rule into question. Indeed, it would give new meaning to the idea that the "enemy of my enemy is my friend."

With a clear, hard-hitting message, the Barr campaign quickly achieved media superiority. Barr had persuaded the Republican National Committee (RNC) and the National Republican Congressional Committee (NRCC) that he stood a chance to win the Seventh Congressional District. As a result, Barr was able to attract local media attention with a cavalcade of GOP dignitaries, including former U.S. Attorney General Edwin Meese, Texas Senator Phil Gramm, news commentator and former presidential candidate Pat Buchanan, and former Vice President Dan Quayle. As each high profile Republican traveled through the district, interest in Barr ratcheted upward, along with the campaign's ability to raise money. The combination of money and media coverage built even greater interest in the race, generating a rising spiral of campaign success.

Barr used his money and press coverage to fix public attention on the link between Darden and Clinton. The central line of attack was repeated time and again: Darden is a close ally of Clinton, and both politicians are too liberal for Georgia. Whether the issue was taxes, gun control, or moral values, Darden was said to be on Clinton's side. The image would soon take literal form.

The previous March, Darden and his son had gone jogging around Washington with President Clinton. A picture of that early morning run, showing Clinton alongside Darden, handed the Barr campaign an irresistible metaphor. Staffers posted an enormous blowup of the photograph on a wall of their campaign headquarters. The picture was circulated on letters, flyers, television commercials, and tee shirts. The tee shirts called Darden "Clinton's 'Buddy'," adding sharply, "Buddy Darden ran for Congress as a southern conservative. But look who he's running with these days." The tee shirts were so popular that, according to Barr's campaign manager, "we sold them to voters who didn't even live in the district!"[36] The photograph was a rarity in American politics, a genuine silver bullet. It encapsulated everything that Barr was trying to say about Darden: the incumbent was in step with the president, not the people.

By the time Barr signed the GOP Contract with America, he was already dominating the campaign agenda. One news account told how Barr was "crisscrossing the 11-county district in northwest Georgia with a vengeance, trying to tie the 10-year incumbent to everything that's dragging down Clinton in public opinion polls: a $30 billion crime bill with social programs such as midnight basketball and limits on assault weapons."[37] Darden was in retreat.

Although the *Atlanta Constitution* endorsed Darden—his opponent "has nothing positive to offer [but] right-wing dogma"[38]—Barr was supported by the *Atlanta Journal*,[39] National Right to Life, the National Federation of Independent Business, the Southern States Police Benevolent Association, and the National Rifle Association (NRA). The NRA endorsement was particularly significant. The organization had supported Darden in previous elections and had given the congressman nearly $5,000 earlier in the year; but after Darden's August vote for the gun-control-laden crime bill, the NRA's financial assistance was thrown to Barr. Conservative efforts went straight to the grassroots. Organized into teams of volunteers—right down to the precinct level—an energized, conservative, anti-Clinton constituency had found its voice in Barr's conservative message.

Barr defeated Darden by four points, 52 to 48 percent. The GOP gained majorities in Georgia, in the southern states, and in the House of Representatives. The anti-Clinton strategy instituted by Republican leaders like Gingrich and implemented by individual challengers like Barr smashed the ranks of an already struggling bloc of moderate southern Democrats. It was a sign of the changing South, where social conservatism was overtaking long-held political attachments to the Democratic Party. Regarding the Seventh Congressional District, *Washington Post* columnist Mary McGrory wrote that Darden's loss was emblematic of the 1994 "Republican Revolution." McGrory attributed Barr's victory to "the alienated white male voter—the kind, [Darden] says, 'who thinks Democrats care only about women and blacks, who thinks his guns are being taken away from him and he feels threatened.'"[40] Wrote McGrory, "While every gun nut went to the polls, the Democratic base didn't bother."[41]

Message Discipline

Incumbency brings communicative muscle. Congressional representatives tout federal projects in public events, raise a disproportionate amount of money for campaign advertisements, and connect with individual voters by way of constituent casework.[42] "Incumbency style" has been defined in terms of the "symbolic trappings of the office," an aura of "legitimacy," a presumption of "competency," and a variety of "pragmatic" essentials that include access to news coverage and the ability to distribute federal largess.[43] To be in Congress is to make one's case for re-election every day—or at least to have the opportunity. Challengers are left to hack away at the edges.[44] If a member of Congress releases a steady flow of positive imagery during the first year of the term, and then molds the resulting impressions into a strong theme, the odds of defeat are slim, though every campaign season brings down at least a few incumbents. A post-election survey of the Seventh Congressional District suggested that Barr's issue-based campaign dampened the communicative powers of incumbency.

Darden was well known and well liked. A full 80 percent of respondents said they were familiar with Darden prior to the election.[45] Half of the sample had read about Darden in mailings or newspaper articles and about the same number had seen him on television. In fact, roughly 15 percent had either met the eleven-year congressman personally or attended a meeting at which he had appeared. (In September, a reporter quoted one constituent, "[H]e's touchable. . . . He's a common man."[46]) Asked if they could "remember anything special that Representative Darden has done for the people of this district," more than a quarter answered "yes." Even Barr supporters recognized Darden's accomplishments. Some 88 percent of those who voted for Barr suggested that Darden had considerable experience, while 60 percent thought he was a hard worker. Barr's own campaign manager would later comment that Darden was "one of the most popular, nicest members of the Georgia congressional delegation."[47]

The people liked Darden, but Darden had offered them no compelling rationale for his re-election. Darden attacked Barr for having a "radical right" agenda. He talked about Barr's seeming flip-flops on gun control and abortion. Reminding voters of his own work for the Seventh Congressional District, Darden said, "I still believe the people in Cobb County and Rome and across the district are interested in what I'm able to do to support the local industry, jobs and values."[48] Darden did not apologize for his 1993 budget vote, and with respect to guns, he asked, "what business does a kid have with a MAC-10 [assault pistol], carrying it to school?"[49] Under fire for supporting a crime bill that sought to restrict such guns, Darden emphasized the local impact of law enforcement funding also contained in that omnibus legislation. Finally, in the closing days of the campaign, Darden showed his Georgia roots. A radio ad featured native son Jimmy Carter, using the tagline, "Buddy Darden is 100 percent pure Georgia."[50] Any one of these disparate messages might have provided a good reason to reelect Darden, but they never came together into a single, consistent, effective campaign theme.

Barr, on the other hand, concentrated his message strategy on a single point. In a year when many voters were looking to oust Democratic incumbents, Barr used Clinton's presidency to focus conservative wrath on Darden. The Contract with America gave Barr's message a national hook. Barr occasionally struck at Darden's work for the district—he called Darden's announcement of local law enforcement grants "misinformation"[51]—but for the most part, Barr simply pressed the Clinton-Darden link. The GOP leaders who traveled through the Seventh Congressional District reinforced Barr's message. Republican surrogates were doubly powerful because, apart from Georgians Jimmy Carter and Sam Nunn, Darden was not in a position to call on national Democratic allies. Barr could count on Clinton while Darden could not. In defeat, Darden would say, "The worst thing I had going for me was that I was an incumbent with a D after my name."[52]

Barr's disciplined offensive was complemented by a masterful defensive operation; indeed, throughout the primary and general elections, Barr showed that the best defense is sometimes a good offense. By sheer tenacity, Barr withstood attacks that would have destroyed most candidates. When Fitzgerald claimed that Barr had soft-pedaled the crime issue, Barr accused Fitzgerald of having performed an abortion in her medical practice and asked, "How can you be pro-choice and against murder?"[53] (Fitzgerald flatly denied the charge.[54]) Later, when the Darden campaign found that Barr had once testified in support of gun control, Barr hit back: "They're flailing around, trying to find a way to divert attention."[55] And when the Darden campaign ran ads stating that Barr had been sued for child support by one of his ex-wives, Barr was able to turn even this lethal political issue to his own advantage.

Barr operatives invited all the media they could find to an upcoming debate, promising a huge story. Just before the candidates were slated to begin speaking, Barr's ex-wife walked up to the stage and proceeded to excoriate Darden for "drawing myself and my sons into his campaign."[56] Barr's campaign manager, Jeff Breedlove, would later recall, "There was silence in the place. You could have heard a pin drop and Buddy had nothing to say in response. It was huge and the cameras were rolling."[57] The next day's headline announced, "Ex-wife Defends Barr as 'Wonderful Father.'"[58]

Shielding itself nimbly while remaining on the attack, the Barr campaign's anti-Clinton message broke through. A full 83 percent of those who had switched their vote from Darden to Barr disapproved of President Clinton's job performance. Asked about the "single most important issue during the campaign," a solid majority of those who supported Barr talked, not about their own candidate, but about Darden: his values, his support for gun control, his vote for new taxes, and his association with Clinton. Many respondents, especially Darden supporters who had shifted their vote to Barr, just saw a "need for a change." Notably, the vast majority of Barr supporters believed that Darden voted with Clinton at least three-quarters of the time, while most Darden supporters thought that their congressman was more independent.

Perhaps the most remarkable finding of the post-election survey was that Darden's message had worked! The Darden campaign never assembled a unified theme, but the congressman was clearly running on the notion that he could deliver for the district. A strong majority of those who voted for Barr thought that Darden was experienced and hardworking. Voters had heard the congressman, and they believed him. But Darden's opponent had argued persuasively that the candidates should be judged on other terms. Barr won because he dominated the agenda, making loyalty to Clinton the criteria against which Darden was to be evaluated.

Some observers had previously believed that Fitzgerald, deemed slightly more moderate than Barr, was better positioned to win the general election. A centrist strategy might have held the partisan base intact while simultaneously attracting swing voters from the middle ground. A few GOP voters did in fact cross over to the Democratic side. Members of "Moderate Republicans for Darden" had seen Barr's campaign "playing to the right wing, religious conservatives . . . and we realized no one even cared about us."[59] If the trend had continued, Barr might have lost.

And yet, Barr's aggressive approach ultimately unseated Darden. Acerbic language made news, helping Barr broadcast his conservative message. Furthermore, Barr was joined in his anti-Clinton campaign by pro-gun and pro-life political organizations, as well as the RNC, the NRCC, and the Republican leadership of the House of Representatives. Converging on a specific weakness—Darden's affiliation with the Democratic president—and repeating their anti-Clinton attacks over and over again, Barr and his allies pounded through heavy layers of incumbent protection. A moderate would have had trouble achieving Barr's strict message discipline. In the Republican Revolution of 1994, strident language helped Barr mobilize the increasingly strong southern Republican base.

Southern Realignment

In a strong sense, Barr's victory was the product of message discipline. Barr had developed a piercing campaign theme that was consistent with a national message formulated by his party, and in this way he was able to use the efforts of the RNC to leverage his own hard work. In another time and place, the Clinton-Darden photograph would have meant nothing. Association with a president from one's own party is not always an electoral liability. But in the context of Georgia politics—given meaning by a larger anti-Democratic message strategy—an innocuous photograph could help dislodge a deeply entrenched incumbent. Barr hammered at his opponent's weak point, and won.

Barr's victory cannot be understood without reference to its geographic and historical context. The 1994 midterm elections were perhaps most significant in their continuation of the long-running Republican thrust into the South.[60] Walter Dean Burnham has called 1994, the year of the Republican Revolution, "probably the most consequential off-year election in . . . one hundred years," predicting that the partisan realignment of the South would continue to strengthen.[61] While the southern realignment may or may not be as deep or as long-lasting as Burnham believed, the GOP's Election Day gains at both the state and national levels were soon fortified by the defections of several southern Democrats to the newly dominant Republican Party.

The 1994 sweep was a complicated affair. It is possible to give too much credit to "angry white males," and it would be misleading to portray the Republican Revolution as a strictly southern phenomenon, since gains in the West and Midwest were almost as great.[62] Ohio's Frank Cremeans was among the beneficiaries. Moreover, a close examination of individual races shows that the force of the Republican Revolution was unevenly distributed. Elections scholar Gary Jacobson has noted that, "although all politics was not local in 1994, the electoral effect of national issues varied across districts and regions, depending on incumbency, the quality of candidates, the level of campaign spending, the partisan makeup of the district, and the behavior of the incumbent."[63] Some Republicans were able to take advantage of the electoral trends while others were not, a fact that tends to highlight the local and strategic factors inherent in seemingly structural change.

Indeed, the Barr-Darden contest might have gone either way. In Darden's favor, the economy had been pulled out of recession, and Darden's status as an incumbent helped to build a strong financial base, maintain an experienced campaign team, and show his concern for the district's well-being; against him, congressional Democrats were all but destined to lose seats in the first midterm election of Clinton's presidential term—a time when incumbents of the president's party almost always lose seats in the House—and in the Seventh Congressional District, the partisan winds that had been gathering for the past half century rendered it increasingly favorable to a Republican challenger. The mixed bag of electoral factors heightened the electoral volatility of the district—or at the very least, it closed the gap between the candidates. The marginality of the district, in turn, amplified the significance of strategic effects.

The close-run politics of the Seventh Congressional District owed much to the deterioration of Georgia's once-powerful Democratic campaign organization. It is interesting to compare Barr's run for the House in 1994 with that of GOP Congressman Fletcher M. Thompson's bid for the Senate in 1972, a presidential election year when Georgians made racial integration and militant patriotism the issues of the day. "During his senatorial campaign," observed one team of historians, "Thompson sometimes seemed to be running less against his Democratic opponent, Sam Nunn, than against school buses, [presidential candidate George] McGovern, and actress Jane Fonda and former Attorney General Ramsey Clark, both of whom had visited North Vietnam and whom, according to Thompson, should be charged with treason."[64] Nixon did well in Georgia—sweeping the white conservative vote that Democrats had left to Wallace four years earlier—but Thompson lost anyway, because the "organizational superiority" of the Democratic establishment ensured Nunn's victory.[65]

A critical difference between Thompson's loss and Barr's win lies in the convergence of two Republican-leaning trends: Georgia voters were increasingly willing to cast their ballots for Republicans, while the state's Democratic Party was losing the firm, county-by-county structure that once characterized southern politics.[66] By 1994, Republican ideology was ready to compete with Democratic incumbency.

The decline of Democratic influence might have been a necessary precondition for Darden's defeat, but party erosion was not sufficient to guarantee Barr's victory. Barr needed a good campaign. He won in 1994 because he skillfully exploited the shifting political terrain. Darden could not effectively cope with the Republican onslaught. As the election progressed, tactical decisions made by the two campaigns had the effect of blunting, even *reversing*, the normally powerful incumbent advantage.

First, Barr organized his campaign around national GOP themes. Challengers are usually hobbled by a relative lack of media coverage—few congressional hopefuls make the network news and even local reporting offers only intermittent attention. But with Republicans across the country singing from the same anti-Democratic hymnal, the GOP message was bound to penetrate. Local campaigns piggybacked onto the national effort. Furthermore, the broad-based Republican message reduced the need for GOP challengers to gain individual attention. Suspicion was heaped on all Democratic incumbents. From the Republican point of view, Clinton and the Democratic Congress had raised taxes, coddled criminals, refused to pass meaningful welfare reform, and placed U.S. troops under United Nations command. Frustrated conservative voters would feel comfortable voting for almost any Republican challenger. (Note that the Darden-Clinton tee shirt attacked Darden without plugging Barr.) On the verge of defeat, Darden summed up his problem: "It's a very strong nationwide tide we're bucking."[67]

Second, Darden offered no unified counterattack. He employed a typical incumbent strategy, talking about his work for the district and suggesting that his opponent was an extremist who had only tenuous connections with the state. The trouble was that Darden's campaign, like the campaigns of many other southern Democrats, never developed a singular message that could sustain itself against the combined GOP offensive. Darden hit Barr for wavering on gun control; he explained that his position on the Appropriations Committee was helpful to the district; and he assured his constituents that he was "pure Georgia"—but these divergent themes never coalesced. Democratic moderates throughout Georgia were all facing the same problem: they offered no clear-cut rationale for continuing the tradition of moderate Democratic representation in the South.

With the exception of Governor Zell Miller (who was endorsed by the NRA) and Congressman Nathan Deal (who would switch to the GOP in April of 1995), the moderate Democrats of Georgia's political leadership were swept from office in 1994 even as the state's liberal Democrats were left standing.

Finally, Barr found a way to negate the powers of incumbency. Although the economy was picking up, Barr argued that the American standard of morality was in decay. As evidence, he proffered gays in the military, the welfare system, abortion rights, and foreign language examinations for U.S. citizenship. Combining two hot-button themes into a single, piercing charge, Barr expressed his concern that "illegal immigrants receive billions in welfare; this should be absolutely prohibited."[68] More than anything else, Barr articulated conservative disdain for Clinton. Barr exclaimed, "You can cut or slice it any way you like, but [Darden's 92 percent agreement with Clinton] is higher than any Georgia member of Congress, including Cynthia McKinney and John Lewis," two liberals in the Congressional Black Caucus.[69] It mattered little that Darden was conservative on many key issues: if the country was in decline, then Democrats must pay.

Like many Republicans in the "Class of 1994," Barr equated Democratic incumbency with deference to the president. According to McGrory, "Barr's motto was 'You can't vote against Clinton right now, but you can vote against Buddy Darden.'"[70] Repeated time and again, it became a persuasive notion.

Barr's campaign manager believes that Darden's loss stemmed from a paradoxical vulnerability of congressional power. Darden had moved up the ranks of the House Democratic Caucus, winning appointment to the Appropriations Committee. The seat came at a price, however. Members of the committee were expected to show party loyalty on important votes. While Darden may have opposed some provisions of Clinton's 1993 budget, the presumption of party support that accompanied his influential committee assignment required Darden to vote for final passage on the House version of the bill. Hence the fatal link: Darden was trying to cooperate with the congressional leadership while the congressional leadership was trying to cooperate with the president. It was a deadly chain of responsibility for a Democratic congressman from Georgia.

During the campaign, Darden defended his party line voting as a matter of legislative obligation. "If you serve on the Appropriations Committee and you help formulate the bills," Darden told a reporter, "you don't turn around and vote against what you've done."[71] To at least one constituent who was worried that the Democratic Party was dragging the nation down the wrong path, Barr's characterization of Darden made more sense: "On every important vote, [Darden] is with Clinton."[72]

It was an ironic twist: rising up through the Democratic ranks, Darden had enhanced his ability to bring federal projects back to the district, but newfound party responsibilities left him ideologically distant. Barr thus turned the dilemma into a no-win situation for Darden. The conventional wisdom had been that the "local" in Tip O'Neill's rule went to economic concerns. On this score, Darden was in good standing. He had done everything that a good congressional representative is supposed to do. Barr, however, understood that the interests of the district had come to be defined in more ideological terms. Darden, a Democrat who tended to vote with his party, could be portrayed as a congressman out of touch with his constituency. Thus, in the Seventh Congressional District of Georgia, Barr's anti-incumbent strategy turned congressional power into an electoral curse.

Barr's win was a product not simply of regional realignment, but of strategy and tactics—or more precisely, a clever line of attack that availed itself of opportunities created by a southern electorate in transition. The southern realignment worked for Barr because Barr and his campaign *made* it work in their part of Georgia. Without a good strategy, Barr could easily have succumbed to a well-liked moderate Democrat who had long brought lucrative federal projects back to his district. But a smart, policy-oriented strategy, tailored to the ongoing southern disaffection with Democratic priorities, would prevail over the power of incumbency. The night that Barr won—helping the Republican Party gain fifty-two seats in the House of Representatives, placing the House in GOP hands for the first time in four decades—the band at Barr's victory party played "Dixie" and "many in the crowded room swayed and sang along."[73] It was a sign of the new Southern Republicanism.

Notes

1. Philip D. Duncan and Christine C. Lawrence, eds., *Politics in America, 1998* (Washington, D.C.: Congressional Quarterly, 1997), 398.

2. Michael Barone and Grant Ujifusa, eds., *Almanac of American Politics, 2000* (Washington, D.C.: National Journal, 1999), 477.

3. Adam Clymer, "House Approves Repealing of Ban on Assault Guns," *New York Times*, 23 March 1996.

4. "Resigned to Losing, Managers Pin Blame; GOP-led Senate Hamstringing Them," *Baltimore Sun*, 28 January 1999.

5. Melinda Henneberger, "The Georgia Republican Who Uses the I-Word," *New York Times*, 9 May 1998.

6. Christopher Caldwell, "The Southern Captivity of the GOP," *Atlantic Monthly*, June 1998, 55–72.

7. Anthony Gene Carey, *Parties, Slavery, and the Union in Antebellum Georgia* (Athens: University of Georgia Press, 1997), 105–23.

8. V.O. Key noted an interesting exception to the area's Democratic lean: in 1928, northern Georgia gave Hoover a stronger vote than the rest of the state—a phenomenon Key attributed to the relative lack of black voters in this part of Georgia. V.O. Key, Jr., *Southern Politics in State and Nation* (New York: Alfred A. Knopf, 1949), 325–27.

9. See Numan V. Bartley, *From Thurmond to Wallace: Political Tendencies in Georgia, 1948–1968* (Baltimore, Md.: Johns Hopkins, 1970).

10. See Joseph A. Aistrup, *The Southern Strategy Revisited: Republican Top-Down Advancement in the South* (Lexington: University Press of Kentucky, 1996).

11. Alan Ehrenhalt, ed., *Politics in America: Members of Congress in Washington and at Home, 1986* (Washington, D.C.: Congressional Quarterly, 1985), 411.

12. "Voting Studies Appendix," in *Congressional Quarterly Almanac, 1984* (Washington, D.C.: Congressional Quarterly, 1985).

13. Michael Barone and Grant Ujifusa, eds. *Almanac of American Politics, 1990* (Washington, D.C.: National Journal, 1989), 311.

14. Carlos Campos, "Legal Group's Action Stirs Concern," *Atlanta Journal & Constitution*, 11 July 1999.

15. Tom Baxter, "Darden Takes Barbs For His Vote," *Atlanta Journal & Constitution*, 31 May 1993.

16. Susan Laccetti, "Barr to Oppose Darden in 7th District Next Year," *Atlanta Journal & Constitution*, 9 August 1993.

17. See "Election '94: Your Voters Guide to Tuesday's Primary," *Atlanta Journal & Constitution*, 14 July 1994.

18. Kathey Alexander, "Fitzgerald, Barr to Debate Tonight; Republican Foes to Meet Last Time Before Primaries," *Atlanta Journal & Constitution*, 14 July 1994.

19. Kathey Alexander, "Fitzgerald, Barr to Debate Tonight."

20. Kathey Alexander, "Accusations Heat Up 7th District Race for GOP Nomination," *Atlanta Journal & Constitution*, 12 July 1994.

21. Kathey Alexander, "Republicans Ready to Salve Wounds, Join in Attack on Incumbent Darden," *Atlanta Journal & Constitution*, 21 July 1994.

22. Terrel L. Rhodes, *Republicans in the South: Voting for the State House, Voting for the White House* (Westport, Conn.: Praeger, 2000), 20–56.

23. Ibid., 20, 56. Notably, Arkansas Governor Bill Clinton had a respectable southern showing in 1992, winning a handful of southern states, including Georgia (which Clinton lost in 1996).

24. See Aistrup, *The Southern Strategy Revisited.*

25. See John C. Green, "The Christian Right and the 1994 Elections: A View from the States," *PS: Political Science & Politics* (March 1995): 5–8.

26. Aistrup, *The Southern Strategy Revisited*, 56–57.

27. Ibid., 56. See also Louis Bolce, Gerald DeMaio, and Douglas Muzzio,

"Dial-In Democracy: Talk Radio and the 1994 Election," *Political Science Quarterly* 111(1996): 457–81.

28. James G. Gimpel, *Fulfilling the Contract: The First 100 Days* (Boston: Allyn and Bacon, 1996), 19–20.

29. Barrie Tron, "Staging Media Events: What We Learned from the 'Contract with America,'" *Campaigns & Election*, December/January 1996, 50.

30. Ibid.

31. Republicans in several states developed their own versions of the Contract with America, effectively drawing the nationalized election down to the local level. See Thomas H. Little, "On the Coattails of a Contract: RNC Activities and Republican Gains in the 1994 State Legislative Elections," *Political Research Quarterly* 51 (1998): 173–90.

32. Gary Jacobson notes that the actual effect, as measured by exit polls, showed that few voters knew of the Contract and even fewer were persuaded by it. Of those who reported that the Contract had made a difference in there vote, "7 percent said it would make them more likely to vote for the Republican House candidate, while 5 percent said it would make them less likely to do so." Gary C. Jacobson, "The 1994 House Elections in Perspective," *Political Science Quarterly* 111 (1996): 203–23, 229. Two percent is a small portion of the electorate, but in a marginal race, small swings can change the outcome. (One analysis found that awareness of the Contract clustered disproportionately among wealthier voters, for whom several of its provisions—for example, capital gains tax cuts—seem to have been designed. Jeffrey M. Stonecash and Mack D. Mariani, "Republican Gains in the House in the 1994 Elections: Class Polarization in American Politics," *Political Science Quarterly* 115 (2000): 93–113.) Furthermore, by setting a national agenda, Republicans generally avoided the sorts of mixed messages that plagued the Democrats during 1994, with moderate and conservative Democrats running away from the legislative agenda of the previous two years as liberal and urban Democrats embraced it.

33. Dick Williams, "Back to Medicine: Negative Ads May Have Killed Fitzgerald's Bid," *Atlanta Journal & Constitution*, 26 July 1994.

34. See Mary McGrory, "Buddy, Can You Spare a Term?" *Washington Post*, 20 November 1994.

35. Kathey Alexander, "Barr Tries to Pin Darden to Clinton Coattails," *Atlanta Journal & Constitution*, 18 September 1994.

36. Jeff Breedlove, telephone interview, 11 December 2000.

37. Alexander, "Barr Tries to Pin Darden to Clinton Coattails."

38. Editorial, "Candidates of Substance," *Atlanta Constitution*, 20 October 1994.

39. Editorial, "Conservatives Needed to Check Administration," *Atlanta Journal*, 26 October 1994.

40. See McGrory, "Buddy, Can You Spare a Term?"

41. Ibid.

42. See Gary C. Jacobson, *The Politics of Congressional Elections*, 5th ed. (New York: Longman, 2001).

43. Judith S. Trent and Robert V. Friedenberg, *Political Campaign Communication: Principles and Practices*, 4th ed. (Westport, Conn.: Praeger, 2000), 77–93.

44. Ibid., 93–101.

45. For a more complete examination of the post-election poll in this district, see Daniel M. Shea, "Issue Voting, Challenger Quality, and the Ousting of a Ten-Year Incumbent," *American Review of Politics* 17 (1996): 395–419.

46. Kathey Alexander, "Three Tough Races for Democrats in Two Districts, Incumbents Try to Hold on to Seat," *Atlanta Journal & Constitution*, 18 September 1994.

47. Breedlove, telephone interview.

48. Alexander, "Barr Tries to Pin Darden to Clinton's Coattails."

49. Ibid.

50. Lucy Soto and Charles Walston, "Endangered Candidates? Johnson, Darden on List," *Atlanta Journal & Constitution*, 1 November 1994.

51. Rebecca Nash, "Initial Crime Bill Grants Allot $5.5 Million in Ga.," *Atlanta Journal & Constitution*, 12 October 1994.

52. Kathey Alexander, "Barr Says He'll Stick to GOP 'Contract,'" *Atlanta Journal & Constitution*, 10 November 1994.

53. Peter Mantanis, "Atlanta Almanac," *Atlanta Journal & Constitution*, 15 July 1994.

54. Ibid.

55. Kathey Alexander, "Barr, Darden Sticking to Their Guns in 7th District Race," *Atlanta Journal & Constitution*, 6 October 1994.

56. Kathey Alexander, "Ex-wife Defends Barr as 'Wonderful Father,'" *Atlanta Journal & Constitution*, 21 October 1994.

57. Breedlove, telephone interview.

58. Alexander, "Ex-wife Defends Barr as 'Wonderful Father.'"

59. Alexander, "Three Tough Races."

60. Jacobson, "The 1994 House Elections in Perspective"; James E. Campbell, "The Presidential Pulse and the 1994 Midterm Congressional Election," *Journal of Politics* 59 (1997): 830–57, 850–53; Marie-France Toinet, "Les élections américaines de 1994: Sont-elles des élections de réalignment?" *Revue France de Science Politique* 45 (1995): 980–1000.

61. Walter Dean Burnham, "Realignment Lives: The 1994 Earthquake and Its Implications," in *The Clinton Presidency: First Appraisals*, eds. Colin Campbell and Bert A. Rockman (Chatham, N.J.: Chatham House, 1996), 363, 385.

62. See Grant Recher and Joseph Cammarano, "In Search of the Angry White Male: Gender, Race, and Issues in the 1994 Elections," in *Midterm: The Elections of 1994 in Context*, ed. Philip A. Klinkner (Boulder, Colo.: Westview, 1996); David W. Brady, John F. Cogan, Brian J. Gaines, and Douglas Rivers, "The Perils

of Presidential Support: How the Republicans Took the House in the 1994 Mid-term Elections," *Political Behavior* 18 (1996): 345–67.

63. Jacobson, "The 1994 House Elections in Perspective," 220–21; See also John E. Owens, "The Importance of Candidate Characteristics and Local Political Conditions in the 1994 US [sic] Mid-Term Elections," *Political Studies* 46 (1998): 766–76.

64. Numan V. Bartley and Hugh D. Graham, *Southern Politics and the Second Reconstruction* (Baltimore, Md.: Johns Hopkins University Press, 1975), 180.

65. Ibid.

66. For a discussion of the county structure in Georgia, see Key, "Southern Politics in State and Nation," 117–29.

67. Kathey Alexander, "Darden Struggles to Hang on to Seat; Anti-Clinton Feelings Give Barr Early Lead in Hard-Fought Race," *Atlanta Journal & Constitution*, 9 November 1994.

68. "How Candidates Stand on the Issues: Crime," *Atlanta Journal & Constitution*, 27 October 1994.

69. Alexander, "Ex-wife Defends Barr as a 'Wonderful Father.'"

70. McGrory, "Buddy, Can You Spare A Term?"

71. Mike Christensen, "Backstage Style Fits Darden; Demo Shrugs off Foe's Strategy," *Atlanta Journal & Constitution*, 20 October 1994.

72. Alexander, "Barr Tries to Pin Darden to Clinton's Coattails."

73. Kathey Alexander, "Error Gave Candidate False Win," *Atlanta Journal & Constitution*, 10 November 1994.

Defy Conventional Wisdom 5

LORETTA SANCHEZ
D-CALIFORNIA
FORTY-SIXTH CONGRESSIONAL DISTRICT

P OLITICAL CAMPAIGNS often take surprising twists and turns. The presidential election of 2000 ended with a recount that left scholars, pundits, and voters scrambling to understand how localities choose their voting equipment, when ballots are discarded, how the absentee voting process operates, and why the basic machinery of American democracy sometimes fails to work as planned. Four years earlier, election observers had been given a primer on post-election politics with the contested victories of two Democratic women. In the Louisiana race for U.S. Senate, Mary Landrieu slipped past her Republican adversary by a handful of votes, and in the contest for the Forty-Sixth Congressional District of California, long-shot candidate Loretta Sanchez defeated nine-term GOP incumbent Robert K. Dornan by an equally slim margin. Both races ended in challenges and recounts, resisting the textbook treatment of American campaigns—one that runs from a primary elections, through a general campaign, on to Election Day and the late-night concession by the loser. In Sanchez' case, the post-election contest would last until early 1998, as Dornan and his supporters tried to oust the congresswoman from her seat by overturning the certified results of the 1996 election.

Dornan's post-election battle was an extreme manifestation of unconventional political warfare. Dornan charged that a large number of ineligible voters had cast ballots for Sanchez. His legal challenge was denied and, in a 1998 rematch, Sanchez beat Dornan by a substantial margin. During the 1996 campaign, Sanchez had used an unconventional strategy of her own. Discounting the accepted rules of electoral strategy, which call for high profile electioneering and widespread exploitation of broadcast media, Sanchez maintained a quiet, grassroots crusade that gambled on the then-unproven power of cable advertising. Her victory shows that strategic rules are made to be broken. Sanchez won the race by rethinking some of the fundamental principles of political strategy.

Unpredictability is a strategic asset. Because resources are limited, a campaign must prioritize its tactical risks. No candidate has the wherewithal to dominate every corner of the electoral battlefield, so opposition defenses often hinge on a capacity to predict where and when a strike will come. The lesson: surprise attacks force opponents off-balance. A stunned opposition must scuttle prearranged strategies and gather new resources in hopes of beating back the assault. If new defenses cannot be emplaced swiftly, defeat may ensue. Summarizing military theorist Carl von Clausewitz, John Pitney writes: "The idea is to get adversaries to forgo opportunities, fall into traps, and do other things that will hasten their own defeat."[1] Dornan's failure to see the danger posed by Sanchez' campaign challenge reveals the power of tactical creativity in electoral warfare.

Dornan's confidence was grounded in reason. He was a leader among right-wing conservatives and he had raised huge sums of money for his many re-election campaigns. From 1977 to 1983, Dornan had represented California's Twenty-Seventh Congressional District in Santa Monica, leaving Congress only after his seat was eliminated by redistricting. A failed attempt at the 1982 Republican nomination for the U.S. Senate only strengthened Dornan's resolve. The former congressman soon shifted operations to conservative Orange County, more than an hour's drive from Santa Monica. He won the Forty-Sixth in 1984. As an outspoken conservative with an uncanny ability to spin quotable quotes—he had been a drama student in college and later found work as a radio talk show host—Dornan had gained a national following. Direct mail solicitations reaped millions of dollars from around the country. As a result, Dornan routinely crushed his opponents under a barrage of well-honed verbal attacks supported by massive advertising budgets. In 1994, Dornan swamped his opponent by spending $2.3 million when the average incumbent spent about a third of that amount.

Dornan's aggressive tactics seemed to demoralize the district's Democratic base. Even though the partisan registration of this formerly Republican district had begun to favor the Democrats, low turnout by Democratic voters had allowed Dornan to maintain his grip on the Forty-Sixth Congressional District.

The Candidate

Sanchez seemed an unlikely candidate to oust Dornan. Born and raised in Anaheim, she was the daughter of Mexican immigrants, both of whom worked at a local manufacturing plant. After high school, Sanchez studied economics at Orange County's Chapman University before moving on to receive a Master of Business Administration in 1982 from American University in Washington, D.C. Sanchez returned home to work as a business consultant. Though she had never held elective office, she had served a short stint in the public sector helping to manage the finances of the Orange County Transportation Authority. Sanchez has said that Pat Buchanan's harsh brand of conservatism prompted her to switch her party affiliation from Republican to Democrat in 1992.[2] In 1994, Sanchez ran for Anaheim City Council under her married name of Brixey. The results were disappointing. She came in eighth among sixteen candidates, netting just 5.8 percent of the overall vote. It was an inauspicious way for Sanchez to start her political career.

At the beginning of the 1996 election cycle, Sanchez still appeared to be a political innocent. The thirty-six-year-old candidate received virtually no press during the first few months of the year. Indeed, Sanchez was all but ignored prior to the March primary, which pitted her against two experienced Democratic candidates (one of whom had received a bevy of endorsements from local, state, and national Democrats). Even after Sanchez' upset victory in the primary election, there seemed to be little reason for Dornan to take his opponent seriously. Looking forward to the general election, one analysis blithely remarked, "Doesn't matter."[3] Dornan would surely win!

Sanchez told journalists that her face-to-face conversations with voters were going well, but the Sanchez team was not floating any positive poll numbers in the press. Sanchez was getting scant funding from national-level political action committees, and the organizers of the Democratic National Convention in Chicago declined to have her speak from the podium. She had no television presence. In fact, there was little evidence that the Sanchez campaign would be able to make the heavy media buys usually required to defeat an entrenched incumbent. Every two years, hundreds of earnest challengers are crushed by professionalized campaign operations, and by all appearances, Sanchez was indistinguishable from any other political novice.

Appearances were deceiving, however. The Sanchez campaign was not an amateur act; rather, it was a professional team led by experienced consultants, including John Shallman, a veteran of Los Angeles politics; Bill Wachob, a respected media advisor; and Lake Research, a top-tier polling firm. Early Sanchez polls showed that Dornan was highly vulnerable. Conventional wisdom would have had the campaign announce its encouraging findings in order to raise voter expectations, media coverage, and campaign money, but the Sanchez organization chose not to release their polling. Instead, political operatives bet on a long-shot political strategy. They kept Dornan's vulnerabilities quiet so as not to wake the sleeping giant. When the time was right, the campaign released its polls and spent nearly all of its remaining cash on a series of hard-hitting cable television ads. Money started coming in. And just as the cable war heated up, the campaign shifted into a massive get-out-the-vote drive, an approach that many Digital Age political consultants deem less important than electronic media. Each tactical move was perilous—and each had its critics—but the ultimate wisdom of the strategy was borne out by electoral victory.

The Sanchez win underscores the power of changing demographics. In the 1980s, Dornan's district was Anglo and Republican; by 1996 it was Latino and Democratic. Businesswoman Loretta Sanchez appealed to Latino voters in ways that a Republican candidate never could. During the late 1980s and early 1990s, California Republicans joined in a backlash against illegal immigration, particularly against the delivery of government services to undocumented aliens and their families. The rhetoric of the backlash seemed to carry a chauvinist edge. Many Latinos were angered by claims that California was suffering from an "invasion" of Mexicans. Many Asians felt that the effort was directed at *all* non-Anglos. By aligning itself with the anti-immigrant cause (albeit without the racist vocabulary of die-hard nativists), California Republicans alienated a growing Latino constituency. The strategy would cost Republicans dearly. George W. Bush's effort to woo Latino voters early in his presidential term was an attempt to mend fences with the Hispanic community.

Many challenger campaigns rely on voter persuasion. In Georgia's Seventh Congressional District, voters went to the polls on a regular basis, so Republican Bob Barr had to find his winning percentage from among Democrat Buddy Darden's supporters: Darden voters were asked to vote for Barr. A low turnout constituency, however, offers an alternative approach: activating dormant supporters. California's Forty-Sixth Congressional District had one of the worst turnout rates in the country, reaching as low as 35 percent. Dornan, meanwhile, was suffering from voter erosion. In 1988, he received 87,690 votes, and then successively lower vote totals each year until he hit 50,126 in 1994. Dornan's numbers were trending steadily downward, but challenger scores had varied widely. If the Sanchez campaign, local Democrats, union organizers, and politically active community groups could maintain past Democratic numbers and increase the anti-Dornan turnout just slightly, Sanchez would have a shot at winning.

Immigration and California Politics

Sanchez ran for Congress at a moment of ethnic instability. Relations between Anglo and Hispanic residents of California had been tense even before the territory was carved from Mexico in the 1840s. Many Hispanic families have southern California roots that predate statehood, and a steady stream of immigrants arrived throughout the 1800s. In the early 1900s, Texas was the primary destination for most Mexican immigrants, but beginning in the 1960s, California was receiving a greater share of Mexican immigration than any other state, a trend that continued through the end of the century.[4] In the early 1990s, opposition to illegal immigration had become a central tenet of Republican ideology in California. In 1994, the issue came to a head with Proposition 187.

Prop 187, the "Save Our State Initiative" (SOS) sought to deny nonemergency public benefits to undocumented aliens. The proposition was debated at all levels of California politics and became a point of conflict in political races statewide, with conservative Republicans strongly supporting the measure. Moderate GOP Governor Pete Wilson was the most visible advocate for SOS.

The arguments that Wilson and others made for Prop 187 were framed in economic, not ethnic terms: illegal immigrants, it was said, paid no taxes, but they used public services and sent their children to public schools. Because California maintained a relatively generous social service system, some feared that the state was becoming a "welfare magnet" for illegal immigrants who did not pay their fair share. Advocates of the proposition further held that California was carrying the burden of weak federal policies. They argued that soft federal enforcement of immigration law had the effect of making California pay for a variety of problems—including a rise in criminal activity and a decline in living wage jobs—that barely touched other states in the union. Prop 187 would be one way to ensure that California did not have to pay for the failures of the national government. By concentrating on dollars and cents, Prop 187 advocates sought to avoid a campaign based on race or ethnicity.

Some GOP leaders opposed Prop 187 and the unusually mean-spirited rhetoric that it generated. Prominent Republicans Jack Kemp and William J. Bennett argued that Prop 187 was constitutionally dubious and politically unwise.[5] Conservative gadfly Ron Unz, who challenged Wilson in the 1994 Republican primary and who later sponsored an initiative to end bilingual education in California, has written about the vitriol that emerged from the debate:

> With even California's "moderate" governor calling for the expulsion of 300,000 children from California schools, implicit sanction was given to far more extreme words and deeds. At one point, Proposition 187 chairman Ron Prince told an audience of conservative activists that "you are the posse and SOS is the rope," while others regularly declared that the measure would finally drive the encroaching hordes of illegal aliens back to Mexico.[6]

Some of the language within Prop 187 lent pause to legal residents and U.S. citizens. Provisions calling for state employees to report anyone merely *sus-*

pected of being an illegal alien led many Hispanics to believe they might face a lifetime of mistrust and persecution. There was little reason for Latinos to think that Prop 187 was anything but an Anglo attempt to harass people of Hispanic origin.

Prop 187 passed with 59 percent of the vote. Wilson, who had entered the 1994 gubernatorial contest with sagging approval ratings, was returned to office in a landslide. Wilson's popularity had skyrocketed and many Republicans urged the Governor to run for president in 1996. The GOP gained a temporary majority in the state assembly and the party's congressional delegation added four new members. In Orange County, Republican candidates swept their Democratic opponents with ease. Dornan earned 57 percent of the vote—seven points higher than his 1992 margin. Statewide, Republican support among Hispanic voters dropped precipitously, but the swelling share of Anglo voters supporting Republican candidates more than erased this deficit.

At least for the short-term, the backlash against illegal immigration boosted the political stock of Republicans in California. It seemed to give the Republican Party a rock-solid issue that divided the electorate in favor of the GOP. But Election Night 1994 was the Republican high-water mark.

Speaker Willie Brown would maintain Democratic control of the state assembly through a series of extraordinary parliamentary maneuvers; Wilson's campaign for the presidency would be short-lived; and Prop 187 would eventually be ruled unconstitutional. The long-term implications of Prop 187 on California's political terrain would prove even more damaging to the state's GOP candidates. Pro-187 arguments highlighting criminality, welfare free-loading, and widespread economic parasitism were directed chiefly at illegal immigrants, and yet many other Latinos—citizens and legal residents alike—came to believe that the broad-brush attacks were directed at everyone of Hispanic descent.[7] Many felt that the seemingly neutral economic arguments merely cloaked old-style nativism. (Indeed, a study of voter preferences later found a strong "nativist link" between economic pessimism and support for Prop 187.[8]) The conservative backlash against illegal immigration thus created a counter-backlash that unified the Hispanic political movement squarely behind the Democratic Party.

Latino voters favored Democrats, but voter registration and Election Day turnout had been comparatively low. Anti-187 mobilization seemed to be changing things. In the aftermath of Prop 187, legal residents were seeking citizenship, new citizens were registering to vote, and new voters were highly motivated.[9] Latino registration drives heavily favored Democratic candidates. Political commentator E. J. Dionne wrote that Prop 187 "gave Latinos a hard shove into Democratic arms."[10] One consultant shared his political math: "In the 1980s, Latinos made up about 7 percent of the state's electorate and voted Democratic by about three to two. And that netted the Democrats a two-point lift in the typical election. Now, Latinos make up 14 to 15 percent of the electorate and are voting four-to-one Democratic, giving Democrats an eight to nine point boost."[11] As a result, "Republicans have to win [the Anglo vote] by fifteen points to win an election."[12]

As more and more Hispanics registered to vote, the Democratic advantage over Republicans would only grow larger. Kemp and Bennett had seen the problem coming. In October of 1994, they had written that "the anti-immigration boomerang, if it is hurled, will come back to hurt the GOP."[13]

The District

A suburban landscape and a history of Republican voting patterns give Orange County its staid, conservative reputation. Its economy centers around Disneyland, in Anaheim, and a variety of corporate headquarters and defense contractors, giving the Forty-Sixth Congressional District a measure of economic stability—a sense of security that seems to be reflected in mile after mile of straight avenues and boulevards, lined by green trees and well-manicured lawns. Strong support for Ronald Reagan in 1980 and 1984, and George H. W. Bush in 1988, made Orange County a bellwether of California conservatism; but in national politics, the county was taking on a more Democratic cast, particularly neighborhoods that made up the Forty-Sixth. By the time Sanchez launched her 1996 congressional campaign, Dornan's district was amenable to a Sanchez candidacy.

Dornan had been elected to the seat in 1984, when his district was very Republican and only one-quarter Hispanic. Redistricting, along with a dramatic transformation in ethnicity, enlarged the pool of potential Latino voters and reversed the district's partisan predisposition. Census data from 1990 showed that Hispanic residents made up half of the Forty-Sixth Congressional District, while Asian Americans accounted for another 12 percent. By 1996, a whopping 40 percent of the district was foreign-born. Democratic registration had grown to a level six points higher than Republican registration. Dornan's district was no longer Anglo and Republican; it was now Latino and Democratic. A Hispanic businesswoman running as a Democrat would be a very attractive candidate in the Forty-Sixth. If Sanchez could motivate the Latino vote without arousing nativist opposition, she might defeat "B-1 Bob."

Bob Dornan

"I'm not a complex person," Dornan once told a reporter; "I say what I believe. People who say I'm out of control mistake passion for temper."[14]

Moral fervor has led Dornan to call Democratic Senator Tom Harkin a "Marxist creep"[15] and to label the financial backers of then-Representative Barbara Boxer as members of the "coke-snorting, wife-swapping, baby-born-out-of-wedlock, radical Hollywood left."[16] Dornan has boasted that "every lesbian spear chucker in this country is hoping I get defeated."[17] It was a remark that seemed to epitomize the congressman's outrageous words and deeds. Once, during a heated debate over military spending, Dornan grabbed a congressional colleague by his necktie and reportedly warned, "Don't let me catch you off the [House] floor, where you are protected by the Sergeant at Arms."[18] In 1995, the congressman accused President Clinton of lending "aid and comfort to the enemy" by protesting the war in Vietnam—intemperate words that got Dornan suspended from speaking in the House chamber for a day.[19] Clinton had once said, "every time I see Dornan he looks like he needs a rabies shot."[20]

Dornan had been born in New York City and moved with his family to Los Angeles. After graduating from high school, Dornan studied acting at Loyola University. In 1952, at the age of nineteen, Dornan enlisted in the Air Force, where he became a fighter pilot. Later, following an undistinguished acting career, Dornan began offering political commentary on a local television public affairs program. The show received two Emmy awards. Riding the popularity of this program, Dornan was elected to the House of Representatives in 1976. His Santa Monica district was soon chopped up by redistricting, but Dornan persevered by running for the U.S. Senate in 1982. He lost all but eight percent of the primary vote, but he gained statewide recognition as a hardcore member of the conservative Right. Two years later, Dornan shifted his sights to the Thirty-Eighth Congressional District in Orange County. Defeating a liberal incumbent in 1984, Dornan would go on to hold the seat (later reshaped and renumbered as the Forty-Sixth) until his own loss in 1996.

While he served, Dornan was one of the most visible members of Congress. His claim to fame, aside from charged rhetoric and impassioned attacks on abortion, was a fervent support for military appropriations—not surprising for an Air Force veteran representing a district filled with defense contractors. Dornan aggressively supported funding for both the B-1 and B-2 bombers, and he actively promoted Reagan's Strategic Defense Initiative. This passion for military hardware earned "B-1 Bob" his nickname, one he bore proudly. With the Republican takeover of Congress in 1994, Dornan gained the chairmanships of both the National Security Committee's subcommittee on Military Personnel and the Select Intelligence Committee's subcommittee on Technical and Tactical Intelligence, but Dornan's political ambitions ran even higher.

Vowing to defend "democracy and decency" against the "moral decay that is rotting the heart and the soul of our country," Dornan announced in early 1995 that he was a candidate for president.[21] The White House bid was never taken seriously. Many conservatives backed Dornan—thanks largely to his animated attacks on liberals and his frequent appearances on C-SPAN, CNN, and a variety of radio and television talk shows—but the congressman spoke to the right wing of his party, and the competition on the Right was fierce. Senator Phil Gramm, radio talk show host Alan Keyes, television commentator Patrick Buchanan, businessman Morry Taylor, and publisher Steve Forbes were all jockeying for position among hard-line conservatives. In his own district, where Dornan appeared on the ballot seeking the GOP nomination for both Congress and the presidency, he garnered only 1,029 votes for his presidential bid.

White House ambitions drew national exposure but threatened electoral prospects back home. It was a strategic trade-off. Dornan tried to distinguish himself from GOP moderate Bob Dole by appealing to the far Right; Dornan's congressional district, however, had never been overwhelmingly conservative, and it was trending ever more liberal. George Bush had netted just 40 percent of the vote in 1992. Dornan's own numbers fell to 50 percent that year, and in 1994, though he earned 57 percent of the vote, he did so by spending heavily against a resource-starved challenger. Many district residents saw the congressman as a demagogue in pursuit of an ever-larger stage and an ever-widening audience. Indeed, to many southern Californians, Dornan's battle for "faith, family, and freedom" sounded like a call for Big Brother to enforce a strict moral code. Furthermore, Dornan's run for the presidency fueled long-standing resentment about the congressman's national aspirations. Some complained that his trips back home had become increasingly rare, suggesting that the congressman's most passionate interests lay inside the Beltway. Dornan's quest for national exposure seemed to violate Tip O'Neill's political advice.

More seriously, Dornan had depleted his financial resources. The congressman was usually a solid fund-raiser. He could pull in millions if necessary, as in 1994, when he spent $2.3 million against a weak opponent. But it is difficult to raise funds for two races at once, and all of Dornan's efforts in 1995 and early 1996 had been directed at the presidential quest. As the campaign season began, one journalist detailed how Dornan had spent all his money and incurred debts of $200,000 by November of 1995. "It appears he has drained much of his personal assets and targeted contributors for his presidential race," the reporter noted, "so there may be little or no cushion to support his 1996 bid for reelection to Congress."[22] In the spring of that election year, contributors were tapped out and Dornan's congressional campaign account was down to $23,000. Dornan appeared to be in serious trouble, even as most observers assumed that the congressman would find a way to get himself reelected.

Approaching the General Election

In November 1995, Bill Wachob, the media consultant, received a call from Sanchez inviting him to lunch.[23] Sanchez wanted to chat about the possibility of running against Dornan the following year. Wachob agreed, reluctantly, to make the drive from his San Diego office to a Denny's restaurant halfway to Anaheim. He was skeptical about Sanchez' chances. During the drive he thought about how tough it would be to defeat Dornan with *any* candidate, much less a relatively unknown and underfinanced party-switcher. The results of Sanchez' 1994 city council run were less than impressive. More significantly, Dornan had consistently risen from adverse circumstances to fight his way back to Washington. Sure, Dornan had made countless outrageous remarks about gays, women, minorities, and political liberals, making Dornan an alluring target for Democrats in California and Washington, but Dornan was a reliable winner. He knew how to raise money and he knew how to fight.

Most political consultants would have been justifiably concerned that a challenge to Dornan would end up diminishing their professional win/loss records. Most would have been wary of getting lured into a false confidence in some new approach, new message, or new candidate. History had not been kind to Dornan's adversaries. Still, the political terrain had an interesting feature that might favor a Democrat. The Forty-Sixth Congressional District had one of the lowest voter registration rates in the state, and indeed the whole nation. As a result, Election Day turnout was abysmally low. In many congressional districts, a candidate who wants to prevail in a competitive election must gather at least 100,000 votes; in the Forty-Sixth, Dornan had shown that he could succeed with just over 50,000. The small electorate would make the race financially manageable, and the large pool of untapped voters left Dornan vulnerable to even a relatively small uptick in Democratic turnout. Indeed, the ethnic cluster that had always proved most reluctant to register and vote in the Forty-Sixth was the Hispanic community. Sanchez could win if she boosted turnout among a few thousand new voters.

Wachob had mixed feelings. Sanchez was excited about the race, but she was vague about her volunteer base and her financial commitment. Charisma and energy are important, but in politics—as in the rest of life—the devil is in the details. Wachob left the meeting agreeing to consider the race, to chat about Dornan with Washington-based operatives, and to take a closer look at the demographics and electoral history of the district. When Wachob and Sanchez met again in January 1996, things were different. Sanchez arrived with specifics about money and organization. She was ready to run and she was prepared to invest in a full-scale campaign. "By our January meeting Loretta was really excited and really focused," Wachob remembers; "I was in."

The first challenge was the Democratic primary. Candidates usually seek to avoid primary elections. Intra-party skirmishes drain resources, divide potential supporters, and they do away with many candidates altogether. But sometimes a primary race is constructive: primaries can strengthen campaign organizations, establish workable themes, and secure media attention for unfamiliar candidates. Sanchez, it turned out, would gain the benefits of a primary bid without incurring the costs.

The March primary pitted Sanchez against three male candidates, all of whom were Anglo. (This time Sanchez would run under her Spanish-origin maiden name.) With one of the opponents backed by key Democrats and another having run in the district before, the Sanchez operation had to assemble its supporters and begin mobilizing dormant voters. The campaign spent $60,000 on direct mail to get its message out. It was clear that Sanchez was a scrappy fighter, willing to do whatever victory required. Indeed, Sanchez earned 7,142 of the 20,599 votes cast in the primary—enough to beat her three opponents. Moreover, she would enter the general election with a spirited campaign organization that had survived a hard-fought battle.

As the general election neared, the Sanchez team considered its options. Congressional challengers like Sanchez frequently go on the attack. This had been Barr's strategy against Darden two years earlier in Georgia. In that race, a relatively moderate Democrat was defeated because he seemed to tilt leftward. If Darden could be brought down just because he went jogging with Clinton, then Dornan, a vocal right-wing extremist, could surely be removed on account of his callous conservatism. Dornan's vitriol seemed to provide plenty of ammunition in the increasingly Democratic Forty-Sixth Congressional District. Women's groups, gay rights groups, environmental groups, and labor groups all prodded the Sanchez campaign to start hammering away. "There was no doubt about it: we were getting heat from Washington to get personal, to take the gloves off," recalls Wachob.

The campaign resisted this well-meaning advice. First, previous opponents had used this very approach, and it had failed. Was there anyone in the Forty-Sixth Congressional District who did not already know what Dornan was like? Second, on the issues, the Sanchez team reasoned that attacks on Dornan's social conservatism would not necessarily help them reach Latino voters. Orange County's Hispanic community was strongly Catholic, and the Sanchez campaign felt that an assault on Dornan's pro-life, pro-family rhetoric might prove counterproductive in a district where traditional family values held sway. More generally, a strictly ideological approach would play to Dornan's strengths, inviting the congressman to dismiss Sanchez as a "radical feminist."

Sanchez needed a less predictable strategy. Like Ted Strickland, Sanchez understood that politics is a local affair. By ignoring the parochial nature of congressional politics, Dornan had left himself vulnerable to charges that he had forgotten about the people of his district. The Sanchez campaign could argue that Dornan was basking in the national spotlight while local schools were deteriorating and local jobs were disappearing. The congressman was working the talk shows instead of listening to his constituents. In fact, Dornan's White House bid seemed to be nothing more than a publicity stunt that demonstrated how little Dornan cared about the district. Who was looking out for Orange County? If the race could be turned into a referendum on district service—a question of who could best get the Forty-Sixth Congressional District its "fair share"—then Sanchez might gain a competitive edge over Dornan. Moreover, by highlighting Dornan's seeming dereliction of duty, Sanchez could build her own image as a longtime Orange County resident who stood ready to fight for the people of the Forty-Sixth. The Sanchez message would concentrate on local jobs, local schools, and local economic development.

Dornan's record might have tempted a lesser campaign organization off course. Political operatives often run on messages that resonate with their own hyperpartisan priorities, particularly when they possess adverse information about the opposition. Political professionals live by the rhythms of the campaign season; supplied with a heavy weapon, their first instinct is to use it. As a result, many political operatives rush into a strategic decision without mulling over the obvious problem with preliminary intuitions. A theme that inspires partisans might not influence swing voters, and a campaign ad can be cute, clever, and ideologically correct without being effective. Dornan's record offered the Sanchez organization a plethora of offensive remarks, and there were even old charges (later retracted) that the congressman had once abused his wife.[24]

Most upstart challengers could not have resisted pressure from well-heeled Washington-based political groups urging them to portray Dornan as a cold-hearted Neanderthal. The Sanchez operation, however, chose a different path. It developed a campaign theme that would ring true with targeted voters in California's Forty-Sixth Congressional District. The media team won no awards for creative advertising, but their efforts helped Sanchez gain a seat in Congress.

Unorthodox Communicative Tactics

The Sanchez campaign had departed from conventional wisdom in its choice of theme, and taking another gamble, the organization decided to convey its message via unorthodox communicative tactics. It would stay quiet at times when most campaigns would have made noise; it would use cable television when others would have paid for broadcast; and in an age of media-driven politics, the Sanchez organization would rely heavily on old-style grassroots efforts. These separate techniques would combine to form a potent electoral strategy—one that was uniquely suited to the campaign of a little-known candidate running in a low turnout district against an incumbent who usually raised his money with direct mail solicitations.

Flying under the Radar

Sanchez began her effort from a disadvantaged position. Party officials, political action committees, and wealthy donors tend to ignore challengers who lack public recognition; but interest is difficult to generate without attention from key players. It is a self-fulfilling prophecy that hurts challengers. "[I]n order to *raise* money," scholars have noted, "challengers must *have* money: to rent the services of consultants, to conduct polls showing the incumbent's vulnerabilities, to do some preliminary advertising to increase their name recognition in order to convince PACs, party officials, and major donors to invest in their campaign."[25] Challengers often fall into a double bind that prevents them from posing any real danger to incumbent candidates.

Wachob recalls an early trip to Washington that was intended to rally financial support behind Sanchez, but which merely exposed the inherent skepticism that political "smart money" holds toward challengers. "Loretta was really frustrated," according to Wachob; "Other candidates were getting attention and this was hard to take. She complained a great deal about this, but I understood it is a fact of political life."[26]

Many challengers seek attention by kicking up as much dust as possible. They air negative television ads and coordinate publicity stunts, and they begin aggressive efforts to reach decisionmakers in the news media. A benchmark survey by a respected polling firm—though it may deplete the campaign treasury—can often pique interest in the challenger's prospects. A finding of incumbent vulnerability helps demonstrate a challenger's strength to reporters, party officials, wealthy donors, political action committees, and to national-level political handicappers like Charles Cook (of the *Cook Political Report*) and Stuart Rothenberg (of the *Rothenberg Political Report*). State-level political newsletters are particularly important. If a race appears on insider "watch-lists," the campaign can expect more productive fundraising and increased public attention.

The Sanchez organization hired Lake Research to perform a benchmark poll. Peter Feld, a seasoned operative, conducted an extensive survey and found that Dornan was in relatively poor standing: only 33 percent of the respondents gave Dornan an excellent or good job approval rating; 44 percent saw his performance as fair or poor. Just 39 percent of the respondents were set to vote for Dornan in November. Dornan's support would surely grow once his campaign got underway, but the early numbers indicated electoral weakness.

Conventional wisdom would call for immediate release of the polling data. But after a long, heated strategy session that included Sanchez, Wachob, Feld, and other key advisors, a decision was made to keep the numbers quiet. The campaign was deliberately forgoing the benefits of a heightened candidate profile. In a high-stakes political wager, the Sanchez team chose to hide the big stick as it walked softly through the first stages of the general election—or, as the Sanchez organization phrased it, to "stay under the radar." "It was a tough summer," Feld recalls, "because the money never came in."[27] The Sanchez team was gambling that Dornan would think himself invincible. "We played into Dornan's enormous ego," notes Feld.[28] The congressman had probably commissioned a survey that showed the same weak findings; but if there was no outside confirmation, Dornan might simply assume the results were faulty.

It would have been a rational assumption on Dornan's part. Democratic challengers had gone after the congressman every election year, and they had all lost. There was no reason for Dornan to suspect that a politically inexperienced woman who lacked any real standing in the community would have a chance to win the general election. The fact that Democrats in Washington were staying out of the race seemed to prove that even Dornan's most vociferous political opponents lacked faith in Sanchez. A dangerous logic suggested itself: because Sanchez did not pose a serious threat, there was no reason for Dornan to exploit his nationwide fundraising prowess, to build up a formidable campaign organization, or to start running his usual negative ad blitz.

Tending to the Grassroots

With a shortage of funds and a strategy that relied on stealth, the Sanchez operation quietly undertook a person-to-person grassroots campaign. The tactic was adopted partly out of necessity—it was a low-cost line of attack— but grassroots electioneering was also a product of Sanchez' personal knowledge of Orange County. "Loretta was extremely hardworking and she had a gut-level feel for the district," Wachob recalls; "She is one of the few candidates that I've worked with that can describe their district block by block. She was indeed the hardworking, hometown gal."[29]

The grassroots campaign focused on voter registration and turnout. Dornan had been able to win the 1994 election with just 50,000 votes due to the district's unusually low voter participation. If a significant number of district residents sympathetic to Sanchez were registered to vote, and if they were persuaded to show up at the polls on Election Day, Sanchez would gain tremendous leverage. The Sanchez organization thus made an assertive effort to sign up new voters. It cultivated a massive grassroots network. Building on the backlash against Prop 187—not to mention new efforts by national GOP leaders to prevent *legal* immigrants from receiving government assistance— the voter registration program worked well among Spanish-speaking residents. As voters were added to the rolls, the Sanchez team appended the new names to its direct mail and telephone lists. Hard work was put into an absentee ballot operation, on which the campaign spent as much as $75,000.

Sanchez herself hit the pavement with discipline and resolve. She believed that tight contests like hers could succeed one vote at a time. In late October, a reporter followed Sanchez as she worked a neighborhood, armed with precinct lists and campaign brochures. After a brief exchange with a young Latina, Sanchez wondered aloud, "Will she come out and vote? She's pretty disinterested. She needs some information and a reason to vote. But she met me and we'll call her. If she does vote, Bob Dornan loses."[30] The degree to which the Sanchez strategy favored grassroots efforts over broadcast media served to distinguish the Sanchez effort from most other successful congressional campaigns. Sanchez understood that a grassroots push could be deployed with a modest financial investment. The low voting history of the district and the simmering anger over Prop 187 enhanced the power of grassroots electioneering.

The campaign got personal. According to both Feld and Wachob, the fact that Washington money was slow in coming had the effect of energizing campaign operatives back in Orange County. If professionals inside the Beltway could not appreciate Sanchez' potential, the folks in the field would simply roll up their sleeves and work even harder for their candidate. A post-election editorial noted that Dornan "was having trouble accepting that so many voters in the district he has represented since 1984 were willing to trade a congressman with a global reputation for an unknown who he said campaigned as if she were running for city council."[31]

Gambling on Cable

Even a grassroots movement requires money. Fundraising demands candidate visibility, and visibility is difficult to achieve with grassroots efforts alone. Seed money can buy early television advertisements, generating name recognition and popularity. By enhancing the perceived competitiveness of the candidate, the campaign becomes more attractive to donors. But as the summer came to a close, Sanchez (1) did not have much cash on hand, and (2) did not have much visibility—byproducts of the under-the-radar approach Sanchez had been using. The Sanchez campaign was largely hidden from public view. Without a high ranking in the polls, the situation seemed desperate: "If we did not [move Sanchez' numbers up quickly], we would not have the resources necessary to wage the fall campaign."[32] With few alternatives, the campaign was willing to hazard yet another risky tactic, this one on its choice of media.

The economics of paid media sometimes augur against broadcast television. Strickland's southern Ohio district was an expensive broadcast environment because it was split into five separate media markets; Dornan's southern California district would be even more costly because it encompassed only a tiny fraction of a sprawling media market that included all of greater Los Angeles. In this sort of environment, broadcast television wastes a great deal of money. Cable advertising, however, can target audiences more precisely than broadcast, because each cable company can insert its own ads. Using cable, the campaign would be able to tailor its viewership to roughly match the boundaries of the congressional district. But cable "narrowcasting" generates problems of its own. Many homes are not wired for cable, so a cable-based ad campaign does not reach the entire electorate. Also, because cable advertising can target individuals with great precision, its value (and therefore cost) per viewer can be relatively high.[33] Finally, few congressional campaigns had relied on cable prior to 1996, so the medium did not yet have an established track record.

The Sanchez team, though divided on the issue, ultimately settled on cable advertising. Believing that grassroots efforts had peaked, the campaign poured scarce resources into an all-or-nothing cable effort that would either advance their cause by generating new income or exhaust their treasury in the effort. Failure at this stage would have signaled to prospective donors that Sanchez could not win.

At mid-cycle, the campaign produced a pair of television ads that "featured Sanchez as a homegrown leader of Orange County, fighting for secure jobs and safe neighborhoods, good schools for our children, and college loans for the middle class."[34] The strategy worked: "In three weeks, the poll numbers moved. Sanchez went from 25 percent of the vote to 43 percent— putting her in a virtual dead heat with Dornan. This rapid movement also worked to convince the Washington, D.C., political action committee community that Dornan was in fact in serious danger."[35] Money started coming in, and with the summer-long cash crunch resolved, the Sanchez organization pressed on with its direct mail efforts and was even able to run a couple of late-cycle television spots. One ad "contrasted the candidates on the issues of education, seniors, crime, and choice [i.e., the abortion issue]" while a "hard-hitting negative . . . defin[ed] Dornan as an out of touch elected official more concerned with his own stature than the needs of the district."[36] The late-cycle ads would not have been possible had the gamble on mid-cycle ads fallen short of expectations.

Combining Tactical Operations

In marketing terms, the Sanchez campaign was seeking "message frequency," ensuring that target voters were exposed to the Sanchez message time and again:

> All good campaigns need a mantra to live by. Tip O'Neill's was "All politics is local." James Carville's was "It's the economy, stupid!" The Sanchez campaign mantra was "Repetition, Repetition, Repetition!" Keep the message local and simple and say it to as many voters as possible and as many times as possible. When you think you have said it enough, say it again.[37]

The campaign would build message frequency through grassroots tactics, cable ads, and a direct mail onslaught. Proper coordination was critical to maintaining consistent message delivery in a campaign that started off with little money, particularly one that was exploiting the tactical value of stealth. If the campaign could build heavy frequency without drawing attention to itself, it could take advantage of a subtle weakness in Dornan's *modus operandi.*

Dornan was accustomed to raising large sums of money via direct mail solicitations. He had a national network of small donors who were enamored of his confrontational attacks on liberal Democrats. If Dornan believed he was safe, he might not fully replenish his exhausted campaign war chest. It would prove to be a treacherous misconception. During her under-the-radar phase, Sanchez maintained a threshold presence through nonpublic voter contact techniques: phone work, door-to-door canvassing, and direct mail. The Sanchez operation spent a great deal of time and money quietly registering new voters, mostly Latino residents. Dornan was lulled into complacency. By the end of the summer, he had yet to fully activate his financial base. After Sanchez aired her cable ads, it was clear that she posed a threat, but Dornan's main fundraising tactic—direct mail solicitation—suffers a time lag. Letters must be produced, delivered, and then acted upon by thousands of recipients. Dornan, who relied heavily on mail-in donations rather than local grassroots supporters, was not in a position to counter Sanchez' person-to-person effort.

Sanchez' combined tactics, meanwhile, had a triple effect. First, after running silently with grassroots techniques, the cable ads drew new attention to

Sanchez. The race had been the subject of only a handful of news reports. In fact, the newspapers would carry more stories about Sanchez in November and December of 1996 than in all the previous ten months put together. Cable allowed Sanchez to break through the surface quickly and with great effect. Second, the cable ads activated PAC donors. By the middle of September the Democratic Congressional Campaign Committee was on board, and so too were a number of labor, environmental, Hispanic, and feminist groups, along with Hollywood entertainers. EMILY'S List soon joined the fray. So much money came in that Sanchez wound up out-raising Dornan by about $75,000.

It was October by the time Dornan began hitting back and by then most polls had the race as a dead heat. When Dornan released a series of negative ads, the Sanchez operation went on the offensive. It highlighted the negativity of the Dornan campaign in order to show, once and for all, that Dornan was not interested in the issues most important to the people of the Forty-Sixth Congressional District. In the final days of the election, Dornan could not raise enough money to counter Sanchez' multipronged assault—and then the clock ran out. Dornan lost to Sanchez by 984 votes, 47,964 to 46,980 (with minor candidates taking another 7,540 votes).

The story was in the math. Democratic turnout increased by 2,529 votes over the 1992 presidential year election and by 15,387 votes over the 1994 midterm. Dornan's totals, which had dropped by about 10 percent from 1992 to 1994, fell yet another 6 percent in 1996. The Dornan trend was well established—Dornan had been losing votes for years—but Democratic challengers had not received this many votes since the district's relatively high turnout in 1988. Increased voter participation among Democrats overtook decreasing support for Dornan, and the result was a startling defeat for one of the most visible conservatives in the House of Representatives. The congressman had walked into his own trap. Democratic strategist Richard Schlackman once observed, "[V]ulnerable incumbents . . . run the same campaign each election."[38] Ed Brookover, former political director of the National Republican Congressional Committee, has said, "There is nothing more pleasing, from the point of view of a strategist, than to work against an incumbent who runs the same campaign again and again."[39] This was the key to the Forty-Sixth district of California. Turnout in Hispanic precincts was not as high as the Sanchez campaign might have hoped, and more than a year would pass before the House of Representatives would officially accept Dornan's loss; nevertheless, Sanchez had scored a major coup. Many called her a "giant killer."

Although forced to use stealth tactics by a lack of financial resources, the Sanchez campaign, in the words of Sanchez pollster Feld, "turned a necessity into a virtue."[40] Understanding the district, knowing the rules of the game well enough to break them, and having a keen understanding of the opposition, Sanchez pulled off one of the most celebrated upsets of 1996.

Candidate Quality

California Republicans had made a serious political error with their full-throated support of Prop 187. In the Forty-Sixth Congressional District, the uproar forged a coalition of Hispanic leaders.[41] The 1996 primary election, in which Hispanic precincts heavily favored Sanchez, showed that Latino unity was a force to be reckoned with.[42] The Hispanic electorate was largely beyond Dornan's reach. In addition, a sizeable Vietnamese community, which had been an important part of Dornan's conservative base, was beginning to falter; here, as in the Hispanic community, the seeming nativism of the California GOP was at least partly to blame.[43] Without an assertive effort to undo the damage of Prop 187, Dornan was almost completely reliant on his Anglo voters, but there was a problem even here: the Anglo population had historically turned out in relatively high proportion, meaning that there was little room for improvement—and the Anglo community was now in the minority. When Sanchez' quiet direct mail campaign started targeting Dornan's "young Republican women, older Democrats and independent voters,"[44] the congressman's electoral coalition was in danger of coming undone. To force the defeat, Sanchez used the power of the unexpected: she defied conventional wisdom with a stealth campaign that brought down an incumbent in the last days of the electoral cycle.

The defeat of a sitting member of Congress is often attributable to a mixture of incumbent weakness and challenger quality. Political scientists generally accept the notion that "other things being equal, a high-quality challenger can make a race against an entrenched incumbent more competitive than can a challenger of lesser quality."[45] But how are challenger qualifications to be measured? One recent study used "politically knowledgeable 'informants'" in each of 200 congressional districts to help identify available challengers. The researchers looked at traits that were both strategic (e.g., the ability to raise money and gain the support of political elites) and personal (e.g., integrity, the ability to speak in public, and a grasp of public policy).[46] Combining personal and strategic attributes, the researchers arrived at an "overall assessment of strength."[47]

Multifaceted evaluations of this sort can help guide future research on challenger success, pushing academic findings beyond easily observable factors such as prior office-holding. Scholars can begin to look at the visceral side of campaign mode. Candidate quality may be found to entail not simply a strategic predisposition for political campaigning, but also an intense personal desire to win.[48]

When an election is being decided by a narrow margin, every feature of the political terrain seems to take on electoral significance. In 1996, voter turnout increased, partly due to interest in the presidential campaign but also because of an Orange County visit from Bill Clinton at the end of the campaign. Democrats had significantly out-registered Republicans. Newly naturalized Latinos voted in high numbers across the state.[49] An improving economy helped Democrats while Latino hostility toward Prop 187 hurt many California Republicans. Further, Sanchez had shown herself to be a quality challenger, even if she did not fit the traditional mold. She had held no public office, had only limited public recognition, and had no great wealth, but Sanchez was willing to throw herself into the election with an enthusiasm that Dornan could neither anticipate nor match.

New York State Democratic operative Jim Murphy once said that he seeks out "candidates who have a big heart—those not afraid to show it. When you are looking for challengers to back, the depth of their conviction says as much as anything."[50] Sanchez' deep personal involvement in the campaign was a source of constant inspiration for unpaid volunteers, and in news coverage— what little there was of it—earnest electioneering helped to differentiate Sanchez from a distant, doom-saying opponent fond of knife-edged rhetoric. Throughout the election, Sanchez' dedication proved valuable in both tactical operations and strategic communications. Six years later, after Loretta Sanchez' younger sister, Linda Sanchez, won the Democratic primary in the largely Latino Thirty-Ninth Congressional District—bringing the pair within striking distance of becoming the first sisters ever to serve in Congress— Linda reflected on the value of political passion. Celebrating her victory on Election Night, Linda said to her sister, "You showed me that this experience was really worth every ounce of energy."[51]

Disciplined enthusiasm had helped Loretta Sanchez court, employ, and work with a top-shelf team. As political parties have withdrawn from the business of putting together candidates' campaigns, congressional challengers have had to learn how to recruit their own electoral organizations. Indeed, the Democratic establishment backed one of Sanchez' opponents in the primary, and then absented itself from the general election until the closing weeks. Sanchez was on her own. Personal vigor forged a committed corps of volunteers and a professional approach to the campaign effort helped to assemble a team of talented consultants. Wachob's firm, the Campaign Group, Inc., had a winning record, and shortly after he signed on with Sanchez, *Campaigns & Elections* magazine named Wachob one of the year's "rising stars"[52]; Feld was a respected member of the polling community; and Shallman, in addition to having a great deal of experience in California, had worked on a couple of presidential campaigns. It was the sort of team one would have expected to find working for a well-known candidate with better odds of raising money. But Sanchez was able to persuade the consultants to risk a dreaded "L" (for "loss") on their career tallies.

Working together, Sanchez and her team developed and implemented an unconventional strategy. The strategy succeeded because the Sanchez team had skillfully deciphered the political terrain. Its dicey plan of attack jeopardized the professional reputations of everyone on board. The Sanchez organization turned down reasonable advice to go after Dornan's character; it chose not to run any early ads; and it deliberately held back poll numbers that might have helped raise desperately needed funds. Shallman believed that Dornan "could have squashed Loretta's campaign early, before it got legs."[53] Had the late-cycle cable ads failed to generate substantial income, Sanchez and company would have been ridiculed for running a thoroughly incompetent campaign. But the Sanchez operatives had predicted Dornan's behavior perfectly—the congressman was strategically lulled into complacency, and the back-loaded media effort took Dornan by surprise.

On the *Today Show*, Sanchez' win was called "the biggest upset of [the 1996] congressional elections."[54] In a meeting of congressional Democrats, Sanchez received a "roar of approval."[55] ("A reporter mentioned this to a Republican House member, who thought a moment and opined: 'She'd get the same reaction in our place.'"[56]) The Sanchez victory drew national attention largely because it defied conventional wisdom. Indeed, Sanchez might easily have lost the election but for a thoughtful campaign strategy, reliant upon stealth, that was calculated to fit the tactical contours of the Forty-Sixth Congressional District of California.

Notes

1. John J. Pitney, Jr., *The Art of Political Warfare* (Norman: University of Oklahoma Press, 2000), 100.

2. John Jacobs, "Latina is Gunning for Dornan's Post in Orange County," *Fresno Bee*, 29 October 1996.

3. "Congress," *California Journal*, 1 May 1996.

4. Jorge Durand, Douglas S. Massey, and Fernando Charvet, "The Changing Geography of Mexican Immigration to the United States: 1910–1996," *Social Science Quarterly* 81 (2000): 1–15.

5. William J. Bennett and Jack Kemp, "The Fortress Party?" *Wall Street Journal*, 21 October 1994.

6. Ron Unz, "California and the End of White America, *Commentary*, November 1999, 21.

7. Ruben Martinez, "Fighting 187: The Different Opposition Strategies," *NACLA Report on the Americas*, November/December 1995, vol. 29, 29–32.

8. R. Michael Alverez and Tara L. Butterfield, "The Resurgence of Nativism

in California? The Case of Proposition 187 and Illegal Immigration," *Social Science Quarterly* 81 (2000): 167–79.

9. Adrian D. Pantoja, Ricardo Ramirez, and Gary M. Segura, "Citizens by Choice, Voters by Necessity: Patterns in Political Mobilization by Naturalized Latinos," *Political Research Quarterly* 54 (December 2001): 729–50.

10. E. J. Dionne, "Democrats Strike Gold," *Commonweal*, February 26, 1999, 7.

11. Ibid.

12. Ibid.

13. Bennett and Kemp, "The Fortress Party?"

14. Philip D. Duncan and Christine C. Lawrence, eds., *Politics in America, 1996* (Washington, D.C.: CQ Press, 1995), 195.

15. "GOP Candidates in N.H. All Claim the Most-Right Stuff," *Los Angeles Times*, 5 July 1995.

16. Leah Garchik, "Personals," *San Francisco Chronicle*, 8 October 1990.

17. Glenn F. Bunting, "Overhaul of State Congressional Delegation Begins," *Los Angeles Times*, 3 June 1992.

18. Lois Romano, "Duel on the Hill; Dornan and Downey: The Blow-by-Blow," *Washington Post*, 6 March 1985.

19. "Rep. Dornan Rebuked for Floor Tirade," *Washington Post*, 26 January 1995.

20. Maralee Schwartz, Kenneth J. Cooper, and Ruth Marcus, "Quotable," *Washington Post*, 24 October 1992.

21. Amy Bayer, "Dornan Joins GOP Presidential Race, Vows to Fight Moral Decay," *San Diego Union-Tribune*, 14 April 1995, 6(A).

22. Rebecca S. Weiner, "Dornan's Debts May Hamper '96 Run for Congress," *Los Angeles Times*, 26 November 1995.

23. Bill Wachob, telephone interview, 13 February 2001.

24. See R. Scott Moxley, "The Secret Lives of Bob Dornan: Inside the Fevered Imagination of O.C.'s Most Infamous Congressman," *OC Weekly*, 18 October 1996.

25. Benjamin A. Webster, Clyde Wilcox, Paul S. Herrnson, Peter L. Francia, John C. Green, and Lynda Powell, "Competing for Cash: The Individual Financiers of Congressional Elections," in *Playing Hardball: Campaigning for the U.S. Congress*, ed. Paul S. Herrnson (Upper Saddle River, N.J.: Prentice Hall, 2001), 46.

26. Wachob, telephone interview.

27. Peter Feld, telephone interview, 1 February 2001.

28. Ibid.

29. Wachob, telephone interview.

30. John Jacobs, "Will Orange County Turn on Dornan?" *San Diego Union-Tribune*, 31 October 1996.

31. Editorial, "Dornan Trails After Absentee Votes Tallied; Democrat Claims Win," *San Diego Union-Tribune*, 14 November 1996.

32. Bill Wachob and Andrew Kennedy, "Beating B-1 Bob: Underdog Ends Conservative's Congressional Career in California's 46th District in 1996," in *Campaigns & Elections: Contemporary Case Studies*, eds. Michael A. Bailey et al. (Washington, D.C.: Congressional Quarterly, 2000), 103.

33. See Daniel M. Shea and Michael John Burton, *Campaign Craft: The Strategies, Tactics, and Art of Political Campaign Management*, rev. and exp. ed. (Westport, Conn.: Praeger, 2001), 162–63.

34. Wachob and Kennedy, "Beating B-1 Bob," 103.

35. Ibid.

36. Ibid.

37. Ibid., 102.

38. Daniel M. Shea and Stephen C. Brooks, "How to Topple an Incumbent: Advice from Experts Who've Done It," *Campaigns & Elections*, June 1995, 24.

39. Ibid.

40. Feld, telephone interview.

41. Gebe Martinez, "Farber: Dornan Wants to Cut Latino Vote," *Los Angeles Times*, 8 October 1994.

42. See Greg Hernandez, "Voter Turnout is Crucial for Sanchez in the 46th," *Los Angeles Times*, 14 April 1996.

43. Dana Parsons, "It Was One Election that Dornan Lost, Not One Race," *Los Angeles Times*, 15 November 1996.

44. R. Scott Moxley, "The Campaign Was in the Mail: How Loretta Sanchez Beat Bob Dornan," *OC Weekly*, 15 November 1996.

45. L. Sandy Maisel, Walter J. Stone, and Cherie Maestas, "Quality Challengers to Congressional Incumbents: Can Better Candidates be Found?" in *Playing Hardball: Campaigning for the U.S. Congress*, ed. Paul S. Herrnson (Upper Saddle River, N.J.: Prentice Hall, 2001), 14.

46. Ibid., 19.

47. Ibid.

48. See Maisel, Stone, and Maestas, "Quality Challengers to Congressional Incumbents," 26, 31–33.

49. Pantoja, Ramirez, and Segura, "Citizens by Choice, Voters by Necessity," 729.

50. Shea and Brooks, "How to Topple an Incumbent," 23.

51. Richard Marosi, Jean Merl, and Claire Luna, "Sister Act in Congress Is Closer to Reality," *Los Angeles Times*, 7 March 2002.

52. "Introducing the Rising Stars of 1996," *Campaigns & Elections*, April 1996, 28–33.

53. Moxley, "The Campaign Was in the Mail."

54. Gebe Martinez, "Unofficial Winner Sanchez Finds She Has Friends in High Places," *Los Angeles Times*, 17 November 1996.

55. Al Kamen, " 'Rush Week' Features and Open House," *Washington Post*, 25 November 1996.

56. Ibid.

Gain the Center without Losing the Base

6

HAROLD FORD JR.
D-TENNESSEE
NINTH CONGRESSIONAL DISTRICT

T ITS 2000 CONVENTION in Los Angeles, the Democratic Party showcased its luminaries. The president and the vice president were scheduled to address the assembly, of course—Bill Clinton gave a rousing speech on Monday and Al Gore was to accept the nomination at the end of the convention on Thursday—but in between Clinton and Gore were a variety of prominent Democrats carefully selected to demonstrate that all segments of the party were united behind Gore's candidacy. On Tuesday, the roster included the Reverend Jesse Jackson, Senator Ted Kennedy, and the thirty-year-old keynote speaker from Memphis, Tennessee, Congressman Harold E. Ford Jr.

Ford, an African American, told the convention, "I recognize that I stand here this evening because of the brave men and women, many of whom were no older than I am today, who fought and stood and oftentimes sat down to help create a more perfect union." Having given history its due, Ford Jr. turned his attention to the coming challenges and opportunities: "I also stand here this evening representing a new generation, a generation committed to the ideals of the past but inspired by an unshakable confidence in our future." Ford Jr. spoke of an "entrepreneurial spirit" and of a "debt-free economy," and most urgently, he asked Democrats to "remember those children, in kindergartens in Memphis and across our nation and remember what this election is really all about."[1]

Although Ford Jr. had been nervous about the speech beforehand, reviews the next day were uniformly positive. Tom Shales of the *Washington Post* called his effort "one of the two best speeches at the convention last night"—on par with Jesse Jackson's.[2] Others drew comparisons between Ford Jr. and Gore: both of them were sons of powerful Democratic Tennessee legislators who started their political careers early in life, pressing more centrist policies than their fathers did. The connection was more than happenstance. Gore had once recommended to Harold Ford Sr., then the congressman from Memphis, that Ford Jr. be enrolled in the prestigious private high school from which Gore himself had graduated. Ford Jr. credited Gore's father, Senator Al Gore Sr., with creating a political environment in which his own father, Ford Sr., could win election to Congress.[3] In fact, Ford Sr. and Gore Sr. had both defeated the same Republican, Dan Kuykendall: Gore Sr. beat him in a 1964 U.S. Senate race and Ford Sr. successfully challenged Kuykendall, elected to Congress four years later, in a 1974 bid for the House of Representatives. Given the intertwining family histories, it is not surprising that Ford Jr. has called Gore Jr. a "role model."[4]

Ford Jr.'s speech at the 2000 Convention was notable for its inclusive message. Indeed, Ford Jr.'s presence on the podium was a message in itself. Once the bastion of southern segregation, the Democratic Party had remade itself in the 1960s and 1970s into a stronghold of diversity politics. It had become a party that courted voters regardless of race, gender, or ethnicity— a response to changes across the political landscape. As African Americans became an increasingly large segment of the voting population, greater and greater numbers were serving in elective office, including Congress. Even among the thirty-seven members of the Congressional Black Caucus (CBC), there was an increasingly diverse ideological mix, with a new generation of representatives more willing than their elders to depart from traditional liberalism.[5] Harold Ford Jr. personified this new diversity.

Ford Jr. was dealing with racial divisions that had long haunted American politics. A history of slavery, failed Reconstruction, Jim Crow culture, a racial caste system enforced by violence, unredressed economic injustice, the assassinations of African American leaders, and the continuing racial frictions that mark everyday life—these burdens continue to affect modern electoral politics. Times were changing, but only slowly. The Voting Rights Act of 1965 initiated significant progress, and yet white majorities continued to swamp the black vote. Scores of black candidates in the 1960s and 1970s were forced to mobilize African American voters, often to the exclusion of white voters, because they found that the white electorate was not willing to cross racial lines.

Even in the 1980s and 1990s, race continued to play a role in American political campaigns. In 1990, Senator Jesse Helms of North Carolina attacked his black opponent with a television spot featuring white hands (wedding ring clearly visible) crushing a piece of paper: "You needed that job and you were the best qualified. But they had to give it to a minority because of a racial quota." Helms' use of the race card was unmistakable[6]; other white candidates, however, have expressed more ambiguous references to race.

Does opposition to "quotas" convey disagreement with a controversial form of affirmative action, or does it suggest blindness to the historic repression of African Americans? The meaning of a campaign message often depends on the listener's racial heritage.

In electoral politics, race matters. At least as far back as V.O. Key's 1949 observation that racial polarization in the South was caused by white supremacy and the black response to it, researchers have noted the power of race in U.S. elections.[7] African Americans vote Democratic in extraordinarily high numbers, and they tend to vote for black candidates over white candidates; white candidates, in turn, receive a disproportionate number of white votes.[8] Although there has always been some degree of "crossover" voting, electoral patterns show a distinct racial bias, almost always to the detriment of African Americans. Many of the black elected officials who came to power in the 1960s and 1970s won office using racial polarization to their own advantage: an African American candidate would mobilize the black community into a solid bloc, emphasizing the importance of civil rights and other social policies that offered direct benefits to black voters. While Ford Sr. sought the white vote in his 1974 bid for Congress by linking his opponent to Richard Nixon, Ford's winning strategy was aimed principally at his African American base of support.[9]

In the 1980s, black candidates across the country began to stress more centrist policies, particularly with respect to education and economic opportunity. In 1989, when several black mayors were elected in major cities and a black governor was elected in the Commonwealth of Virginia, it appeared that African American candidates were able to win in majority-white jurisdictions. Subsequent victories tended to reconfirm the power of broad, race-neutral messages in electoral campaigns.

The strategy behind biracial coalition building was simple: a candidate who speaks only to a minority constituency will be less likely to win than a candidate who broadens the message to attract some portion of the majority population.[10] Sociologist William Julius Wilson argued in 1990:

> [The Democratic Party] needs to promote new policies to fight inequality that differ from court-ordered busing, affirmative action programs, and anti-discrimination lawsuits of the recent past. By stressing coalition politics and race-neutral programs such as full employment strategies, job skills training, comprehensive health care, reforms in the public schools, child care legislation, and prevention of crime and drug abuse, the Democrats can significantly strengthen their [electoral] position.[11]

Because these programs do not discriminate on the basis of race or economic class, majority publics might be more likely to accept them.[12] Acceptance, it was hoped, would lead to electoral victory and social power.[13]

The passing of Tennessee's Ninth Congressional District from Ford Sr. to Ford Jr. marked a dramatic shift from the politics of mobilization to the politics of cross-racial coalition building. A powerful black congressman steeped in the politics of the civil rights movement, Ford Sr. had gained and maintained power by marshaling his African American base with tactics that one analyst has called an "us-against-them style of politics."[14] Ford Sr.'s supporters "remember what it was like to be a repressed minority, and the only way they were able to make any progress was through confrontation," so "Harold Ford [Sr.] earned the right to be considered a kind of folk hero in Memphis."[15]

Ford Jr., while preserving the base of support his father built, expanded traditional mobilization with a New Democrat approach that emphasized economic opportunity over left-leaning liberalism. Departing from his father's proven strategy of mobilization carried risk. The strategic shift might well have imperiled his relationship with the African American base, and few white voters could have been expected to vote for a Ford. Ford Jr.'s electoral success, however, would exceed all expectations. In 1996, Ford Jr. won office by maintaining his father's constituency. In 1998, Ford Jr. extended his majority by forging a coalition that transcended racial lines. In 2000, the congressman ran for re-election without opposition. It was a position of power that many veteran incumbents never enjoy.

The Candidate

Harold Ford Jr. is a study in cool. He drives a 4 × 4, listens to the artist Prince, and in 2001 he was named one of the "World's Most Beautiful People" by *People* magazine.[16] His personal style is low-key—serious and urgent, as though the problems facing his district are so important that there is no time for idle chitchat. He is constantly in motion, absorbing what his constituents tell him after a public event, handing out business cards to those who need help from his office, and keeping a schedule that many in the private sector would find too punishing. Still, Ford Jr.'s speeches are smooth and self-assured, always mindful of his relative youth.

Talking to school kids, Ford Jr. sounds like an older brother. He does not assume that children know how the Social Security system works, but neither does he talk down to his junior high school audience. Echoing Newt Gingrich, Ford Jr. tells children that he looks forward to the day when every child carries a laptop to school, but he gives the idea a twist that sounds more like the policies of Jesse Jackson. He says it just makes good economic sense to invest in education over incarceration. Thus Ford Jr. states his "selfish" reason for promoting high quality schools: the only way to get a good job someday is to get a good education now, and if you don't do that, then we all end up spending money on your prison cell. Ford Jr. says he does not want to foot the bill for dropouts. The congressman therefore challenges students to do their homework and to think about the question, "Would you hire yourself?" At the end of the hour, Ford Jr. has his attentive students raise their right hands and repeat after him, in a Jackson-style give-and-take, "I Am—*Somebody*," an educated citizen who will "work hard and play by the rules."

These "congressional classrooms" began during the 1996 congressional campaign, when Ford Jr. visited a hundred or so schools. In a daring departure from standard campaign theory, he spent much of his time stumping before nonvoters: high school, middle school, and elementary school children. The reason was partly a matter of practicality. Ford Jr. needed as many speaking engagements as he could find, and he was receiving scores of invitations from local schools. He began to call himself the "king of the kindergarten graduation circuit." Press reports on the congressional classrooms highlighted Ford Jr.'s commitment to education. Fathers and mothers learned that a congressional candidate—the son of renowned congressman Harold Ford Sr.—was preaching personal responsibility to their children, and this might prompt the parents to offer their support on Election Day.

Half of a decade after he first announced his bid for Congress, Ford Jr. was still teaching his congressional classrooms. High school students are likely to have seen the congressman in junior high; new eighteen-year-old voters probably saw Ford Jr. in their high schools. In a sense, Ford Jr. was building a powerful base of future support from the ground up.

In front of senior citizens, Ford Jr.'s style is that of a secular preacher. He honors his elders by agreeing with them on fundamental values, but then he challenges senior citizens to ensure that their values are reflected in daily life. The young congressman earns applause by pointing to the roots of criminal culture in the breakdown of traditional families. A child needs a parent, not just a friend, he says; friendship is conferred by default, but what kids really need is parental guidance. The approach is relatively bipartisan. Ford Jr. is ready to accuse the GOP of endangering Social Security and Medicare, but in the next breath he will say there is no Democratic or Republican way to teach arithmetic. Both points are made with equal vigor.

Ford Jr. brings his high-energy style to a district accustomed to personal contact. When a constituent he meets on one of his bus tours tells of a problem with a Social Security payment, a caseworker will be pulled into the conversation to get the details; back on the bus, the caseworker will get on her cell phone to begin untangling the problem with a federal agency liaison. The congressman himself has an astounding ability to remember names and faces, and he offers bear hugs to almost everyone he knows, going out of his way to introduce himself to those he does not. He will linger after an event and listen to those who want to speak their mind or to just say "hi." Indeed, the congressman can move instantly from an enthusiastic conversation with a constituent to a taped interview for the local news, taking only a moment to straighten his suit and collect his thoughts before speaking calmly into the television camera. Lug-soled shoes help Ford Jr. zigzag down the street to make contact. Along the way, his press secretary takes digital pictures that will be uploaded to his official Web site. All this in an election year when no opponent had filed to run against the congressman.

The idea that a young African American would be seeking re-election in Memphis without opposition would have been unthinkable at the turn of the twentieth century. For that matter, the idea that a member of the Ford family would be running as a centrist, drawing substantial support, as Ford Jr. does, from the white community in the suburbs, would have been unthinkable ten years earlier. Ford Jr.'s style of representation symbolized a dramatic shift in the racial politics of Memphis, Tennessee.

The District

A long-segregated city of the Old Confederacy, Memphis has a bleak history of racial oppression. Even after slavery, few social, economic, or political opportunities were open to African American citizens. Jobs and neighborhoods were separated by race, and white elected officials dominated city power. For much of the twentieth century, the white political machine of Edward Hull Crump enforced a suffocating brand of segregation on the black community of Memphis.[17]

Elected mayor in 1909, this businessman-turned-politician was soon ousted by charges of corruption, but Crump's real power (legal and otherwise) came from his political machine, an organization that selected the city's elected officials until Crump's death in 1954. Key ranked Crump's machine among the "most thorough" in the South.[18] The Crump organization did not permit the election of black officials—indeed, Crump supported the segregationist Dixiecrats in 1948—though it did offer minimal government services in return for the black vote, which the machine actively registered.[19] As one scholar put it, "Crump recognized [black Memphians only] out of some feudal sense of *noblesse oblige*."[20] Because the Crump machine barred independent black representation, it perpetuated the economic and social problems of racial segregation.

The city remained racially polarized after Crump's demise, and with African Americans constituting only about a third of the population, the task of electing black officials would prove difficult. Black political organizations were thwarted by a lack of numbers, a shortage of funds, active white resistance, and even legislative restructuring of electoral procedures that guaranteed victory by the white majority.[21] In 1967, a relatively promising African American ran for mayor, but a belief that the black candidate could not win office led many black voters to support a white moderate rather than risk the election of a white conservative.[22] Frustrated with electoral politics, the community moved toward social protest. Most notably, Memphis saw a 1968 strike by city sanitation workers seeking better pay, employee benefits, and recognition that "I Am a Man." The arrival of the Reverend Martin Luther King Jr. was not enough to keep the peace. The sanitation workers' concerns were heard only after King was assassinated at a Memphis motel.

The 1970s saw a reversal in the fortunes of black candidates in Memphis. The transformation resulted partly from a strategic move by the Ford family. With Memphis still majority-white and racially polarized, the prospect of electing a black candidate in a citywide election seemed remote. Better odds could be found in the city's majority-black legislative districts. In 1970, Ford Sr. and his brother John each successfully ran for office—Harold in the Tennessee House and John as a district representative on the city council. When congressional district lines were redrawn in 1972, the Eighth Congressional District was left with a roughly even racial split. Two years later, in 1974, Ford Sr. won the seat, ousting Kuykendall by a slim margin. Through careful political organization and sheer force of personality, Ford Sr. held his congressional seat with strong majorities. Over the years he would assist another six family members into office, including his son, Harold Jr. For many aspiring black candidates, a Ford endorsement was a precondition for elective office.

Ford Sr.'s victory, however, did not signal the end of racial polarization so much as a re-weighting of racial power. While Ford Sr. received a small percentage of the white vote, he gained the black vote in overwhelming numbers.[23] After his first few years in office, he routinely won elections with about 70 percent of the vote, picking up some white support through strong constituent service. He was unopposed in the 1980 general election. In his last three elections, however, Ford Sr. had dipped to 58 percent. The vote was not overwhelming, but it was a solidly held majority that easily protected his seat from serious opposition.

The key to victory was African American mobilization. Because black candidates drew few white votes, internal splits in the black vote spelled almost certain defeat. If, however, the African American community rallied behind a single candidate, racial polarization could actually *help* win a citywide election by translating the black majority into a black victory. From the 1970s into the 1990s, the Ford organization was the center of African American political leadership. Infrequently challenged from inside the community and roundly criticized outside of it, Ford Sr. chipped away at the white power structure that had consistently and effectively suppressed black political participation.

In 1991, the African American community took extraordinary measures to find consensus. A "People's Convention" chose school superintendent Willie W. Herenton as its candidate for mayor, and rival black political factions fell in line behind the Herenton candidacy to ensure that the black vote would not split.[24] The result was a razor-thin, racially divided, one hundred forty-two-vote win that gave Memphis its first black mayor.[25]

As powerful as Ford Sr. was, his seeming invincibility was tested in the early 1990s by the rise of Mayor Herenton as a rival black leader as well as a federal indictment on charges of political corruption. Given the oppressive history of Memphis politics, many of Ford Sr.'s supporters assumed that the indictment was racially motivated. This impression was reinforced by the prosecutor's effort to move Ford Sr.'s trial from Memphis to a nearby suburban community that would have fewer black residents in the jury pool. In 1993, Ford Sr. was acquitted, but the congressman had become an increasingly powerful symbol of racial division in Memphis. Despite a strong record of constituent service and a range of moderate, family-oriented legislative accomplishments, support from the white community collapsed. Reelected in 1994, Ford Sr. announced his retirement in April of 1996, after more than two decades in Congress.

Emergence

Harold Jr.'s electoral challenge was different from the one that had originally faced his father. The Eighth Congressional District had been reconfigured in 1972 to include a heavily black constituency inside the Memphis city limits. In the years after Harold Sr.'s 1974 election, the Eighth would become majority-black. Decennial redistricting in 1982 gave Tennessee an additional House seat, and transformed and renumbered Ford Sr.'s district into the new Ninth, which had a slightly higher white population than the old Eighth; but the new demographics did not seriously threaten Ford Sr. Redistricting in 1992, however, raised some concerns. A declining population in Memphis forced the district to expand beyond the city's boundaries, pushing the Ninth south and east, outside its urban core and into Shelby County. New precincts from the affluent white neighborhoods to the east made the new Ninth somewhat less black, less liberal, less Democratic, and less downscale than the old Ninth. The new district had a 59 percent black population, but only 55 percent of the total population was comprised of voting-age African Americans.[26]

A race-based mobilization strategy, by itself, would leave only a small margin for error. In 1992, the Memphis *Commercial Appeal* noted that Ford Sr. would "have to run harder and spend more money to win another two years in Washington."[27] Ford Sr.'s powerful organization prevailed in 1994, but there was no guarantee that Ford Jr. would inherit his father's political base intact.

When Ford Sr. announced his retirement, Ford Jr. was finishing law school at the University of Michigan. His youth was palpable. Some recalled that, at four years old, Ford Jr. had cut a radio spot for his father, saying, "I want a better school to go to, I want a better house to live in, and I want lower cookie prices." Ford Jr. raised his own right hand to take the oath of office when his father was sworn into Congress. When Ford Jr. announced his candidacy in April 1996, he was, at twenty-five years old, just four years younger than Ford Sr. had been in his first run for Congress; but unlike Ford Sr., Ford Jr. had not yet held elective office.

A prep school education in Washington led some to protest that Ford Jr. had not paid his Memphis dues. (Ford Sr. filed election papers for his son as Ford Jr. was taking final exams in Michigan.[28]) Responding to critics, Ford Jr. pointed to his management of two previous Ford Sr. campaigns and his work on justice-related issues during the 1992 presidential transition. A series of town hall-style meetings held by Ford Sr. made clear that the elder Ford thought his son was ready for the job. Ford Sr. thanked his constituents for the backing he had received over the years and urged that this support be transferred to Ford Jr. Just as important, Ford Sr. vowed to raise large sums of money on his son's behalf, a move that would make other potential candidates think twice before getting into the race.

The first test came during filing season. Mayor Herenton did not want to see Ford Jr. get the nomination unchallenged. A "Committee for Better Government," Herenton said, would search for alternatives. The mayor wanted a candidate with "more experience and maturity."[29] The Ford-Herenton rivalry got ugly. Ford Sr. hinted that Herenton should be recalled; Herenton questioned whether Ford Sr.'s tenure in Congress had brought any real benefits to Memphis. The public dispute boiled over into the press: "It's a war in the city of Memphis and we might as well face that," Ford Sr. declared at a public housing forum in South Memphis. To applause and shouts of approval, Ford Sr. said he stood by his plan to step down and to support his son Harold Ford Jr. as his successor. Herenton, speaking to reporters at City Hall, said he was determined to seek an alternative candidate because Ford Jr. lacked experience. "Ford [Jr.], with his audacity and his arrogance, thinks that this community is going to be blindsided with a lot of empty rhetoric. This isn't going to be a cakewalk," the mayor said.[30]

The battle lines were drawn. At one point, Herenton appeared to have found an opposition candidate in Lois DeBerry, a respected state legislator with close ties to the Ford family, Tennessee Democrats, and Vice President Gore. DeBerry, however, declined the opportunity, not wanting to get in the middle of the increasingly hostile Ford-Herenton dispute. With DeBerry out of the running, the Democratic field was left to second-tier candidates, including state legislator Rufus Jones and state senator Steve Cohen.

It was the Cohen candidacy that posed the greatest danger. While Cohen was no less liberal than Ford Jr.—in fact, he was probably *more* liberal than

Ford Jr.—he was white, and he was not a Ford. A political columnist for *The Commercial Appeal* noted that "Republicans . . . will cross over into the Democratic primary and vote for Cohen, no matter how much they dislike this Kennedyesque liberal."[31] Voting in sufficient numbers, Republicans might have the opportunity to choose Cohen as the Democratic nominee. The *Nashville Tennessean* offered its own strategic analysis: "If the split between Ford [Jr.] and Jones is close enough, Memphis political watchers figure, Cohen could slip through and win the race if he is able to attract as little as [10 to 15 percent] of African-American voters."[32]

Tensions mounted. In early June, Ford Jr. charged that Cohen was "position[ing] himself as the great Republican hope in the Democratic primary."[33] Cohen alleged that this was "code language for race," a reference to the bigoted ideal of a "great white hope" in the sport of boxing. The potential for Republican crossover voting appeared greater after Cohen received the *Commercial Appeal's* endorsement, an editorial which unabashedly played to Republicans by highlighting the conservative side of Cohen's political philosophy.[34]

Ford Jr.'s obstacles were his youth, inexperience, and the double-edged sword of his father's reputation. Unable to deny the obvious, Ford Jr. embraced it. Ford's young age implied a "New Vision" for the Ninth. His formative years, the candidate would point out, were spent watching his father's hard work for the district, an education that taught him the ways of Washington. Ford Jr.'s challenge was to build strong connections with his father's loyal constituency. While some children of prominent officials would be eager to run on their own hook, "Junior," as he was coming to be known, unapologetically identified with his father: "He has been a provider, he has been a father, he has been a daddy, he has been a best friend, he has been an adviser, he has been a counselor, he has been a consoler, he has been a parent, and if I have to make excuses for someone being all that to advance myself to run for elected office, then you keep the seat. You keep the seat."[35]

Any policy differences that might have separated father from son went unnoticed by the press. Ford Jr. addressed time-honored Democratic issues like education, economic opportunity, crime, Medicare and Medicaid, labor rights, and health care, and he garnered endorsements from labor unions, Jesse Jackson, and a long line of big-name representatives from the Congressional Black Caucus. When Rosa Parks, heroine of the civil rights movement, came to town, her limousine sported a Harold Ford Jr. bumper sticker.[36]

Ford Jr. was mobilizing his base. The strategy made sense. He was up against a white candidate and a black candidate—and the white candidate was likely to pick up Republicans who would vote in the Democratic primary just to spite Ford Sr. Jones, on the other hand, who was to gain Herenton's endorsement, could be expected to reap the small anti-Ford vote that resided in the black community. If Ford Jr. could hold his father's constituency—many of whom had met the congressman personally, and many of whom had been assisted by his office—Ford Jr. would win the nomination. The father's connections could quite possibly be passed on to the son as a sort of political primogeniture.[37] There was little reason to retreat from the identity, issues, or alliances of Ford Sr., even as Cohen called on Republicans to vote in the Democratic primary to "End the Ford Machine."

Election Day bore out the wisdom of Ford Jr.'s approach. Republicans voted in the Democratic primary in unprecedented numbers, but Ford Jr.'s Democrats crushed the Republican crossover. Ford Jr. received 60 percent of the vote to Cohen's 34 percent. Jones trailed with just five percent. On Election Night, Cohen, a lifelong defender of civil rights, lashed out at the results: "It is impossible for a person who is not African-American to get a large vote in the African-American community . . . against a substantial candidate. The fact is I am white, and it doesn't seem to matter what you do."[38] At least one analyst thought the election was defined by family ties more than racial divisions. Black Memphians, it was said, viewed "Ford Sr. as the man who, more than two decades ago, challenged an oppressive establishment and won"—and Ford Jr. had assured the voters that he would continue to serve them as well as his father had done for so many years.[39]

The general election was over before it began. Ford Jr.'s opponent was computer professional Rod DeBerry (no relation to State Representative Lois DeBerry), a black Republican who had run against Ford Sr. and lost by a 16 percent margin. Ford Jr. charged that DeBerry was a Gingrich-style Republican, while DeBerry railed against the "Ford machine." Ford emphasized the responsibility of the public sector to help educate the children of the Ninth Congressional District, while DeBerry argued that small-scale government meant greater economic opportunity. The conclusion was forgone.

Cohen and Herenton lined up behind Ford Jr.'s candidacy, as did a string of leading lights from the Democratic Party, including Jesse Jackson, Al Gore, and Bill Clinton. Signs and bumper stickers around the district simply said, "Jr." Even the *Commercial Appeal* endorsed Ford Jr., though they said the result was a "close decision" that rested partly on the Ford family's tradition of constituent service.[40] With Ford Jr. vastly outspending DeBerry in a naturally Democratic district, observers were not surprised when Ford Jr., who celebrated his twenty-sixth birthday during the campaign season, won the race and became the youngest member of the United States Congress. But the margin was truly unexpected: Ford Jr. beat DeBerry with 61 percent of the vote, a slightly larger share than Ford Sr. had received in the past three elections. Said the "proud daddy" to his assembled constituents, "I leave here tonight, but leave you in good hands."[41]

Expansion

Immediately after the election, Ford Jr. began putting a measure of distance between his father's convictions and his own. He said, "I respect my dad and love my dad and admire my dad a great deal. But I don't think he would respect me if I didn't have the fortitude to disagree with him if I felt he was wrong."[42] A close review of Ford Jr.'s 1996 campaign showed that there was some divergence from the start, if only in emphasis. Ford Sr. had long worked to maintain the social safety net, making sure the government took care of the poorest of the poor; Ford Jr. stressed the need for increased opportunity, which he believed could be cultivated by education and hands-on computer training in Memphis schools. Furthermore, while Ford Sr.'s campaigns were criticized for having a racial appeal, Ford Jr. repeatedly expressed a desire to bring the black and white communities together. Ford Jr. was his father's son, but he was ready to lead Memphis in new directions.

The changing demographics of southwest Tennessee had created a more complicated political environment than the one Ford Sr. had entered in the 1970s. Racial divisions persisted, but they had changed. On one hand, the city remained racially segregated, in practice if not in law. A prominent black businessman called Memphis "the most race-conscious place I've ever seen," and a black pastor saw a city where "[r]ace informs almost everything that happens"—"[w]here housing projects are built or not built; where new schools are built or not built; whether the school budget is funded or not funded; how neighborhoods develop; the makeup of the city council."[43] And yet, on the other hand, this was no longer a city where the Crump machine openly practiced racism. Some segments of the black community had begun to enjoy the fruits of national prosperity. Ford Jr., noting that his "dad grew up without running water," confessed that a "bad day for me was the movie place not having the movie I wanted to rent."[44]

Changing demographics meant changing politics. When Ford Sr. first ran for Congress in the mid-1970s, a race-based strategy made perfect sense. In 1994, the venerable congressman, who once was the only southern member of the CBC to stand for re-election, seemed to grasp the new dynamics of the district when he endorsed a white independent candidate for Shelby County mayor in a field that included a Democratic Party endorsee and one of the congressman's own brothers. In mayoral politics, the percentage of white voters casting ballots for Herenton increased from 4 percent in 1991 to 40 percent in 1995.[45]

One columnist argued that Ford Sr.'s endorsement against his brother was a strategic move to help his son: "As the growing number of black political leaders fragment [Ford Sr.'s] once-solid base of support, it has become a political reality that black politicians who want to win in the future must court the white vote."[46] A shift of some kind seemed inevitable. Growing political influence in the black community brought the threat of division. In the late 1970s, Ford Sr. was just about the only game in town. By the 1990s, there were a number of active players. Herenton, as mayor of Memphis, had his own stake in the black vote. While Ford Sr. and Herenton had often helped each other's electoral efforts, and while the two could work together as needed, they remained bitter rivals speaking to overlapping constituencies. Disagreements about government projects and local political personalities generated a feud that would last throughout the 1990s.

Ford Jr. continued his father's rivalry with Herenton—a political scrap over the funding of a summer jobs program became a major flashpoint—but more noteworthy than local political intrigue was Ford Jr.'s alliance with the New Democrat version of the political center. On one hand, Ford Jr. continued to fight for the key tenets of Democratic liberalism, standing up to Bill Clinton's White House for negotiating away funds for local school construction; on the other hand, Ford Jr.'s education agenda was identified more and more with a centrist brand of reform. In his first days in office, Ford Jr. called for policies that would "challenge, empower and propel our young people into the 21st Century, equipped with the skills needed to keep America competitive."[47] To Ford Jr., education was a "national security" issue. Without technological training, students lack opportunity; the poverty cycle continues; and the nation's standing in the world economy is weakened.

So powerful was the congressman's commitment to New Democrat ideals that his own father seemed to fear misplaced priorities: "Nothing wrong with doing [policy] the first two years, but you'll make all kinds of mistakes, and you aren't going anywhere with it."[48] The proven path toward success, according to Ford Sr., lay in the hard work of constituent service.[49]

Ford Sr. was right that Ford Jr., a freshman legislator, would have difficulty enacting policy—the House of Representatives operates on the basis of member seniority—but a centrist policy agenda would help Ford Jr. make a name for himself. The manner in which Ford Jr. linked school funding to economic opportunity illustrates his overall approach to social and economic policy. To channel students out of poverty, Ford Jr. believed, the federal government should increase school funding but test for results. As the American economy moved into the Digital Age and becomes increasingly tied to global markets, individual success demands public commitments to develop skills suited to the new economy. Charter schools (i.e., private institutions that receive public money subject to strict standards) represented one way to provide this sort of accountability. But knowledge without opportunity only empowers by half. Ford Jr. therefore tried to use governmental leverage to bring the international marketplace to Memphis. (Vice President Gore gave Ford Jr. a large share of the credit for securing tens of millions of dollars to

construct an intercontinental runway at the Memphis International Airport.)
To Ford Jr., "It isn't about race or party or gender. . . . In the next century
it will be about access. Access to education, technology. That will determine
who can compete and who can't."[50]

Ford Jr.'s strategy did not ignore race—the congressman actively promoted minority business development and spoke out against racial injustice—but his line of attack did not rely strictly on the mobilization politics
that often characterize elections in racially polarized constituencies. Ford Jr.'s
market-based approach lent itself to small and big business alike. The new
runway would help expand the shipping capacity of the airfreight giant,
FedEx, a major employer in Memphis. Small business, which Ford Jr. aggressively courted, would benefit from other federal projects announced by the
congressman, including a business "incubator" to help new ventures. At the
same time that Ford Jr. was acquiring the confidence of local employers, he
was gaining a solid reputation in Washington, even among Republicans. A
GOP House colleague who had once tried to send Ford Sr. to jail called Ford
Jr. "a pleasure to work with."[51] Gone was the atmosphere of confrontation
from Ford Sr.'s time; in its place was a policy of strategic cooperation.

Ford Jr.'s New Democrat approach departed from 1960s-era civil rights
liberalism, and the new style was not always welcome. While *People* magazine
focused on the congressman's attractiveness to "Generation Next,"[52] *Ebony*
named Ford Jr. alongside "members of the generation [who] seem to lack a
sense of history and a sense of connectedness to the major figures of the
past."[53] To *New York Times Magazine*, Ford Jr. symbolized a new cohort of
black lawmakers who have embraced a more moderate approach to politics
than their elders in the Congressional Black Caucus.[54] Congressman Bill Clay
of Missouri, who came to public service through his work for the National
Association for the Advancement of Colored People, has called Ford's theory
of government "the oldest type of philosophical witchcraft": "It's closer to
Republican ideology than anything I've heard in recent years."[55] A letter to
New York Times Magazine complained that "there is no message and no
vision other than political expedience behind the junior Ford's drive to help
move the Democratic Party to the center."[56]

Ford Jr. does not apologize for his centrist politics—he is a true believer—
and there was electoral benefit in his centrist approach to public policy. Using
Ford Sr.'s support and organization as his base, Ford Jr. has carried his message to Memphians who did not vote for his father:

> I was blessed with the foundation [that Ford Sr.] built. . . . I believe
> strongly in holding and expanding that base of support. Ways to
> expand that base are to talk about things that a lot of people can
> relate to [and] to show folks how similar our issues are. That is one

of the things I've attempted to do, and my dad attempted to do throughout his tenure but [he] faced a different set of obstacles. If I do nothing but maintain [the base], I think I've failed [his] legacy. I need to build on it.[57]

Ford Jr. believed his father's generation of leadership "only had a hammer, but I have a screwdriver and a wrench."[58]

Ford has supported Democratic initiatives to bring computers to classrooms in low-income areas, but he has also supported traditionally Republican positions on free trade and capital gains tax cuts. The result of Ford Jr.'s bid to simultaneously hold his liberal base while seeking new sources of support resulted in a political fusion unusual for congressional politics in Memphis, Tennessee: broad organizational support from his father's black constituency and financial backing from white neighborhoods in East Memphis.

The 1998 election was anticlimactic. Ford Jr. had been making grant announcements; speaking to schools, churches, and civic groups; cutting ribbons; pressing for campaign finance reform, railing against youth-oriented tobacco advertising; dealing with a major strike by airline pilots; calling for affordable housing; escorting a string of Clinton administration officials through Memphis; and despite occasional spats with local leaders, using congressional power to assist development projects initiated by the city and county governments. Memphis mayor Herenton and the GOP mayor of Shelby County both had good things to say about Ford's first year in Congress.[59]

As the election approached, Ford Jr. had no challenger within his own party and had given the opposition party little reason to mount an assertive effort of their own. The congressman's Republican opponent in 1998 was an artist who had failed in two previous attempts to get the nomination. The *Commercial Appeal* gave Ford Jr. an unambiguous endorsement, declaring that the congressman had "demonstrated the ability, intelligence and energy to help his constituents."[60]

Election Day brought a commanding victory. Ford Jr. received 79 percent of the vote, a share that approached his father's high water mark. As he had hoped, the African American community had held firm while the white suburbs added a substantial number of votes to the final tally.

Facing a National Audience

Strong victories raised Ford Jr.'s public profile. Immediately after his 1998 win, Ford was considered a potential candidate for the Senate in 2000, and there was even talk of an eventual bid for the presidency.[61] *George* magazine included Ford Jr.'s views on education in its book, *250 Ways to Make America Better*,[62] and *The New Yorker* profiled the congressman as a leader of the "Next Generation."[63] *Ebony* listed Ford Jr. among the "100 + Most Influential Black Americans" (Ford Jr., Jesse Jackson Jr., and other "new generation names . . . will play a major role in the power dialogues of the new century").[64]

Back home, however, the Ford-Herenton feud was growing to near-mythic proportions. Joe Ford, chairman of the city council and brother of Ford Sr., had filed to run against Herenton in the 1999 mayoral elections. The campaign became so heated that local political observers expressed only mild surprise when an off-duty member of Herenton's security detail retrieved a firearm from his vehicle during a clash over a yard sign between opposing operatives. (The competing organizations later agreed, in writing, that "no campaign worker shall carry a weapon on his or her person while engaged in public campaigning."[65])

Herenton soundly defeated Joe Ford; another Ford brother, Edmund, took Joe's place on city council; and Herenton said that he might endorse GOP Senator Bill Frist over Ford Jr. if Ford Jr. joined the Senate race. Indeed, political loyalties were crisscrossing Memphis as never before. Not only was Herenton ready to back Frist's bid for re-election, but both Herenton and Ford Sr. had supported Republican governor Don Sundquist the previous year, and the Shelby County Democratic chair had sent money to the campaign of Shelby County's Republican mayor. Endorsements had become so politically convoluted that county Democrats announced that they wanted to expel party officers who helped Republicans. Even the racial lines that had long dominated Memphis were showing signs of decay, as Herenton in 1999 was able to gain a large segment of the white, East Memphis electorate, a repeat of his performance in 1995 and of Ford Jr.'s success in 1998. Divisions were still present, but voting patterns in the late 1990s were, without question, less segregated than they had been when Harold Ford Sr. first ran for Congress.

After consulting with Vice President Gore, Ford Jr. opted out of the Senate bid in February 2000, but even without the Senate bid, Ford Jr. was making news. On April 7, 2000, another milestone was reached: election petitions were due, and no candidate—Democrat or Republican—had filed to run against Harold Ford Jr. The following August, the vice president invited Ford Jr. to keynote his nominating convention. Asked why, Gore said of Ford Jr., "He's a rising star. He has a bright future. And he's from Tennessee."[66] Ford Jr.'s reaction to Gore's request, which he said he accepted in a "nanosecond,"[67] suggested the weight that newfound leadership had placed on his shoulders. In the congressman's view, "Not only am I representing the Ninth District and my state, but I'm also representing my generation. . . .

I will try my hardest not to let them down."[68] Before he delivered the keynote address, Ford Jr. asked his father whether he would like to review the text. Ford Sr. replied, "It's your speech."[69]

Coalition Strategies

Ford Jr. had become an uncontested candidate in large part because he was able to move to the center without losing his base. Scholars sometimes distinguish between the strategic effects of inclusive political messages (on which there is general consensus) and of divisive issues (that pit one group against another).[70] The mathematics of electioneering usually advises a candidate to avoid divisive issues rather than risk alienating a large portion of the electorate—but not always. Frank Cremeans and Bob Barr used Bill Clinton, a divisive political figure in 1994, as a campaign issue, making their respective elections into referenda on the president. Likewise, Ford Sr. had used the preexisting racial divisions within Memphis as the foundation for a strategy of black mobilization. Ford Jr., however, defied expectations and strengthened his political grip on Memphis politics by dislodging the monopoly power of racial issues on Ninth district electioneering.

Ford Jr. built a new political consensus in Memphis. His father, lacking support from the white community, solidified his political power by mobilizing African American voters. Ford Sr. attended to the needs of the poor families and he stood up for the rights of minorities. As the racial composition of Memphis elections consistently showed, white voters rejected Ford Sr.'s approach. Ford Jr., however, shifted the political debate. He spoke to low-income black constituents and upper-income white constituents about economic opportunity. Ford Jr. did not see his centrist message as an abandonment of traditional civil rights politics, but an extension of it. In Ford Jr.'s mind, African American children, like all children, must be given the chance to compete in the modern economy. It was an approach that allowed Ford Jr. to talk about racial inequality without being painted as a left-wing radical.

Some scholars have misgivings about biracial electoral strategies. One concern is that black candidates elected with the support of biracial coalitions may not fully serve their black constituencies. Although there is no conclusive evidence in either direction, the question leads to heated debate.[71] In addition, some have misgivings about the pursuit of a race-neutral approach that builds on race-conscious legislation, fearing that it neglects the accomplishments of the past. "Th[e] explosion in African-American participation was made possible," it has been argued, "by the Voting Rights Act of 1965, a race-specific piece of legislation on the heels of a civil rights bill that helped to stabilize an emerging African-American middle class through its affirmative action, education, and equal opportunity provisions."[72] A third concern holds that the approach is not always the best path to electoral victory. The benefits of mobilizing the black community may sometimes outweigh the value of a more broadly cast message. In Memphis, for example, mobilization brought the city its first black mayor in 1991; earlier coalition-based attempts had failed, but an African American won office that year because pent-up demand for black representation forged a solid voting bloc in support of an African American candidate.[73]

Ford Jr.'s politics have not been universally popular among black political officials—or even his own family. "Harold Jr. and you young people are standing on the shoulders of those who brought you the [twenty-first] century," Harold Sr. once said; "We can't let America off the hook."[74] Political scientist Huey L. Perry writes:

> [While the use of race-neutral strategies] is an important ingredient in the fabric of successful African American electoral politics, the importance of traditional black politics has not diminished. For the foreseeable future, deracialization and traditional black politics will exist as twin pillars in black electoral politics, with the former being more successfully deployed in majority white districts and jurisdictions and the latter being more successfully deployed in majority black districts and jurisdictions.[75]

According to Perry, one result of "this dual structure in African American politics may be the emergence of ideological and class divisions in the structure of black politics."[76]

Ford Jr. has built his strategy on *both* pillars. He won his seat in 1996 by mobilizing the base that his father built; he dominated the 1998 and 2000 elections because he held the base and reached beyond it. The powers of incumbency, shown to increase a minority congressional representative's margin of victory,[77] seem insufficient to explain the breadth of Ford Jr.'s support. The congressman did not simply widen his lead—he fundamentally changed his electoral constituency, creating a biracial coalition of supporters in a city that remains deeply divided by race.

While Perry speculated that coalition strategies would be most successful where there is a white majority, and that race-conscious strategies would be most useful where there is a black majority, Ford Jr.'s dominance of the Ninth Congressional District tends to suggest the occasional utility of a biracial coalition strategy in majority-black districts. Observers of differing ideological persuasions have been impressed by Ford Jr.'s ability to forge a biracial coalition so strong that he could, after just four years in office, be reelected to Congress without opposition—this in Crump's Memphis, where electing a black mayor in 1991 required a powerful effort within the African American community because little help could be expected from outside of it. Under such circumstances, the electoral heights attained by Ford Jr. represented a genuine personal triumph.

Notes

1. "Keynote Speech by Harold Ford Jr., D-Tenn., as Prepared for Delivery to the Democratic National Convention in Los Angeles on Tuesday," *Associated Press*, 15 August 2000 (corrected to reflect speech as delivered).

2. Tom Shales, "The Networks Blink and Miss the Best Parts," *The Washington Post*, 16 August 2000.

3. *Hardball with Chris Matthews*, CNBC, 18 June 1999.

4. Jessica Wehrman, "Young Keynoter Looks to Role Model Gore," *Scripps Howard News Service*, 15 August 2000.

5. See Jeremy Derfner, "The New Black Caucus," *American Prospect*, March 27–April 10, 2000, 16–19. See also Robert Singh, *The Congressional Black Caucus: Racial Politics in the U.S. Congress* (Thousand Oaks, Calif.: Sage, 1998).

6. Republican media consultant Alex Castellanos, who produced the spot, denies that Helms' campaign was playing the race card: "The message in that spot's very clear and that is nobody should get a job, or be denied a job because of the color of their skin. . . . [W]hen a conservative Republican says the same words that Martin Luther King says, somehow he's racist. And I just don't buy that. I think you're proscribed from talking about quotas and things like that because you're a, you're a white guy. . . . I don't give a damn if I'm white, black, or whatever, if I can't say that, that giving somebody a job or denying them a job because of the color of their skin, if I can't say that's wrong, this is not America. I believe that." Alex Castellanos, interviewed for PBS, *The :30 Second Candidate*, 1998 (transcript at http://www.pbs.org/30secondcandidate [last accessed 24 April 2002]).

7. V.O. Key, Jr., *Southern Politics in State and Nation* (New York: Alfred A. Knopf, 1949), 648.

8. See Thomas F. Pettigrew, "When a Black Candidate Runs for Mayor: Race and Voting Behavior," in *People and Politics in Urban Society*, ed. Harlan Hahn (Beverly Hills, Calif.: Sage, 1972); James M. Vanderleeuw, "The Influence of Racial Transition on Incumbency Advantage in Local Elections," *Urban Affairs Quarterly* 27 (1991): 36–50; Monika McDermott, "Race and Gender Cues in Low-Information Elections," *Political Research Quarterly* 51 (1998): 895–918.

9. Sharon D. Wright, *Race, Power, and Political Emergence in Memphis* (New York: Garland, 2000), 88.

10. See Charles S. Bullock III, "Racial Crossover Voting and the Election of Black Officials," *Journal of Politics* 46 (1984): 238–51.

11. William Julius Wilson, "Race-Neutral Programs and the Democratic Coalition," *The American Prospect*, Spring 1990, 74–81, 74.

12. Ibid., 81.

13. Some scholars call the strategy "deracialization." The strategy was first propounded by Charles V. Hamilton, who, in 1977, called on African Americans involved in electoral politics to emphasize issues that could not easily be characterized according to race. "[F]ull employment, a meaningful national health insurance law, and a sound income maintenance program would (or at least ought to) appeal to broad segments of the electorate across racial lines." Charles V. Hamilton, "De-Racialization: Examination of a Political Strategy," *First World: An International Journal of Black Thought* (March/April 1977): 3–5, 3. Hamilton felt that Democratic losses in 1972 were caused by a Republican strategy of "racialization"—talking about "zero-sum" issues like "busing" that served as a code-language to divide the electorate along racial lines, with the African American community as victim. Racialization should be fought with "deracialization." The strategy was not considered a permanent solution to problems of discrimination, but rather a strategy that could work in a 1970s electoral context. See also Huey L. Perry, "Introduction: An Analysis of Major Themes in the Concept of Deracialization," in Huey L. Perry, ed., *Race, Politics, and Governance in the United States* (Gainesville: University Press of Florida, 1996), 1–11; Joseph McCormick II and Charles E. Jones, "The Conceptualization of Deracialization: Thinking Through the Dilemma," in *Dilemmas of Black Politics*, ed. Georgia A. Persons (New York: HarperCollins, 1993), 66–84; Huey L. Perry, "Deracialization as an Analytical Construction in American Urban Politics," *Urban Affairs Quarterly* 27 (1991): 181–91; Raphael Sonenshein, *Politics in Black and White: Race and Power in Los Angeles* (Princeton, N.J.: Princeton University Press, 1993).

14. "'Jr.' Making Strong Bid for Congress," *Associated Press*, 9 October 1996.

15. Political scientist Kenneth Holland, in "'Jr.' Making Strong Bid for Congress."

16. "The 50 Most Beautiful People in the World, 2001," *People Monthly*, 14 May 2001, 73–194, 116.

17. See William D. Miller, *Mr. Crump of Memphis* (Baton Rouge: Louisiana State University Press, 1964).

18. Key, *Southern Politics in State and Nation*, 398.

19. Miller, *Mr. Crump of Memphis*, 102–104.

20. Ibid., 206–207.

21. Wright, *Race, Power, and Political Emergence*, pass.; Christopher Silver and John V. Moeser, *The Separate City: Black Communities in the Urban South, 1940–1968* (Lexington: University Press of Kentucky, 1995), 181–82; David M. Tucker, *Memphis Since Crump: Bossism, Blacks, and Civic Reformers, 1948–1968* (Knoxville: University of Tennessee Press, 1980), pass.

22. Wright, *Race, Power, and Political Emergence in Memphis*, 61–64.

23. Ibid., 90–91.

24. See Marcus D. Pohlmann and Michael P. Kirby, *Racial Politics at the Crossroads: Memphis Elects Dr. W.W. Herenton* (Knoxville: University of Tennessee Press, 1996).

25. Wright notes that Herenton's narrow 49.446 percent to 49.376 percent plurality would have offered a hollow win if two-way runoff elections had still been required in the event that no candidate received a majority of the vote. The federal courts eliminated the runoff requirement earlier in 1991: "Because black voter turnout in past runoffs has been substantially lower than in general elections, a high probability existed that Herenton would have lost the runoff election, mainly because of a higher white voter turnout rate and racially polarized voting." Wright, *Race, Power, and Political Emergence in Memphis*, 140.

26. The local media closely followed the racial composition of the new district designs. Analysis of the various plans was simplified by voter registration rules that asked voters to identify themselves by race. All but 5 percent do so. See Charles Bernsen, "Sundquist, Ford Face Tougher Re-Election Test in New Districts," *The (Memphis) Commercial Appeal*, 10 May 1992.

27. Ibid.

28. Terry Keeter, "Ford Hands in Son's Qualifying Petition," *The (Memphis) Commercial Appeal*, 24 April 1996.

29. Tom Humphrey, "Rep. Ford Weighing Re-Election Bid; Bid by His Son an Alternative," *Knoxville News-Sentinel*, 1 April 1996.

30. Nate Hobbs and Debra Elliott-Tenort, "'It's War,' Ford Says to Herenton," *The (Memphis) Commercial Appeal*, 2 April 1996.

31. Susan Adler Thorp, "Ford Jr. Finds Inside Track in Primary," *The (Memphis) Commercial Appeal*, 26 May 1996.

32. Larry Daughtrey, "An Opening for Cohen House Win?" *The Tennessean*, 30 June 1996.

33. Nate Hobbs, "Cohen to Ford Jr.: Retract 'Great Republican Hope' Remark, *The (Memphis) Commercial Appeal*, 4 June 1996.

34. Editorial, "Cohen's Record Tops Ford's Inexperience," *The (Memphis) Commercial Appeal*, 21 July 1996.

35. Nate Hobbs, "Ford Jr. Shines in His Dad's Shadow," *The (Memphis) Commercial Appeal*, 2 June 1996.

36. David Waters, "Ford Sr. Legacy Defines Congressional Race, Son's Youth Irks Veterans Cohen, Jones," *The (Memphis) Commercial Appeal*, 21 July 1996.

37. A small-sample *Commercial Appeal* poll (that drew 10 percent of its sample from outside the Ninth District) found that Ford Jr. had 86 percent name recognition. Nate Hobbs and Anna Davis, "Voters Unsure on 9th District, Fewer than Half See Ford Win," *The (Memphis) Commercial Appeal*, 9 June 1996.

38. Susan Adler Thorp, "Cohen Just Knew It, and Yet. . . ." *The (Memphis) Commercial Appeal*, 11 August 1996.

39. Ibid.

40. Editorial, "For Congress: In a Close Decision, Ford Edges DeBerry," *The (Memphis) Commercial Appeal*, 30 October 1996.

41. Aissatou Sidime, "Ford Dynasty Motors on as Son Takes over Seat," *The Tennessean*, 6 November 1996.

42. James W. Brosnan, "He Won't Be 'Puppet,' Ford Jr. Vows, Back's Dad's Urban Agenda but Plans Education Push," *The (Memphis) Commercial Appeal*, 7 November 1996.

43. David Waters, "A Deep Racial Divide, a Deeper Need to Unite," *The (Memphis) Commercial Appeal*, 4 April 1993.

44. Dana Milbank, "Harold Ford Jr. Storms His Father's House," *New York Times Magazine*, 25 October 1998, 40–43.

45. Wright, *Race, Power, and Political Emergence in Memphis*, 166–67.

46. Susan Adler Thorp, "Can Ford Pull off Bet on Sammons?" *The (Memphis) Commercial Appeal*, 27 July 1994.

47. Terry Keeter, "Businesses and Schools Will Host Ford's Meetings," *The (Memphis) Commercial Appeal*, 14 January 1997.

48. Terry Keeter, "Ford Gives Jr. an A but Not an A-Plus; Freshman Congressman Still Learning," *The (Memphis) Commercial Appeal*, 17 March 1997.

49. Ibid.

50. David Waters, "The New School of Leadership; Rep. Harold Ford Jr. Makes Moves on the Hill," *The (Memphis) Commercial Appeal*, 10 August 1997.

51. Rep. Ed Bryant, quoted in James W. Brosnan, "Fellow Politicians Hail Harold Ford Jr.'s First Year as a Success," *The (Memphis) Commercial Appeal*, 30 November 1997.

52. "Generation Next," *People Weekly*, 18 November 1996, 51.

53. Joy Bennett Kinnon, "The Hot Generation," *Ebony*, January 1998.

54. Milbank, "Harold Ford Jr. Storms His Father's House."

55. Ibid., 42.

56. Thomas G. Allen, Letter to the Editor, *The New York Times Magazine*, 15 November 1998, 30.

57. Kriste Goad, "Ford, Rival Seek Niche with Voters," *The (Memphis) Commercial Appeal*, 13 October 1998.

58. Milbank, "Harold Ford Jr. Storms His Father's House," 43.

59. James W. Brosnan, "Fellow Politicians Hail Harold Ford Jr.'s First Year as a Success," *The (Memphis) Commercial Appeal*, 30 November 1997.

60. Editorial, "Rep. Ford; He Clearly Has Earned Another Term in Congress," *The (Memphis) Commercial Appeal*," 17 October 1998.

61. See Kriste Goad, "Rising Star of Ford Jr. Shines Bright in D.C.," *The (Memphis) Commercial Appeal*, 9 November 1998.

62. Carolyn Mackler, comp., *250 Ways to Make America Better* (New York: Villard, 1999), 154–56.

63. Elizabeth Kolbert, "Next Generation: Harold E. Ford, Jr.," *The New Yorker*, 18–25 October 1999, 135.

64. "100 + Most Influential Black Americans," *Ebony*, May 1999.

65. Kriste Goad, "TBI Looks at Sept. 3 Campaign Ruckus," *The (Memphis) Commercial Appeal*, 16 September 1999.

66. James W. Brosnan, "Gore Picks 'Rising Star' Ford Jr. as Keynote Speaker," *The (Memphis) Commercial Appeal*, 4 August 2000.

67. Nancy Zuckerbrod, "Democrats Showcase Youngest Congressman," *Associated Press*, 14 August 2000.

68. Woody Baird, "Congressman Ford Jr. to Speak at Demo Convention," *Associated Press*, 4 August 2000 (bracketed text omitted).

69. Bill Dries and James W. Brosnan, "Despite Short TV Shrift, Democrats See Ford in Prime Time," *The (Memphis) Commercial Appeal*, 17 August 2000.

70. See Stephen A. Salmore and Barbara G. Salmore, *Candidates, Parties, and Campaigns: Electoral Politics in America*, 2nd ed. (Washington, D.C.: Congressional Quarterly, 1989), 112–13, 121.

71. See Robert D. Starks, "A Commentary and Response to 'Exploring the Meaning and Implications of Deracialization in African-American Urban Politics,'" *Urban Affairs Quarterly* 27 (1991): 216–22; Huey L. Perry, "Toward Conceptual Clarity Regarding Deracialization: A Response to Professor Robert T. Starks," *Urban Affairs Quarterly* 27 (1991): 223–26.

72. Starks, "A Commentary and Response," 218.

73. Sharon D. Wright, "The Deracialization Strategy and African American Candidates in Memphis Mayoral Elections," in Huey L. Perry, ed., *Race, Politics, and Governance in the United States* (Gainesville: University Press of Florida, 1996), 151–64.

74. Milbank, "Harold Ford Jr. Storms His Father's House," 42.

75. Huey L. Perry, "Preface," in Huey L. Perry, ed., *Race, Politics, and Governance in the United States* (Gainesville: University Press of Florida, 1996), xi–xii.

76. Ibid., xii. Perry was concerned that the division "may compromise the ability of African American politicians to produce benefits for black constituents."

77. See James M. Vanderleeuw, "The Influence of Racial Transition."

Preempt the Challenge

RICK SANTORUM
R-PENNSYLVANIA
U.S. SENATE

7

OLITICAL OBSERVERS tend to highlight the most dramatic moments of an electoral campaign. Silver bullet advertisements and "killer" campaign themes often take center stage. Sometimes the focus will be held on the sheer quantity of money that one side or the other poured into a heated contest. It will be said that the message or the money was the deciding factor, as the search for causal explanations in the vast constellation of issues and events, personalities and personal interactions are grossly oversimplified. Thus, George Bush's 1988 presidential victory is often attributed to the attack ads leveled at Michael Dukakis—images of revolving-door prisons and of the Democratic candidate's head poking through the top of a tank—but the cause-and-effect relationship between aggressive television spots and electoral victory is far from clear. In the multifaceted world of politics, even a highly effective ad like the "Dukakis-in-the-tank" spot might ultimately prove to be nothing more than a "vivid" memory that "forges an illusory correlation between going negative and winning."[1] Reductionism provides observers with useful shorthand for describing complex phenomena, but the vastness of a political campaign cannot be summed up by any single political moment.

In Pennsylvania, Congressman Paul Kanjorski's 1984 campaign is remembered for its clever use of television: his "boiling water" ad illustrated the incumbent's neglect of the district's problem with giardia contamination. Kanjorski's chief of staff, however, argues that the ad did not create public sentiment so much as it crystallized a campaign message. The important part of the story, from her perspective, was Kanjorski's long record of public service, which allowed Kanjorski to be compared favorably with his seemingly hapless opponent.[2] The "boiling water" ad would have meant little had Kanjorski not been laying the groundwork through years of assistance to the people of northeastern Pennsylvania. Seven years after Kanjorski entered Congress, Democrat Harris Wofford, appointed to the Senate upon the death of Republican John Heinz, won re-election with an ad that called for universal health care. "If criminals have the right to a lawyer," Wofford argued, "I think working Americans should have the right to a doctor."[3] It was clever phrasing, but again, the message would have meant nothing out of context: only by understanding the dire economic situation of many Pennsylvania voters—where pink slips threatened to devastate family finances, and where the Reagan-Bush era seemed to have left mid-Atlantic manufacturing behind—can one fully appreciate the power of the message. Politics is a complicated business.

The Republican Revolution of 1994 swept scores of Democrats from Capitol Hill, Pennsylvania's Wofford among them. Wofford was defeated by a brash, hard-driving Republican congressman three decades his junior: Rick Santorum. Although Wofford's short stay in the Senate did not seem to afford much electoral advantage—his staid, professorial style did not always fit the sharp-edged world of Pennsylvania politics—Santorum would make the most of his own incumbency. Over time, the new senator would learn to use the power of legislative institutions to broadcast his political message, deliver public goods to his home state, and raise large sums of campaign cash for his re-election. As the incumbent, Santorum was his party's presumptive nominee for the 2000 election, by which time the senator had built a solid base of support across the Keystone State. No single factor delivered Santorum his commanding re-election victory; rather, each element was part of a larger political whole.

Incumbents *do* lose—Ted Strickland temporarily lost his seat in 1994—but incumbent losses are usually attributable to events that are equally complex. In Strickland's case, the district's ideological bearing shifted with the national tide, while conservative groups like the Christian Coalition targeted the congressman for defeat—a loss that appeared to be sealed when Strickland remarked that Congress might have to raise taxes to pay for an unpopular health reform initiative. Any one of these factors might have been sufficient to defeat the congressman, but none of them work in isolation. The power of the Christian Coalition stemmed largely from the religious traditions of southern Ohio; the tax remark that hurt Strickland in 1994 might have gone unnoticed in 1992, a year friendlier to the Democratic point of view; and the multiplicity of factors behind the rightward shift of the American electorate in 1994 will be debated for years to come, but passage of President Clinton's 1993 deficit reduction package, for which Strickland cast a critical vote, was surely part of the mix.

The role of incumbency in congressional elections is so complicated that scholars have difficulty sorting through all the factors that give incumbents their edge. Still, some of the outlines have become clear. Office bureaucracies staffed by press secretaries, legislative assistants, project managers, and case-workers, among others, help representatives claim credit for the good work that the federal government does.[4] The news media give sitting office-holders a reasonable amount of public attention, introducing the incumbent to voters who do not ordinarily follow political events. And, as many challengers are painfully aware, incumbents are bankrolled by interest groups perpetually seeking access to the halls of congressional power. While the prospect of scandal always looms—public officials are subject to stories about public corruption—incumbency allows congressional representatives to commence an upward spiral of media visibility, campaign fundraising, and congressional accomplishment that can help sitting members weather political hard times. Even the Republican Revolution of 1994 left the vast majority of incumbent Democrats standing.

Santorum's commanding victory in 2000 illustrates the electoral power of incumbency. Santorum provides a particularly interesting example of this phenomenon, insofar as he had gained political fame in the House of Representatives by attacking Congress. Santorum portrayed the institution as a corrupt organization in need of radical change. During his first six years in the Senate, however, Santorum deftly used his office to communicate his message to the people of Pennsylvania. Institutional criticism was replaced by legislative action. It is true that the Senate he joined was being remade in the Republican mold, but it is also true that Santorum learned the political value of congressional incumbency. In the 2000 elections, Santorum, one of the most conservative members of that body, survived his bid for re-election even as Al Gore won Pennsylvania's electoral votes and several Senate Republicans across the country went down to defeat.

The Candidate

In *The United States of Ambition*, journalist Alan Ehrenhalt suggests that a new breed of legislator has radically transformed legislative politics.[5] Ehrenhalt argues that the type of person willing to undergo the rigors of modern-day electioneering has changed. An emerging group of people are eager to jump into the fray—not simply for a few terms, but as a career. They know early in their lives that they want to be elected, and they calculate every move in accordance with that goal. "The skills that work in American politics at this point in history are those of entrepreneurship. . . . Who sent us the political leaders we have? There is a simple answer to that question. They sent themselves."[6] Few politicians exemplify Ehrenhalt's model of a hard-hitting, entrepreneurial politician better than Santorum.

Santorum's rise to power followed a direct route. A political science major at Pennsylvania State University, Santorum worked on John Heinz' 1976 campaign for U.S. Senate. He was elected to the state chairmanship of the College Republicans, widening his political network by helping the 1978 congressional campaign of Bill Clinger, for whom he would serve as a district office intern. Santorum went on to earn a Master of Business Administration at the University of Pittsburgh and he would later graduate from Dickinson School of Law in Carlisle, Pennsylvania. Thereafter, Santorum worked as an entry-level staffer in state politics and as a lawyer in private practice. In 1990, at the age of thirty-two, Santorum ran for Congress in the Eighteenth Congressional District of Pennsylvania, on the outskirts of Pittsburgh. With little support—or even recognition—from national-level Republicans, Santorum defeated a well-funded seven-term Democrat.

Santorum had run a solid grassroots effort using highly motivated conservative activists. His message was that of radical reform in the style of Newt Gingrich, who, in 1990, was challenging his party to be uncompromising in its dealings with the Democrats. Gingrich's strategy hinged on exposing the purportedly scandalous nature of the Democratic leadership of the House. He charged that the congressional insiders had been on the inside so long that they had grown arrogant, aloof, and apart from the American people. To make his point, Gingrich had, in 1989, brought down House Speaker Jim Wright over a relatively minor financial scandal. In 1992, Gingrich helped push a variety of indignities into public awareness, including the House Bank scandal that toppled Ohio Republican Bob McEwen. Because the larger strategy was to show that Congress needed to be brought under new management, the new, hard-edged Republican strategy was ready-made for institutional outsiders like Santorum.

Santorum helped form the self-described "Gang of Seven"—a group of freshman conservatives ready to force change by any legislative means necessary. The Gang pressed to have a federal prosecutor review detailed bank records for all congressional representatives who used the House Bank, even those who did not write overdrafts. Members of the House Ethics Committee pleaded that the data not be released in raw form. Iowa Republican Fred Grandy likened the issue to "some nightmare out of Franz Kafka." But with public opinion moving solidly into the Gingrich camp, the House of Representatives not only released the records to the prosecutor, but it also divulged to the voting public the names of all who had written overdrafts to the public at large, notwithstanding the possibility that many overdrafts were caused by shoddy banking policies. The Gang of Seven had become a major force in the House of Representatives.

An angry Democratic Party targeted the Gang of Seven's membership for defeat. In Pennsylvania, Democrats in the state legislature redrew Santorum's Eighteenth Congressional District to give the Republican an electorate with

70 percent Democratic registration. George H. W. Bush received only 30 percent of the vote in the new Eighteenth; Santorum easily won his election with a full 61 percent of the vote—a credit to the congressman's political acumen and the failure of his opponent, a former Republican, to energize the Democratic base. Within a few months, Santorum was exploring a possible challenge to Wofford. He was ready to pursue the U.S. Senate in a statewide effort.

The State

Pennsylvania defies easy description. Its state lines encompass urban decay, suburban shopping malls, and a rural expanse that holds widely scattered steel mills and manufacturing plants. There is a world of difference between the prosperous neighborhoods outside of Philadelphia and the aging coal towns a few hours' drive to the north. The cities of the Keystone State reach out to every corner of the Mid-Atlantic: Erie is a close neighbor to Cleveland; Pittsburgh lies near the northern tip of West Virginia; Philadelphians live just beyond commuting distance to Baltimore; and in northeastern Pennsylvania are bedroom communities serving New York City. Throughout, one finds an amalgamation of interests, from agriculture to industry, hunting to environmentalism. A long immigrant tradition has left a variety of ethnic neighborhoods in the urban and industrial areas of the state.

Pennsylvania's diversity is reflected in its partisan volatility. Although mostly Republican since the Civil War, Pennsylvania has a sizable labor community that was brought into the Democratic fold by New Deal reforms. The result is a political teeter-totter, complete with partisans who frequently play against type. Republican Senator John Heinz made his mark by way of protectionist trade legislation and government benefits to the elderly; Democratic Governor Bob Casey, on the other hand, was one of his party's staunchest abortion opponents. In the 1960s, the Republicans held the governorship; in the early 1970s, the governor's office fell to Democratic control, only to return to the Republican fold in 1978; in 1986, Casey took the office back with a conservative campaign; in 1994, Pennsylvania handed the reigns to moderate Republican Tom Ridge. As the 2000 elections neared, Santorum was running in a state that had more registered Democrats than Republicans and that had voted for Clinton in two consecutive presidential elections, but which had put Republicans in the governor's office and both Senate seats. "If Pennsylvania is a bellwether," says the *Almanac of American Politics*, "it strikes an atypical note."[7]

Pennsylvania politics are, in many ways, premised on the state's urban-rural split. James Carville, who ran a series of campaigns for Casey and Wofford, has called Pennsylvania "two big cities with Alabama in the middle."

The industrial corners of the state—Pittsburgh in the southwest and Philadelphia in the southeast—had become strongly Democratic by the 1940s. The central region together with the state's northern tier is sometimes known as the "Rural T," which provides solid support for Republican candidates. Yet voting patterns vary by contest. "It's difficult to pin down Pennsylvania voters," says Terry Madonna, Director of the Center for Politics and Public Affairs at Millersville University. "The Republican coalition for gubernatorial contests is different than for U.S. Senate races," Madonna says, where a separate cluster of issues and personalities come into play: "Rather than there being two Pennsylvanias, some might suggest four or five."[8]

The complexity of Pennsylvania politics makes Santorum's 1994 electoral triumph all the more impressive. Unlike Casey, a pro-life Democrat, or Senator Arlen Specter, a pro-choice Republican, Santorum was an outspoken conservative on almost all issues, economic and social. "It was a stunning victory," Madonna suggests: "It was the first time in Pennsylvania state history that the voters would elect a truly conservative statewide candidate into office."[9]

Beating the Incumbent

Santorum's outsider approach was evident from the start. Among those considering a run for Wofford's seat was Santorum's former boss, Bill Clinger, then an eight-term congressman. Santorum, a second-term representative in the tight-knit Pennsylvania delegation, might have been expected to defer to his senior colleague out of respect for political protocol. Most elected officials would not run against their mentors. But even as Clinger declined to seek the Republican nomination, Santorum implied that he would have run for Senate even if Clinger had received the nomination. "It would have been difficult to run a campaign against him," Santorum revealed; "It's not something I was looking forward to."[10]

Santorum won his party's nomination handily. Turning his sights toward Wofford, Santorum commenced a stunning barrage of attacks on Democratic politics. He said that the election would be "a referendum on all the promises made and not kept" by Wofford—most obviously, the senator's continuing failure to guarantee universal health care.[11] Like Frank Cremeans in Ohio and Bob Barr in Georgia, Santorum claimed that his opponent had voted for the largest tax increase in history, and with a special dig at Wofford, Santorum charged that the Democratic health care reform proposals inspired by Wofford's 1991 campaign promise would bring about "socialized medicine." In rural counties that the senator had not yet visited, Santorum ran ads suggesting that Wofford's absence showed the degree to which the incumbent had become a "Washington insider."[12] When Wofford began to run his own negative ads, Santorum used a routine shovel-in-the-sand photo-op to berate the incumbent: "Why is it, Senator? Why haven't you run one positive ad? Don't you have anything to offer the people of Pennsylvania?"[13]

The construction-site fracas violated the standard rules of political warfare, which demand cordial relations at nonpartisan events. Some of the public officials in attendance were embarrassed by the display, but Wofford's reaction exposed the tactical effectiveness of Santorum's approach. As reported in the *Pittsburgh Post-Gazette*, "Wofford, whose professorial style is much less suited to confrontations than his much younger challenger's, never seemed to get an answer in. [Wofford] described the five-minute exchange as 'jarring.'"[14] Santorum had won the round.

Wofford's failure to respond aggressively symbolized the Senator's lack of success with the mechanics of congressional politics. While the senator's calm, studied demeanor often played well on the national stage, it could not counter the fierce attacks that Santorum was ready to mount county-by-county. Moreover, there was a general sense among Pennsylvania politicos that Wofford's ground-level staff was not taking care of constituent business. While the Senator and his top advisors were doing their best to link constituent concerns with broad policy objectives, staffers down the chain of command did not seem to have a full grasp of day-to-day constituent contact: letter-writing, responding to phone calls, and holding one-on-one meetings with key local players. (At one point, Michael John Burton, then working domestic policy issues for Kanjorski, schooled members of Wofford's staff on the basic concerns of Pennsylvania veterans.) As the general election began, a substantial number of Pennsylvania voters did not know their Senator's name.[15]

Ironically, the health care issue was working against Wofford's drive to maintain a money advantage. Wofford's defeat would likely mean the end of comprehensive health care reform efforts; Santorum thus closed the gap in financial resources with generous help from segments of the health care community fearful of Democratic proposals. (Santorum was the leading recipient of money from political action committees representing health and insurance interests.[16]) By the end of the campaign, some polls were giving Santorum a double-digit lead, threatened only by late-cycle ads charging that a Santorum win would limit retiree access to Social Security, as well as a sharp denunciation of Santorum's belligerent style leveled by the widow of John Heinz—but neither attack was sufficient to stem the anti-incumbent tide. Santorum's outsider message, pressed with vigorous assistance from the Christian Coalition and the NRA, brought the Republican Revolution to Pennsylvania. In the end, Wofford lost by two points, 49 to 47 percent.

On the Job

The Rick Santorum of 1994 would say, "No one has ever accused me of being cautious"[17]; over the course of his first term in the Senate, however, Santorum had become not cautious, exactly, but at the very least, integral to a famously cautious institution. Indeed, over time, Santorum would grow into his newfound Senate role in unexpected ways.

Santorum's tenure in the Senate began with an episode reminiscent of his time in the House: the junior senator picked a fight with a senior member of his own party. A constitutional amendment to balance the federal budget—a key provision of the Contract with America—prompted Santorum to help lead a rebellious effort aimed at disciplining the Republican chairman of the Committee on Appropriations, Mark Hatfield, perhaps by stripping Hatfield of his chairmanship. Hatfield suffered no punishment, but Santorum remained defiant. "I think we got the message across to the leaders and to the chairman . . . that we're not a bunch of kids that are going to go away," Santorum proclaimed; "We're going to be coming at you . . . and eventually if you don't change and move things we're going to get you."[18] Many thought that Santorum's Gang-of-Seven tactics were out of place in the United States Senate, which styles itself "the world's greatest deliberative body."

The Hatfield fight earned Santorum a firebrand's reputation. Over time, however, Santorum seemed increasingly aligned with his Senate colleagues and the institution they all served. He was among the few elected officials to stand with his senior colleague from Pennsylvania, Arlen Specter, during Specter's short-lived run for the 1996 presidential nomination. After Bob Dole left the Senate to pursue his own, more serious bid for the White House, the new majority leader, Trent Lott, came to rely on Santorum's counsel. Lott's exclusive "Council of Trent" would hold meetings ("informal, irregular, and often hastily called") to thrash out "ways to advance the GOP agenda."[19] And in 1997, when the Senate had to decide the scope of its campaign finance hearings—aimed principally at airing allegations of wrongdoing by Clinton and Gore—Santorum opposed efforts to extend the investigation to congressional campaigns. It was a position that seemed to conflict with Santorum's call for full disclosure in the 1992 House Bank scandal, but one that helped maintain the unity of the Senate Republican cause.

Santorum did not neglect constituent service. When *Inc.* magazine profiled the Senator's management style, it noted that Santorum had mastered "sanity through efficiency." Santorum "insist[ed] that his staffers craft original and personal responses" to the "[n]early 4,000 pieces of mail [that] arrive at Santorum's Senate office each week."[20] In fact, "To save time and money (and make life easier for all involved), Santorum and his staff disseminate information every way possible, hoping that Pennsylvanians will find answers to their questions before they think of writing. . . . An E-mail version of . . . weekly columns [posted on the Web site], the 'Rick Report,' goes to 'anyone who gives [Santorum] an address.' "[21]

Santorum's outreach effort went beyond E-mail. A report by the conservative Heritage Foundation profiled the senator's efforts to use his Senate office to promote public-private partnerships:

> Senator Rick Santorum has assigned nine staff members throughout his regional offices to community and economic development (CED). CED staff members offer a variety of constituent services. For instance, they build working relationships with private and quasi-governmental organizations, including major employers, universities and colleges, chambers of commerce, community development corporations, and industrial development authorities. . . . CED staff attend community meetings held by local non-profits and government agencies to find out how the Senator can encourage community revitalization.[22]

Unlike Wofford's office, which seemed to have trouble responding to basic constituent inquiries, the Santorum operation made every effort to engage in the everyday business of constituent relations.

In legislative politics, Santorum was becoming a key player. He was instrumental in forging a compromise on welfare reform and he led the Senate fight against partial birth abortion. Santorum was careful to pay attention to national issues having a critical impact on his home state, often positioning himself at the center of the ideological spectrum. For example, when the importation of cheap foreign steel threatened Pennsylvania jobs, he opined, "There's the left that would like to see quotas, the middle that would like to see a more reasonable piece of legislation and the right who want nothing."[23] Even the Senate impeachment debate was quiet for Santorum, at least in comparison to the old days: Santorum argued in vain that Monica Lewinsky should testify on the Senate floor, but he accepted defeat gracefully.

Few classified Santorum as a moderate, but some on the right wing found themselves disillusioned, wondering if Santorum would be able to muster the legions of ideologically motivated activists that would be necessary to "deliver the fliers and do the fundamental things that really propelled him to office."[24] Such concerns reflected a broad political shift that had Santorum, a strict fiscal conservative, voting to increase the minimum wage and working to protect a local Army depot from closure. At the end of 1999, with the 2000 election looming on the horizon, Santorum supported a multi-billion-dollar farm relief package for the first time in his congressional career.[25] In fact, Santorum even tried to *enlarge* the aid package. When his efforts failed, he vowed to continue the fight for more federal aid.[26] One could still see flashes of the Gang of Seven in Santorum's sharply pointed rhetoric, but as the former congressman gained stature in the Senate, he evinced a persona more suitable to the upper house. In Madonna's words, Santorum was "crawling to the middle."[27]

The Democratic Primary

In 1994, Rick Santorum established himself as an alternative to the old-style liberalism of Wofford. Santorum had attacked Wofford for his vote on Clinton's deficit reduction package and for his advocacy of government-sponsored health care. Madonna notes that the Santorum-Wofford race had given voters a clear ideological choice: "the Reagan view vs. the New Deal view."[28] Pennsylvania voters ultimately chose the new conservatism pressed by Santorum, just as Bob Barr's Georgia saw fit to move beyond the politics of the solid Democratic South. Furthermore, the Wofford operation could never figure out how to repeat the stellar performance of 1991.

If it was true that Wofford had run a bad campaign, then perhaps a more aggressive Democrat could beat Santorum. Indeed, as the 2000 electoral cycle approached, Santorum looked vulnerable. A small-sample poll conducted in mid-1999 suggested that the electorate was not yet sold on the incumbent: only 34 percent believed that Santorum deserved re-election.[29] Partly out of sentimental attachment to Wofford, partly out of a dislike for Santorum's conservatism, and partly out of a rational strategic calculation that Santorum was an ideological and temperamental mismatch with his state, Democrats were eager to do battle. One commentator wrote, "Outspoken and controversial in his freshman and sophomore years in the Senate, Santorum was viewed . . . as red meat that could be thrown to Pennsylvania's Democratic wolves."[30] At the national level, the Democratic Senatorial Campaign Committee (DSCC) made Santorum a fixture on its political hit list. With a modest Democratic edge in registration, and with a presidential election predicted to boost turnout in Pennsylvania's cities, a Democrat might have a real shot at winning.

Four-term congressman Ron Klink emerged as the Democratic frontrunner. A former Pittsburgh television reporter, Klink had been elected to the House in 1992. He had strong appeal to union households in his western Pennsylvania district. With only a high school education, Klink was a homegrown populist. His personal style fit labor halls and factory gates better than the trendy cafes of Washington, D.C. During his time in Congress, Klink had emerged as a strong opponent of the Contract with America, the North American Free Trade Agreement, and the General Agreement on Tariffs and Trade. Like many other legislators from industrial states, he feared that environmental regulation could cost jobs. And like Kanjorski, from the opposite corner of the state, Klink's support for the Democratic leadership was tempered by his opposition to abortion and gun control.

The Democratic primary would be an exercise rooted in political geography. It pitted Klink, the only candidate from Western Pennsylvania, against five Philadelphia-area contenders. Klink's two main rivals were Allyson Schwartz, a state senator, and Tom Foley, a former state secretary of labor. Starting the electoral season with the Pittsburgh area in his pocket, Klink used conservative social values to win the "Rural T. Schwartz" and Foley wound up splitting a surprisingly small number of Philadelphia voters (the lowest turnout since World War II), leaving Klink with 47 percent of the vote. It was a strong win, but within Klink's primary election victory were the seeds of his general election defeat. The primary election depleted Klink's treasury—the congressman had to take out a $300,000 mortgage on his own house just to keep the campaign afloat—and without benefit of deep-pocket support, Klink was never able to break into the pricey Philadelphia television market. Still relatively unknown outside of his home base, Klink would have difficulty raising his profile among Democratic voters in the Philadelphia area. Klink's lack of visibility and scarcity of resources would prove to be a fatal combination.

Routing the Opposition

Klink was caught in a vicious circle: because he did not *have* money, the odds of winning diminished, and as a result, Klink could not *raise* money. The campaign was all but broke. Santorum, meanwhile, was pulling in a lot of cash. Within two months of the 1994 election, political action committees had given over $127,000 to Santorum—more than they had given to any other Senate freshman.[31] By the end of 1998, Santorum had raised $1.5 million; a year later, he had twice that amount. And Santorum was better known to begin with. Klink, a congressman from western Pennsylvania, was not widely recognized outside his home region, whereas Santorum, through his "Rick Reports," countless personal appearances, and of course, the regular news coverage all senators receive, had communicated with a wide range of Pennsylvanians. A lesson appeared to have been learned from Santorum's predecessor. Wofford had failed to take full advantage of his incumbent status—and as a result, he had allowed a second-term congressman to reach parity in fundraising and message volume. Santorum would not let Klink eat away at his lead. He would use his incumbency to preempt the Democratic challenge, skillfully combining media and money to do so.

As Klink's prospects fell, Santorum's rose, partly because the incumbent Senator was spending his money well. For polling, Santorum hired Public

Opinion Strategies, with political veteran Neil Newhouse at the helm; fund-raising responsibilities fell to Urban/Tsucalas; and media work was handled by the consulting firm of Brabender Cox Mihalke, founded in Erie, Pennsylvania—a respected consultancy that had handled a long list of distinguished Republican clients.

Santorum had used John Brabender's firm in 1994; for 2000, Brabender believed that the key to winning Pennsylvania lay in suburban Philadelphia, where the electorate leaned toward the center. Pro-choice Republicans had voted for Democrats like Bill Clinton, and Brabender was concerned that the opposition party had done a good job painting Santorum as a radical conservative. To Brabender, this was a false impression: "If you look closely at his voting record, he's a real moderate. Sure, he voted against strict gun control, but he also voted for tougher penalties for gun-related crimes and for mandatory gun locks."[32] To help the public understand Santorum's moderation, the senator's team began a massive direct mail program and a heavy television ad blitz, both of which ran early in the campaign. Klink, short on cash, could only watch from the sidelines.

Santorum ran a smart strategy, carefully calculated for maximum effect. He advertised heavily on Klink's turf in Pittsburgh, forcing the lagging Klink campaign—badly in need of forward movement—to sink its already-scarce resources into a purely defensive battle. "When you challenge a candidate in his home base," says Brabender, "all his friends, neighbors, and family take it personally. They push the candidate to respond even when his money is better spent elsewhere. It's real hard to let go."[33] By keeping Klink pinned down in the Pittsburgh market, Santorum prevented the congressman from moving into Philadelphia.

The message Santorum conveyed was meant to soften the hard edges of the senator's public image, and the basic concept for one important television spot came by accident. Brabender's team had decided to film family-centered ads at the senator's home, trying to make the spots seem cozy and relaxed. The approach was well-worn—simply showing that the politician was a "real person"—but it was known to be effective. As Brabender tells the story, the scripted filming had completed and the senator began playing around with his wife and kids. Brabender told the camera crew to continue filming, thinking that he would simply give the tape to the Santorums as a post-election offering. "It was just for fun," Brabender recalls. But when Brabender returned to the studio to edit the scripted footage, he realized the value of the spontaneous material: it was the real senator and his family, "[s]o we used this goofy footage for our commercials."[34]

But how could this candid action be used to convey the incumbent's record of legislative achievement? Brabender borrowed a trick from the VH-1 music program, *Pop-Up Video*, in which goofs and spoofs are pointed out in the middle of well-known music videos. In Santorum's version, the senator is wrestling with his children on their lawn, and as the kids try to run away, Santorum awkwardly throws a tennis shoe at them as a pop-up bubble explains, "Rick is a lot better at passing legislation—such as the historic welfare reform act." Another pop-up notes, "The filming of this ad was interrupted by lunch and two naps." The response was overwhelming. Says Brabender, "[The ads] were fun, they were entertaining, and they got our message across. I've been in this business for twenty years and have done hundreds of races, but never have I seen such a positive reaction to a spot."[35] Brabender says that tracking polls showed a significant bump just after the ads were released, and the *Pittsburgh Post-Gazette* observed that "Santorum's numbers [rose] 15 points in the Pittsburgh market, an area with love-hate feelings toward the candidate."[36]

Expectations were beginning to drive the race. Santorum had accumulated a strong money advantage and the news media started writing early obituaries about Klink. When the Klink operation dismissed its finance director, the press aired "complaints from state Democrats that Klink [had] not aggressively raised the money he need[ed] to challenge Sen. Rick Santorum."[37] Some talented young political professionals, given the opportunity to raise money for Klink's campaign, were leery of jumping on board a sinking ship. In July, the *New York Times* headlined a story about the race, "Hoping for Easy Win, But Reality Intrudes." The paper reported that optimism "slumped . . . with the release of a poll that showed Mr. Santorum with a [two to one] lead over Mr. Klink. And they sagged even lower on Thursday with release of a campaign finance report that showed Mr. Santorum with nearly an [eight to one] lead in campaign funds, $4.3 million to $564,500."[38] Around political Washington, Democrats were beginning to write off the Klink campaign so as to concentrate on Senate races that seemed more winnable.

Klink's money problems lay in stark comparison to other Senate bids. Wofford raised over $6 million against Santorum for the 1994 election—and, with the power of Senate incumbency behind him, Wofford *still* lost. In the 1999–2000 campaign finance cycle, Klink would never quite reach $4 million, while Santorum's fundraising exceeded $9 million. Nearly all of Klink's money came from individuals and political action committees, as is typical of most Senate campaigns; but Klink was receiving only a small amount of cash from the Democratic Party. Paul Herrnson notes that a typical Senate candidate can expect to receive roughly 7 percent of his or her money from party sources,[39] but Klink received only 3.5 percent of his overall budget from the Democratic Party. Another 11 percent usually comes from the war chests of other candidates, but Klink was only able to bring in 1.4 percent from his peers.

Decisions made by the Democratic Party are revealing. Given that Santorum was on everyone's target list in 1999, most-insiders, including Klink, had assumed that the party would invest heavily in Pennsylvania's 2000 campaign for the Senate. But bad poll numbers and the failure of the Klink organization to raise much money on its own gave pause to Democratic decision makers. Coordinated expenditures benefiting the Klink campaign totaled only $700,000, compared to the $7 million that helped Hillary Rodham Clinton's candidacy in New York. As for soft money expenditures, the Democratic Party sent $1.5 million into Pennsylvania, compared to sums exceeding $4 million sent to help Democratic efforts in Florida, Michigan, Missouri, and New York. In midsummer, the chairman of the DSCC, Senator Robert Torricelli, neglected to mention the Klink campaign among the DSCC's "top priorities": "This is one where the DSCC will monitor it very closely and make a judgment about putting greater resources into it."[40] (When Torricelli corrected himself, saying that Klink was in fact a top priority, a skeptical reporter noted that Torricelli "declined to commit to a specific level of financial support [to] help Klink in the fall."[41]) Klink was furious. After the election, he said that the DSCC "broke their word to us."[42]

The lack of DSCC money hurt the Klink campaign in raw, practical terms—less money meant less visibility—but it also sent a cautionary message to potential Democratic donors. Individuals and political action committees look to the parties for guidance. Party committees base their decisions on good political intelligence and cold-blooded electoral interests; other funding sources tend to follow the party lead. A clear party endorsement in the form of a large cash infusion would have been particularly helpful to Klink's mission because the congressman's pro-gun, pro-life views left many liberal Democratic donors unmoved. When the Democratic Party declined to get actively involved, Klink's fundraising operation, which had a poor track record to begin with, was hard-pressed to make up the difference.

The end was near. Santorum's center-leaning strategy, his early fundraising, and his close attention to constituent needs over the course of a six-year Senate incumbency—all these factors were combining to check Klink's strategic options. And it was beginning to look like a check*mate*. In order to surmount Republican strength in Pennsylvania's suburbs and the Rural T, Klink would have to run well in the Philadelphia market; in order to be more competitive there, he would have to buy expensive television time; but with finances in a downward spiral, Klink could not get into the game. Lacking substantial evidence of strong Philadelphia support, there was little chance that the money problems could ever be resolved. At the end of the race, few believed that Klink had any chance to defeat Santorum.

Expectations proved themselves right: Santorum beat Klink by nearly 7 percent—52.4 to 45.5. Klink understood the power of the expectations game, blaming it for his loss. "The media went beyond reporting the news in this race and ended up making news, because they convinced everybody that we had no opportunity to win this race," Klink later said; "And, in fact, they had these polls that showed us over [twenty] points down and I knew better than that, but it became a self-fulfilling prophecy. We couldn't raise any money because the media kept saying that. We couldn't get beyond that."[43] In truth, Klink had been up against an even larger foe. He was fighting an incumbent senator who knew how to deploy a preemptive strategy: by maintaining a commanding position from the outset—greater visibility, more money, and a message that resonated with Pennsylvania voters—Santorum denied Klink any firm political foothold.

Preemption

To those not directly involved in its conduct, the 2000 race for Pennsylvania's seat in the U.S. Senate was uninspiring. It was overshadowed by Hillary Rodham Clinton's celebrity status in New York's Senate race as well as Democrat John Corzine's $60 million bid to represent the state of New Jersey. When Klink needed media attention the most—at the end of the campaign season—Al Gore and George W. Bush were running neck-and-neck among Pennsylvania voters, drawing nearly all of the state's political news coverage. But most importantly, the race seemed uneventful because Santorum had skillfully executed a smart electoral strategy. Wofford had failed to use his position in the Senate to build strong connections with his constituency, whereas Santorum made every effort to reach out. Wofford had not been able to shake the impression that he was an old-style liberal, but Santorum found ways to dampen his own archconservative reputation. By connecting with the electorate, tempering his conservatism, and raising a lot of money (especially early money), Santorum did his utmost to ensure that there would be no serious race for the seat. In other words, he used the powers of incumbency to preempt the opposition.

Political scientists have long speculated on the source of the incumbency advantage. David Mayhew has argued that congressional representatives are principally driven by the need to be reelected, and that they can further that interest by claiming credit for legislative action.[44] Morris Fiorina has argued that congressional representatives have organized Washington politics—everything from the functioning of their office staffs to the operation of federal agencies—around their personal electoral interests, and a number of studies have supported this claim.[45] Some have speculated that the power of incumbency is on the rise because partisan attachments have fallen away.[46] Still, while incumbency brings a number of important resources, electoral victories are not automatic. Santorum's official position brought funds and visibility, to be sure, which the senator parlayed into *more* money and *more* visibility, but his immediate predecessor had found himself unable to take advantage of incumbency. The difference lay in political skill: Santorum managed his political resources in the service of electoral success, whereas Wofford had failed to do so.

No single factor brought about Santorum's victory; rather, the senator aligned the variegated elements of his political operation to work together as a single unit. He had, in effect, constructed a powerful circle of strategic initiatives: a tempered conservative message that sought pro-life policies, a restrained approach to government spending, and economic development that sought partnerships between the public and private sectors. Santorum did his best to bring federal money back home, and through his regional offices, he attempted to coordinate a wide range of private initiatives and public support. Anyone interested in the senator's accomplishments could learn about them through his constant presence in the news media, or in a more personal way, through his Rick Reports. When, during the campaign season, it became clear that Santorum's image needed to be softened, a tactically intelligent media campaign filled in the gaps. Each element of the Senator's political operation supported all the others.

Incumbency provides resources, but it takes a good electoral strategy to make them work on Election Day. While some portion of the electoral advantage may well be conferred without tactical intervention—coverage in the news media, for example, boosts an incumbent's name recognition almost without effort—a strategically smart incumbent will figure out, as Santorum did, how to maximize the benefits of incumbency, merging them into a mutually reinforcing strategic unit.

In its most commanding form, the power of preemption scares off quality politicians who might otherwise challenge the congressional incumbent. Gary Jacobson has noted that strong incumbents discourage strong challengers: "If an incumbent can convince potentially formidable opponents and people who control campaign resources that he or she is invincible, he or she is very likely to avoid a serious challenge and so will be invincible."[47] Santorum benefited from a less robust form of preemption—but one that, in the end, proved no less effective. The quality challengers were not all scared off—Klink was a good candidate by almost any measure—but Santorum had created a political environment in which a quality challenger simply was not viable. Santorum had made himself so formidable that (1) just pulling even with Santorum's pre-campaign advantage would have required any challenger to spend great sums of political cash, while (2) the diminished prospects for success meant that the political "smart money" was looking to invest elsewhere.

Klink was not scared; he was cornered—and he was hedging his own bets.

Forced to take out a second mortgage on his home to fund last-minute television ads during the primaries, he had to make a decision about the $300,000 loan he had made to his campaign: either require the campaign to repay the debt or let it hang onto the money and enhance the prospects of victory. If Klink won, his campaign treasury would easily be replenished and Klink could be repaid; if he lost, the $300,000 debt would likely have to be written off. Klink played it safe. "When I saw that the party was not going to live up to its obligation—they had promised me $1.2 million in hard money—when I realized that was not coming, I paid off the debt."[48]

A month after the 2000 election, Santorum defeated a senior GOP colleague to become chairman of the Senate Republican Conference—a position that would enable the young senator to build an even higher platform from which to scare off Democratic opponents, reduce opposition fundraising, and to elevate his own media visibility, all at the same time. Were it not for the Republican Party's loss of the Senate in mid-2001—the result of Vermont Republican Jim Jeffords' departure from the GOP—Santorum would have received greatly enhanced powers to steer government benefits to his home state. But even still, Santorum's shift from outsider to insider status is remarkable. In a span of just ten years, Santorum had gone from anti-congressional firebrand in the House of Representatives to loyal member of the Republican leadership in the Senate, giving himself an opportunity to further augment the electorally preemptive powers of his incumbency.

Notes

1. Richard R. Lau et al., "The Effects of Negative Political Advertisements: A Meta-Analytic Assessment," *American Political Science Review* 93 (1999): 860.

2. Karen Feather, telephone interview, 12 January 1999.

3. Dale Russakoff, " 'The Right to See a Doctor When You're Sick'; Wofford's Appeal for Access to Medical Care Creates 'Wildfire' in Senate Race in Pennsylvania," *Washington Post*, 19 November 1991.

4. See Morris P. Fiorina, *Congress: Keystone of the Washington Establishment*, 2d ed. (New Haven, Conn.: Yale University Press, 1989).

5. Alan Ehrenhalt, *The United States of Ambition: Politicians, Power, and the Pursuit of Office* (New York: Times Books), 1991.

6. Ibid., 17, 19.

7. Michael Barone and Grant Ujifusa, *Almanac of American Politics, 1998*, (Washington, D.C.: National Journal, 1997), 1197.

8. Terry Madonna, telephone interview, 13 October 2001.

9. Ibid.

10. Jack Torry, "Clinger Shies from Senate Race; Decision Leaves Santorum as Top Republican Challenger to Wofford," *Pittsburgh Post-Gazette*, 28 July 1993.

11. Harry Stoffer, "Senate Race Shapes up as Referendum on Clinton, Health Reform," *Pittsburgh Post-Gazette*, 12 May 1994.

12. Brett Lieberman, "Santorum Targets Wofford on Airwaves for not Visiting Counties," *States News Service*, 8 July 1994.

13. David Michelmore, "The Senate Race, In Your Face; Santorum Confronts Wofford over TV Attack Ad Campaign," *Pittsburgh Post-Gazette*, 28 October 1994.

14. Ibid.

15. Robert Shogan, "Wofford Swept in on Health Issue, and May Be Swept out with It," *Los Angeles Times*, 7 September 1994, referencing April 1994 poll.

16. Eric Weissenstein, "Big Health PACs Bet Heavily against Reform," *Modern Healthcare*, 21 August 1995.

17. See David L. Michelmore, "Santorum Attacks Wofford in Person with Snarls, Sneers," *Pittsburgh Post-Gazette*, 29 October 1994.

18. Andrea Foster, "Santorum Looks Back on First 100 Days of Senate," *States News Service*, 7 April 1995.

19. Matthew Rees, "The Council of Trent," *The Weekly Standard*, 17 March 1997, 18.

20. Sarah Schafer, "Legislator's Agenda," *Inc.*, July 1998, 31–33, 32.

21. Ibid.

22. April Lassiter, *Congress and Civil Society: How Legislators Can Champion Civic Renewal in Their Districts* (Washington, D.C.: Heritage Foundation, 1998, text available on LEXIS-NEXIS).

23. Anick Jesdanun, "Steel Industry Faces Hurdles in Congress," *Associated Press*, 12 January 1999.

24. Clay Mankamyer, Executive Director of the Christian Coalition of Pennsylvania, quoted in Anick Jesdanun, "Conservative Senator Faces Some Discontent from the Right," *Associated Press*, 25 January 1999.

25. Anick Jesdanun, "Santorum Supports Emergency Spending for First Time," *Associated Press*, 6 August 1999.

26. Ibid.

27. Claude R. Marx, "Pennsylvania GOP Is Diverse—Moderately So," *Associated Press*, 13 September 1999.

28. Judi Hasson, "PA's Anti-Incumbent Mood Sends Santorum to Senate," *USA Today*, 9 November 1994.

29. "Poll Suggests Santorum's Support Is Soft; Bush Enjoys Head Start in PA," *Associated Press*, 28 July 1999.

30. William J. Green, "Ron Klink's Hard Road Ahead," *The Pittsburgh Post-Gazette*, 9 April 2000.

31. "Santorum, Frist Lead Freshman Senators in Post-Election PAC Money," *Associated Press*, 24 February 1995.

32. John Brabender, telephone interview, 25 September 2001.

33. Ibid.

34. Ibid.

35. Ibid.

36. Christina Rouvalis, "Right-Hand Man; Consultant's Ads Boost Santorum and Other Republicans into Winner's Circle," *Pittsburgh Post-Gazette*, 9 November 2000.

37. Jack Torry, "Klink Fires Campaign Finance Director," *Pittsburgh Post-Gazette*, 21 June 2000.

38. B. Drummond Ayres, Jr., "Hoping for Easy Win, But Reality Intrudes," *The New York Times*, 16 July 2000.

39. Paul S. Herrnson, *Congressional Elections: Campaigning at Home and in Washington*, 3rd ed. (Washington, D.C.: Congressional Quarterly, 2000), 176.

40. Claude R. Marx, "Top Democratic Strategist Not Certain of Klink's Prospects in the Future," *Associated Press*, 29 June 2000.

41. Claude R. Marx, "Torricelli Calls Pennsylvania Senate Race a "Top Priority," *Associated Press*, 1 July 2000.

42. James O'Toole, "Klink Has No Regrets about Senate Run; He Won't Rule out a Return to Politics," *Pittsburgh Post-Gazette*, 21 January 2001.

43. Ibid.

44. David R. Mayhew, *Congress: The Electoral Connection* (New Haven, Conn.: Yale University Press, 1974).

45. Fiorina, *Congress: Keystone of the Washington Establishment*; A.D. Cover and B.S. Brumberg, "Baby Books and Ballots: The Impact of Congressional Mail on Constituent Opinion," *American Political Science Review* 76 (1982): 347–59; Diana Evans Yiannakis, "The Grateful Electorate: Casework and Congressional Elections," *American Journal of Political Science* 25 (1981): 568–80; John R. Johannes, *To Serve the People: Congress and Constituency Service* (Lincoln: University of Nebraska Press, 1984), 87.

46. See John A. Ferejohn, "On the Decline in Competition in Congressional Elections," *American Political Science Review* 71 (1977): 166–76; Albert D. Cover, "One Good Term Deserves Another: The Advantage of Incumbency in Congressional Elections," *American Journal of Political Science* 21 (1977): 523–41.

47. Gary C. Jacobson, *The Politics of Congressional Elections*, 5th ed. (New York: Longman, 2001), 36.

48. James O'Toole, "Klink Has No Regrets about Senate Run; He Won't Rule out a Return to Politics."

Conclusion: Campaign Mode Revisited

I N THE STUDY of campaign strategy, politics is largely a matter of who does what, when, and how.[1] Victory often demands not just a preponderance of political assets, but their skillful deployment as well. Smart strategy leverages the power of scarce resources. Ideally, a candidate's time is well spent, the message is carefully targeted, financial resources are shrewdly budgeted, and tactical operations are meticulously planned. If the campaign shows strength, it gets a shot at new endorsements, more money, increased prominence in the news media, and perhaps even a sense of inevitable victory. Success tends to beget success. Conversely, a haphazard approach can produce a cycle of failure. Scheduling is uncoordinated, money is wasted, the appearance of imminent collapse dries up resources—and disappointment ensues. Competitive campaigns require strategic thinking.

To win, political professionals view the political terrain in campaign mode, a state of mind that combines visceral drive with strategic thinking. To Harold Ford Jr., campaign mode is "something intangible." Is it keeping your eye on the big picture? Not getting distracted by the details? Maybe, "but it's important to pay attention to the little things," such as casework, personal contact, and the day-to-day labors expected of a congressional representative.[2] At the ground level, where Ford Jr. works everyday, the importance of the little things seems obvious, and the basic rules of electioneering—like knowing your district, building strong connections, and preempting the opposition—help a political professional visualize the electorally significant features of a given political terrain. Although the rules might differ in application from one campaign to the next, they provide a benchmark from which a political professional may calculate strategic operations.

Campaign mode presupposes that individuals make a difference in the world. In politics, it is believed, life is nasty, brutish, and short; the impediments to victory are often monstrous. But it is assumed that smart strategy can bring triumph. Come-from-behind victories such as Loretta Sanchez' 1996 Orange County win and Harris Wofford's 1991 Pennsylvania victory seem to reveal the strength of carefully directed political ambition. Machiavelli spoke to this idea. "I think it may be true that fortune is the ruler of half our actions," he instructed the Prince, "but that she allows the other half or thereabouts to be governed by us."[3] An operative who does not believe in the power of human intervention lacks any reason to pursue electoral victory.

If political professionals could foresee all possible outcomes for all possible tactics, then strategic choices could be reduced to simple calculation. Yet judgments must be made from imperfect knowledge. The Sanchez campaign's decision to stay under the radar generated controversy within the organization, where some had faith and others were less than sure. Bob Barr won office because Democratic incumbent Buddy Darden assumed that a friendly personal style and a strong record of public service would win in 1994, just as it had in the past; but in the end, the strategy was no match for Barr's aggressive, issue-based campaign. Sanchez' novel approach succeeded against the odds; Darden's proven strategy failed. Those who look for the secret of electoral success will discover many workable campaign rules, but they will also find an abundance of well-laid plans gone awry.

A Cautionary Tale

Heidi Behrens-Benedict rushed the political stage in 1998. In May, she was a self-employed interior designer, a recently widowed mother of two adult children who had never played a role in public life. In June, she was a candidate for Congress, firing up delegates at the state Democratic convention. Behrens-Benedict was set to take on a firmly established Republican with a national reputation: Jennifer Dunn. "Jennifer," she told convention-goers, "Get up. You're in my seat."[4]

A shooting at an Oregon high school had motivated the impromptu candidacy. Shocked by the news, Behrens-Benedict wrote an impassioned letter to the *Seattle Times.* "I am sick to death of children living such desperate lives and having so few options and abilities to cope that their only response to their frustration and pain is murder or suicide," the letter read; "I am sick to death of my elected officials being so afraid of the NRA and so greedy for its blood money that they allow our children to be slaughtered rather than risk the wrath of the NRA."[5] Behrens-Benedict urged readers to contact their representatives "and require them, as a condition of your vote, to reject the NRA and adopt a national policy on gun control."[6]

The letter brought an enthusiastic response from anti-gun liberals. Within days, Behrens-Benedict decided to run for Congress. She phoned the state Democratic Party to discuss her plans, but she received only a polite response. After some persistence, party officials referred Behrens-Benedict to an experienced campaign activist.[7]

The gun issue seemed a natural choice for an electorate that one popular magazine has called "granola-crunchy but conservative on the economy."[8] The Eighth Congressional District of Washington comprises the eastern sections of King and Pierce counties, with its population concentrated in upscale suburbs east of Lake Washington. The "Eastside" has the look and feel of young money, much of it derived from information technology. Beyond the suburbs are a scattering of small towns that mix agriculture, light industry, and retail sales. Although the district lies outside the bounds of Seattle proper, its constituents are inextricably tied to the city's social and economic structure.

Dunn, a former chair of the state Republican Party, was elected to represent the Eighth Congressional District in 1992, and she soon gained a seat on the influential Ways and Means Committee. Easily winning every bid for re-election, Dunn has been able to pursue a wide-ranging policy agenda, even counseling the GOP leadership to begin closing the gender gap by "projecting the soft side of the conservative message."[9] In 2000, she helped George W. Bush strategize his presidential victory. Democrats reportedly set their sights low, believing that Behrens-Benedict needed only 45 percent of the vote—a showing just large enough to "bolster [Democratic] chances for filling the seat if Dunn leaves to work for a Bush administration."[10]

The key to victory in 1998, as Behrens-Benedict saw it, was ideology: the district was not as conservative as it appeared to be. It had voted for Bill Clinton and Democratic Governor Gary Locke in recent elections, owing partly to the efforts of union employees at the local Boeing aircraft plant, in the building trades, and in service industries. Behrens-Benedict needed to do what Clinton and Locke had done.[11] The foreshortened campaign season, however, left Behrens-Benedict without much time to make her case. Rallies were held and mail was sent, but early enthusiasm did not translate into broad support. One newspaper called Dunn "a highly skilled political tactician and vote-getter who will have little trouble dispatching her inexperienced Democratic challenger."[12] On Election Night, Dunn was more concerned about her GOP colleagues than she was about her own re-election, as two of the state's Republican seats switched to Democratic control.[13] Behrens-Benedict earned only 40 percent of the vote, compared to Dunn's 60 percent.

It was a wide margin, but as challenger defeats go, this was a respectable loss. The Behrens-Benedict campaign was a shoestring operation run almost entirely by the candidate herself. Starting late and spending only $172,000 against Dunn's $1.5 million, Behrens-Benedict handed Dunn her lowest re-election margin in six years.

Behrens-Benedict was not ready to give up. After the 1998 loss, she kept herself in the public eye, continued to build her political network, and sought endorsements from friendly interest groups. She got a quick start on her campaign war chest, and by mid-1999 she had hired a professional campaign consultant. Labor endorsed early. Support from the Women's Campaign Fund caught the attention of *Mirabella* magazine, which ran a six-page profile; *Ms.* magazine called Behrens-Benedict a "solid feminist."[14]

The 2000 campaign would focus on moderate women, environmentalists, and pro-choice voters, an effort to take advantage of shifting demographics. As Seattle sprawled across Lake Washington, Democrats were moving to the Eastside. In 2000, a presidential election year, the Democratic Party and organized labor could be expected to activate base constituencies, leaving Behrens-Benedict to concentrate on swing voters. The swing vote would be targeted "demographically and by issues."[15] It would "identify newly registered voters," who, it was assumed, would be "less likely to be social conservatives and [who would] have no history with [Dunn]."[16] The campaign would focus its attention on precincts that had "voted for both Democrats i.e. Governor Gary Locke, and Attorney General Christine Gregoire and Republicans Jennifer Dunn and [U.S. Senator] Slade Gorton."[17]

The strategic math centered on abortion politics. In 1998, Behrens-Benedict received 40 percent of the vote; that same year, a conservative ballot initiative to ban late-term abortions garnered 42 percent. If the 1998 "Heidi vote" would hold in 2000, and if the pro-life vote was made up of die-hard Republicans who would never choose a Democrat, the middle 18 percent could provide Behrens-Benedict her margin of victory.[18] Professionally compiled electoral data identified the district's most persuadable precincts. One wall of campaign headquarters was covered with maps showing where Behrens-Benedict won in 1998, which precincts voted for statewide Democratic candidates, and which precincts voted against the pro-life ballot initiative. An "older and more educated" cohort of absentee voters was targeted as part of the campaign's direct-mail strategy.[19] If Behrens-Benedict could show Eastsiders that Jennifer Dunn was an anti-abortion conservative, then she could pull this Republican stronghold into the Democratic column.

But "the media's favorite challenger"[20] from 1998 drew little notice in 2000. All attention converged on a close Senate race and the presidential campaign. Behrens-Benedict was left out of the picture, and her $375,000 treasury could not begin to make up the difference. (Dunn raised more than $1.7 million for herself and another $500,000 for George W. Bush.) When the *Seattle Post-Intelligencer* rendered its endorsement, it said, "Dunn's political skill, experience and clout in Congress . . . make her the stronger choice."[21] The *Seattle Times* had a similar appraisal: "[Dunn] has become a leader of her party nationally and an influential member of the state's [congressional] delegation. She receives our enthusiastic support."[22]

In November 2000, defeat came by an even wider margin than it had in

1998: 62 to 36 percent. Once again, the Democratic base voted for Behrens-Benedict, but the swing did not.

Understanding Campaign Mode

Behrens-Benedict was in campaign mode, yet she lost anyway. She and her supporters had surveyed the political terrain; they had reverse-engineered a strategic plan; and throughout the electoral season, they had demonstrated an intense commitment to winning the race. Campaign mode demands victory, but cannot always deliver it.

Faith in victory is important to campaign mode, not simply because it motivates the troops, but also because the notion establishes a strict logic of personal accountability. When victory is achievable, defeat might show that the campaign organization was not up to the task. The loss would be everyone's fault. Hence, campaign mode fosters an exacting, outcome-based standard of responsibility: everyone has to make sure they get the job done. The race is worked all day, through mealtimes, and into the night. There are no excuses; assigned duties *must* be completed. Blame cannot be laid on unforeseen obstacles, even if all reasonable steps were taken to avoid them—because "reasonable" is the wrong standard: in campaign mode, the measure of a person lies in the completion of difficult missions.

From the final outcome of an election to all the details that precede it, up and down the chain of command, political professionals demand perfection. Hence, when James Carville ordered an operative to ensure delivery of a taped campaign ad, he drilled home the idea that the mission had to be completed, no matter what:

> I want to know, at every point, when this is happening and who is doing it. Because if it doesn't f---in' get there and they don't see this f---in' spot, it's going to be your f---ing ass, you understand? You. Personally. If that thing doesn't get there, if that plane is late, it's gonna be your fault. If there's a thunderstorm, it's your fault. If that f---ing thing crashes, it's your fault. Okay? You got that? Now go do it. Get out of my sight and then come back and tell me when I know it's there.[23]

In campaign mode, every error is magnified. Particularly when margins are slim, when political resources are stretched to the limit, the domino effect looms large and the weight of each assignment can seem crushing.

This aspect of campaign mode resembles a philosophy of personal responsibility inherent in more lethal pursuits. Behrens-Benedict's father worked with Air Force test pilots on the X-15 rocket planes. In *The Right Stuff,* Tom

Wolfe described a theory of failure common among pilots who pushed the "outside of the envelope."[24] By definition, a test pilot had the right stuff only if he could survive. There could be no shifting of responsibility. Each pilot had to play the hand he was dealt. The brutal logic: if faulty controls sent a test pilot to his death, his fellows did not blame the machinery; instead, they agreed that "when the malfunction in the controls put him in a bad corner, he didn't know how to get out of it."[25] No mission was impossible. Some pilots had the right stuff, it seemed, while others did not.

Test pilots had to believe that survival was likely—true or not. John J. Pitney, a former political operative, notes that inviolable confidence is important to military and political affairs. "When signs point to defeat," writes Pitney, "speakers invariably remind listeners that Truman beat Dewey and David slew Goliath."[26]

Political faith often runs counter to electoral reality. When Behrens-Benedict learned that an independent pollster had found Dunn's numbers slipping badly, the news electrified the candidate and her staff. Although the survey sample was minuscule—a wide margin of error rendered the poll almost useless—optimistic findings renewed hopes that Behrens-Benedict could win. It is a critical irony. On one hand, political faith denies the reality of the situation. False optimism can set in. "When you live in your own election cocoon, you really think you're going to win," said Tennessee state representative Rufus Jones after he received a mere 5 percent of the vote against Ford Jr. in the 1996 congressional primary, a race that Jones never had a chance of winning.[27] On the other hand, resignation to an inevitable loss becomes a self-fulfilling prophecy. Just as a well-positioned campaign might suffer from crippling overconfidence, poor prospects can leave a campaign demoralized. When a campaign organization sees no way to get the job done, then nothing gets done—and the candidate loses.

Some elections simply cannot be won; sometimes strategy does not matter. And yet, any effort to win a race puts faith and fear into the strategic equation. Political professionals do not merely accept political conditions as they come; rather, they seek hidden opportunities wherever the breaks may lie. Campaign mode often demands ill-founded flights of fancy (for underdogs) or a haunting sense of impending doom (for projected winners). Because elections are driven by confidence and fear, self-deception is sometimes a necessary cost of doing business. In campaign mode, politics is the art of the plausible.

Nevertheless, strategic effects are usually marginal and strategic achievements are difficult to specify. Scholarly models predict the bulk of congressional elections without reference to strategy. When surprises occur, alternative explanations are explored: an upset victory might represent nothing more than a statistical fluke or a methodological failure. Even if strategy *does* matter, it is difficult to quantify the impact of any given strategic decision. Did the stealth campaign that Sanchez employed perhaps decrease her margin of victory? Would the increasingly Republican character of southern politics have allowed Barr to use a more positive message without ill effects? The present research has concluded that stealth worked in Sanchez' favor and that Barr ran a smart campaign, but without the capacity to rerun elections for the benefit of political science, the impact of any particular campaign decision is difficult to measure.

But there are clues. Paul Herrnson has calculated the electoral significance of campaign spending, partisan bias, contested primaries, incumbent scandals, issue choices, and media favoritism. For example, a 1998 challenger increased his or her vote share by .34 percent for every $100,000 spent on campaign communications.[28] If increased funding means a larger vote share, a challenger who maintains a strong fundraising operation stands a better chance of winning than a challenger who neglects this aspect of electioneering. Of course, money can be spent well or it can be spent poorly. A campaign organization that fritters away its cash on engraved pens and colorful key fobs will probably fare worse than a campaign that spends the same amount on narrowly targeted radio advertising.[29] Better yet, the campaign might choose to invest in direct mail fundraising, thereby spending money to bring a higher return. Herrnson has shown that the amount of money a challenger spends is related to its vote share; reason suggests that the manner in which a challenger spends the money can be expected to make a difference as well.

Herrnson accounts for tactical factors like strategic targeting, but the strategies of successful electioneering generally resist analytic capture. To fully appreciate a particular strategy is to know both its power and its weakness. When vulnerabilities are discovered, the strategy loses its competitive edge. Textbook campaigns risk textbook defeat. Many uninspired political operatives have learned that strategies become outdated the moment they are pulled into view. In politics, strategic measures are followed by countermeasures, and countermeasures are confronted with wholly new lines of attack. The entire business of strategic interaction is at war with statistical modeling: scholars seek to calculate electoral probability while political strategists try to beat the odds.

In the world of politics, outlier cases like Wofford's 1991 victory float into political lore, stirring political professionals to do their utmost. The vague possibility of an upset links the intellectual side of campaign mode with its visceral complement. In a competitive election, the underdog knows how hard it is to move voters, while the likely winner knows that there is an outside chance of shameful defeat. The result is a spirited dynamic that brings out the competitive nature in candidates, operatives, and volunteers. Indeed, the fear factor is sometimes rampant in campaign organizations that, by all outside appearances, are destined to win. Political favorites must do everything possible to avoid mistakes—and humiliation. Long-shot campaigns, for their part, must seek any possible advantage in an electoral environment that augurs against victory. Doomed campaigns sometimes show an amazing ability to keep hope alive. When both sides are running even, the drama is intensified. Because everyone believes that there is no room for error, the election devolves into a cutthroat competition of skill and will. Thus, campaigns "demand much, usually too much."[30]

Why are political professionals so desperate to win? Ego, perhaps. Surely part of the equation is a sense of high mission; another part may be a quest for political power; yet another might be the thrill of electoral victory (or the fear of an agonizing defeat). For paid consultants, win/loss records affect personal income. Beyond ego, mission, power, thrill, fear, and wealth, many operatives talk about an "addiction to adrenaline." Political journalist Joe Klein, in his (anonymously published) novel about a fictional presidential campaign, had one of his book's characters speculate that the reward inside any political problem is "the pleasure of a challenge": "[Y]ou work at it, you sweat over it, you become a little crazed by it. Then, suddenly, *it falls into place*—and you're still a little crazed by it, you can't stop doing it. You're in love with your ability to do it. It feels so damn good."[31]

The deepest psychological motivations of candidates, consultants, operatives, staffers, and volunteers lie beyond the scope of *Campaign Mode*. For our present purposes, it matters only that political professionals have a clear purpose—Win!—and that, in the heat of battle, most political professionals shift into campaign mode, concentrating on the essential features of the political terrain. Indeed, the political professional who lacks that clear purpose is not in campaign mode.

Robert Rogers understood the need for strategic focus. A Ranger had to keep his "musket clean as a whistle . . . and be ready to march at a minute's warning." Under Rogers' command, Rangers were taught the military value of a copse of trees or a shallow depression in the ground. They learned to see a battlefield through tactical eyes. In this regard, Carl von Clausewitz spoke of the *coup d'oeil*—literally, a "glance," but for Clausewitz it was a "quick recognition" of strategic possibility. Generals look at battlefields in terms of the opportunities they present and those that they foreclose, catching sight of the military resources that should be brought to bear on one's adversary.[32]

Strategic vision in campaign mode is the electoral equivalent of Clausewitz' *coup d'oeil*. Political professionals learn to isolate the electorally significant features of a geographic unit from the elements that will not count toward the final vote tally. In Washington's Eighth Congressional District, for example, a visitor finds Mount Rainier, a volcano lifting more than two miles from the surrounding flatland. Its presence is critically important to a tourist or a seismologist, but the mountain is of only passing curiosity for a political strategist. The most visually prominent feature of the Eighth's physical landscape recedes from view as electorally significant attributes come to the fore: local political personalities, the district's social demographics, its partisan composition, its economy, current issues, voter ideologies, and the political resources available to campaigns on both sides. Where do the swing voters live? Are Democrats more numerous in the suburbs than on the farms? How much does it cost to reach the rural parts of the district by television advertising? By door-to-door leafleting? By radio? By mail?

This sort of vision allows for penetrating analysis. Strickland could see the long-term advantages of constituent service over ideological appeals in southern Ohio; Barr saw the value of the opposite strategy in northwest Georgia. In Orange County, California, Sanchez and her campaign team found a narrow window of opportunity that permitted one of the most celebrated congressional victories of the 1990s. Ford Jr. could see that his father's strategy of mobilization had its limits; what had worked in the past was not guaranteed to work in the future—and he acted accordingly. In Pennsylvania, Santorum's strength came from the senator's insight into preseason electoral politics.

There is no shortage of advice in the world of professional electioneering. One prominent consultant has offered his "100 Greatest Hints": a political professional is told, among other things, "Start early," "Don't panic over mistakes," "Dominate the dominant medium," "Do not fool yourself or your candidate," and "Know when to use bold strokes and when not to."[33] Campaign rules help political professionals reflect on prospective strategies. If, like Strickland, candidates should build strong connections with the electorate, then political operatives ought to find ways to put their candidate in front of the people. If smart campaigns hammer at the opponent's weak point, like Barr's operation did in Georgia, then operatives should begin researching the voting record of the opposition. Santorum, by the very success of his strategy, tells fellow incumbents to make sure the many pieces of their political operation work as a single unit. Each rule highlights a distinct feature of the political terrain, sketching the outlines of strategic thought.

It is interesting to note, however, that many losing candidates have scrupulously followed proven strategic rules. Nancy Hollister believed that she could capture the center without losing her southern Ohio base, but she was defeated anyway. Buddy Darden had done his best to connect with his constituents in the Upper Piedmont of Georgia, to no avail. And Steve Cohen of Memphis hammered away at his opponent's lack of political experience, and was trounced. From the professional perspective, they all lost not because the rules that they tried to apply were wrong, but rather, because they were unworkable—or not worked well—in the time and place in which they were applied. From 1994, the Republicans learned the importance of nationalizing the midterm election; in 1998, they learned that local issues can still hold sway. In the professional world, victory is not found in political rules; the rules merely help strategists to conceptualize the political terrain and to map out an electoral victory. Of course, sometimes, the old rules simply do not work.

Formulating new rules of combat, Rogers counseled, "Don't forget nothing"—but strategic thinking is precisely the art of ignoring all that is not relevant to one's objective. A wise general need not apprehend every feature of the terrain, just the important ones—and indeed, military strategists and political professionals cannot afford the time or energy required to think about extraneous matters. As a philosopher once noted, "The art of being wise is the art of knowing what to overlook."[34] Lacking the capacity for total recall, political professionals must concentrate on the most electorally significant features of the political terrain. Professionals in campaign mode, whose world is governed by strategic vision, and whose failure can be brought about by the smallest error in judgment, nonetheless feel compelled to follow Rogers' first rule of strategy.

The paradoxical need to remember every detail and to forget that which is not relevant prompts those who strategize American elections to constantly review, revise, and reassess the rules of electoral strategy. There is a constant need to close the gap between the political world as it is and the political world as it could be. Sometimes the differences between present and future are worked out in the off-season between campaign cycles; more often, they are handled week-to-week, day-to-day, and moment-to-moment as the electoral contest moves inexorably forward. A political professional must absorb arguments and counterarguments, gather up a broad range of potential strategies, churn through the tactical options presented by a given political terrain, and then confine his or her perception to a narrow tunnel vision (while remaining prepared to reevaluate the chosen strategy). Indeed, the essential tension between strategic perception and the vast, ever-shifting political terrain creates many seemingly intractable dilemmas. Some problems truly defy resolution. But it is precisely the difficulty of a problem (soluble or not) that focuses the strategic mind.

There are no perfect rules, no formulas for success. Good strategic thinking is always a matter of judgment—and luck—and in the merger between wisdom and fortune lies the essence of campaign mode.

Notes

1. Compare to Harold D. Lasswell, *Politics: Who Gets What, When, How* (New York: Whittlesey House, 1936).

2. Harold Ford Jr., personal interview, 25 April 2000.

3. Niccolò Machiavelli, *The Prince*, Ricci translation (Oxford: Oxford University Press, 1935), 120.

4. Robert T. Nelson, "Instant Candidate for Dunn's Seat," *The Seattle Times*, 7 June 1998.

5. Heidi Behrens-Benedict, Letter to the Editor, "A Special Sampling of Responses to Violence in Our Nation's Schools—Where Is Our Indignation at this Senseless Carnage?" *The Seattle Times*, 31 May 1998.

6. Ibid.

7. Heidi Behrens-Benedict, personal interview, 24 August 2000.

8. Nina Burleigh, "Ms. Heidi Goes to Washington," *Mirabella*, June/July 2000, 79–81, 79.

9. David Quigg, "Newcomer Tries Again to Unseat Dunn in 8th; Power Play: Heidi Behrens-Benedict says Jennifer Dunn Isn't in Tune with Constituents in 8th District," *The (Tacoma, Washington) News Tribune*, 27 October 2000.

10. Mike Lindblom, "Rep. Dunn, a Force in 8th District: Candidate's Views Are Right Down Party Lines," *The Seattle Times*, 25 October 2000.

11. Behrens-Benedict, personal interview.

12. Editorial, "Election Endorsements: Our Endorsements for the U.S. House," *The (Tacoma, Washington) News Tribune*, 22 October 1998.

13. David Schaefer and Robert T. Nelson, "Congress—Adam Smith Re-Elected to 9th District—Middle-of-the-Road Philosophy Wins Democrat a Second Term," *The Seattle Times*, 4 November 1998.

14. Burleigh, "Ms. Heidi Goes to Washington," 78–81, 104, 109; Melissa Silverstein, comp., "Races to Watch," *Ms.*, August/September 2000, 30–33, 32.

15. Heidi for Congress, *Campaign Prospectus*, undated.

16. Ibid.

17. Ibid.

18. Behrens-Benedict, personal interview.

19. Ibid.

20. John Carlson, "U.S. House Races Take Shape around State," *The (Tacoma, Washington) News Tribune*, 15 July 1998.

21. Editorial, "Return Jennifer Dunn to the U.S. Congress," *Seattle Post-Intelligencer*, 8 October 2000.

22. Editorial, "For Congress: Inslee, Smith, Dunn, Dicks, McDermott," *The Seattle Times*, 30 October 2000.

23. Mary Matalin and James Carville, with Peter Knobler, *All's Fair: Love, War, and Running for President* (New York: Random House, 1994), 355–56.

24. Tom Wolfe, *The Right Stuff* (New York: Farrar, Straus & Giroux, 1979), 12.

25. Ibid., 13.

26. John J. Pitney, Jr., *The Art of Political Warfare* (Norman: University of Oklahoma, 2000), 94, 95.

27. Susan Adler Thorp, "Cohen Just Knew It, and Yet. . . . ," *The (Memphis) Commercial Appeal*, 11 August 1996.

28. Paul S. Herrnson, *Congressional Elections: Campaigning at Home and in Washington*, 3rd ed. (Washington, D.C.: Congressional Quarterly, 2000), 232. Note that Herrnson's data does not prove causation, though it is safe to assume a cause and effect relationship. In fact, incumbent spending is *inversely* related to vote share. The more an incumbent spends, the lower the vote share, because incumbents usually raise money in earnest only when the race gets close (Ibid., 229).

29. See ibid., 235–36.

30. Ron Faucheux, "Introduction," in *The Road to Victory*, 2nd ed. (Dubuque, Iowa: Kendall/Hunt, 1998), ix.

31. [Joe Klein], *Primary Colors* (New York: Random House, 1996), 351.

32. Carl von Clausewitz, *On War*, ed. and trans. Michael Howard and Peter Paret (Princeton, N.J.: Princeton University Press, 1976), 102–103, 578.

33. Joseph Napolitan, "Joseph Napolitan's 100 Greatest Hints," in Faucheux, ed., *The Road to Victory*, 2nd ed., ed. Ron Faucheux (Dubuque, Iowa: Kendall/Hunt, 1998), 13–35.

34. William James, *The Principles of Psychology*, vol. 2 (Cambridge: Harvard University Press, 1981 [1890]), 992.

Index

81–84; Eighth Congressional District (Tennessee), 119; Eighth Congressional District (Washington), 159–61, 164–65; Ninth Congressional District (Tennessee), 12, 116, 118–20; Eleventh Congressional District (Pennsylvania), 14–16; Eighteenth Congressional District (Pennsylvania), 140–41; Twenty-Seventh Congressional District (California), 90; Thirty-Eighth Congressional District (California), 96; Thirty-Ninth Congressional District (California), 108; Forty-Sixth Congressional District (California), 12, 95, 102–3; knowledge of, 16–17, 106–7, 157; redistricting, 90, 95, 96, 120; significant features, 8–9. *See also* political terrain
Dixiecrats, 118
Do Campaigns Matter? (Holbrook), 30
Dole, Bob, 55, 68, 97
donors, 30, 149, 150
Dornan, Robert K., 89, 94, 104–5; financial resources, 97–98, 105–6; personal qualities, 95–98
DSCC (Democratic Senatorial Campaign Committee), 146, 150
Dukakis, Michael, 137
Dunn, Jennifer, 158–61

Ebony, 126, 128
economic issues, 8, 15, 23, 28–29, 49, 58, 81, 145–46; immigration and, 93–94
economic opportunity, 125–26, 129
Edelman, Murray, 29
Ehrenhalt, Alan, 139
Eisenhower, Dwight D., 25
EMILY's List, 9, 106
entrepreneurship, 139
expectations, 150–51

failure, theory of, 161–62
Faucheaux, Ron, ix, 9–10
fear factor, 163–64
Feld, Peter, 101–2, 106, 108
Fenno, Richard F., 12, 35–36, 39–40, 62, 63
Fiorina, Morris P., 12, 26, 39, 151
Fitzgerald, Brenda, 71, 74, 79, 80
Flood, Daniel J., 14–15
Foley, Tom, 147
Forbes, Malcolm S. "Steve," 55, 97
Ford, Edmund, 128
Ford, Harold E., Jr., 19, 37, 113–35, 157, 162, 165; 1996 election, 120–23; 1998 election, 127; career path, 120–24; constituent service, 116–17; expansion of base, 124–27; financial resources, 121, 123; issue-based strategy, 124–25; national audience, 127–29; personal qualities, 37, 116–18; speeches, 113–14, 116; supporters, 113, 122
Ford, Harold E., Sr., 114, 115, 119–20, 123; changes in strategy, 124–25
Ford, Joe, 128
Ford, John, 119, 124
forward planning, 6
Friedenberg, Robert V., 35
Frist, Bill, 128

game theory, 35
"Gang of Seven," 140, 144
Gaudet, Hazel, 24–25
Genovesi, Anthony, 3–4, 10–11, 16
George, 127–28
Germond, Jack, 28
Gingrich, Newt, 52, 55, 60, 67, 73, 116, 140
global economy, 125–26
Gore, Al, 2, 17, 23–24, 41, 67, 68, 113–14, 151; Ford, Jr., and, 125–26, 128

ABOUT THE AUTHORS

Michael John Burton is assistant professor of political science at Ohio University. He previously worked in the office of Vice President Al Gore as special assistant to the chief of staff and assistant political director (1993–98). Prior to the White House, Michael worked in the Justice Cluster of the Presidential Transition (1993), the office of Congressman Paul E. Kanjorski (1991–93), and the Congressional Research Service (1991). He is the coauthor (with Daniel M. Shea) of *Campaign Craft: The Strategies, Tactics, and Art of Political Campaign Management* (rev. and exp. ed. 2001).

Daniel M. Shea is associate professor of political science and director of the Center for Political Participation at Allegheny College. He worked as Campaign Coordinator for the Democratic Assembly Campaign Committee (1986–89). He is the author of *Transforming Democracy: Legislative Campaign Committees and Political Parties* (1995), and *Campaign Craft* (1996). With John C. Green, he has edited three editions of *The State of the Parties* (1994, 1996, and 1999). Recent books include *Mass Politics: The Politics of Entertainment* (1999), *New Party Politics: From Hamilton and Jefferson to the Information Age* (2000), and *Contemplating the People's Branch: Legislative Dynamics in the Twenty-first Century* (2000).

Burton and Shea both received their doctorates in political science from the State University of New York at Albany.